THE STARTUP GAME

INSIDE THE PARTNERSHIP BETWEEN VENTURE CAPITALISTS AND ENTREPRENEURS

WILLIAM H. DRAPER III

To the entrepreneurs of the world

THE STARTUP GAME
Copyright © William H. Draper III, 2011.

All rights reserved.

First published in 2011 by
PALGRAVE MACMILLAN®
in the US—a division of St. Martin's Press LLC,
175 Fifth Avenue, New York, NY 10010.

Where this book is distributed in the UK, Europe and the rest of the world,
this is by Palgrave Macmillan, a division of Macmillan Publishers Limited,
registered in England, company number 785998, of Houndmills,
Basingstoke, Hampshire RG21 6XS.

Palgrave Macmillan is the global academic imprint of the above companies
and has companies and representatives throughout the world.

Palgrave® and Macmillan® are registered trademarks in the United States,
the United Kingdom, Europe and other countries.

p. 217: Harbor Lights
Words and music by Jimmy Kennedy and William Grosz
© 1937 (renewed) Peter Maurice Music Co., Ltd.
All rights in the U.S. and Canada administered by Chappell & Co.
All Rights Reserved
Used by permission of Alfred Music Publishing Co., Inc.

ISBN: 978–0–230–10486–0

Library of Congress Cataloging-in-Publication Data

Draper, William H., 1928–
    The start up game : inside the partnership between venture capitalists and
entrepreneurs / William H. Draper III.
        p. cm.
    Includes index.
    ISBN 978–0–230–10486–0
    1. Draper, William H., 1928– 2. Capitalists and financiers—United States—
Biography. 3. Venture capital. 4. Entrepreneurship. 5. New business enterprises—
Finance. I. Title.

HG172.D73A3 2010
332.092—dc22   2010025518

A catalogue record of the book is available from the British Library.

Design by Newgen Imaging Systems (P) Ltd., Chennai, India.

First edition: January 2011

10 9 8 7 6 5 4 3 2 1

Printed in the United States of America.

Contents

Acknowledgments

WHEN I MENTIONED MY thought of writing a book about the three generations of Draper venture capitalists and the entrepreneurs we met along the way, Phyllis, my lovely wife of fifty-seven years, immediately exclaimed, "You have to do it!" She has supported me enthusiastically at every step of the way. Her encouragement and editorial advice have been more important to me than any other factor in taking on this challenge and following it through to completion.

My three children, Becky, Polly, and Tim, have all helped to keep me motivated by reading my drafts and urging me on. Tim, of course, supplied significant content by his remarkable contribution to the industry and also provided a thoughtful afterword. Eric Schmidt wrote an extraordinary foreword, and through his leadership at Google, he reminds all of us every day of the essential role entrepreneurship plays in making the world a better place.

Yasemin Denari, who is now pursuing her MBA at the Stanford Graduate School of Business, has been involved in this project more than any other individual. When she joined me at Draper Richards, she was eager to learn about the venture capital business—and she certainly did. She interviewed some of the best minds in the business, conducted superb research, and truly helped to shape, write, and edit this book. She has done an exceptional job of managing this endeavor from start to finish. I am deeply indebted to her.

Jeff Cruikshank was my editor in chief, and he supplied me with many words, much-needed guidance, and some very creative structuring. His excellent grasp of how business works was of real value to this project.

I would never have received the credentials to write as an authority about venture capital without the support of my many partners along the way. When I was a young associate at Draper Gaither & Anderson, I learned the basics by trial and error with the other young associates and senior partners, including my father. To all of them, I will be eternally grateful. My dear friend Pitch Johnson and my wonderful partners at Sutter Hill—particularly Paul Wythes—taught me a great deal and together we made a significant impact on an embryonic industry. This book could never have been written without them. Robin Richards Donohoe and I pioneered the venture capital thrust into India, and her consistently sound judgment, solid encouragement, and insightful ideas continue to be an inspiration for me. Her contribution to this book and to my life cannot be overemphasized. Howard Hartenbaum and Cynthia Lam have helped me in innumerable ways and have advised me at every stage of the development of this book. Of course the administrative support, which Jenece Sales, Linda Rheem, Rhonda Meier, and Jeannelle Luber have given me, has made my crazy life seem easy breezy.

If Jim Levine, my stellar agent at the Levine Greenberg Agency, or Laurie Harting, my executive editor at Palgrave Macmillan, had not seen a glimmer of hope early on in my proposal, I would have been practicing my trade more and writing about it less over this past year and a half. I am very appreciative of their faith in me. Laurie's direct involvement in balancing the complexities of my story have been particularly helpful.

Hats off to the many venture capitalists and entrepreneurs who agreed to be interviewed by Yasemin or me. They had a lot to say, and I am only sorry that we could not put all of their ideas, experiences, and wisdom in the book. I would also like to thank Anne Marie Burgoyne, Steve Jurvetson, Brook Byers, Mickey Butts, Jenny Shilling Stein, Thomas Foley, and Breanna DiGiammarino for their editorial contributions. And of course, thank you to Bill Bowes, Charles Ewald, Stuart Davidson, John

Fisher, Matt Scott, and all of my other friends who read early drafts of the manuscript and provided helpful commentary.

Most of all, I am in awe of and thankful to the entrepreneurs who were with me in the startup game. We've participated in a great game—not always successful, not always fun, not ever easy, but a great game nonetheless. Most of my career was spent with these extraordinary individuals, and I came to admire every single one of them, regardless of the outcome of our venture. Together, we took on the task of building great companies, but it was these gutsy and energetic visionaries who did the real work.

The startup game is hazardous and exhausting, but often exhilarating. When an entrepreneur crosses the finish line a winner and I am at his side, I know his story has to be told. When an entrepreneur stumbles, and I, as his partner, am unable to get him back on his feet, I know his story must also be told. That is why I wrote this book and why I dedicated it to the entrepreneurs of the world.

Foreword

FUTURIST ALVIN TOFFLER ONCE SAID, "Change is not merely necessary to life—it is life." He believed that the great engine of change is technology, which builds on itself and thus makes the next advanced technologies possible.

Gutenberg's printing press, Edison's lightbulb, and Bell's telephone are all examples of early technological innovations that dramatically transformed the ways in which people lived, learned, and communicated. Truly disruptive technologies such as these actually change the social norms as richer and more pervasive models emerge. As Henry Ford said, "If I had asked people what they wanted, they would have said faster horses." Ford's ability to upend the status quo and create a new category is a good example of what fuels the continuous engine of change.

Technological change is certainly not new. What is new is the exponential increase in the rate of technological advancements, and the result is our growing interconnectedness as a global society.

History has demonstrated the direct correlation between the amount of information available to an average citizen and the economic progress in that citizen's country. Each day, more and more people around the world gain access to new information and additional tools to help them collaborate, communicate, formulate ideas, and dive instantaneously into the live stream of knowledge. There are roughly 3 billion Google searches conducted each day; Facebook's 500 million users post about 700 status updates per second; Twitter's 190 million users tweet 65 million times a day; and since it was introduced in 2003, 250 billion minutes of free Skype-to-Skype calls have been made. These are today's figures; by the time you read this, all of them will have grown.

So Google, Facebook, Twitter, and Skype are similar in that they are rapidly transforming our world. But they also share another common element: all four of these companies are venture backed. If the venture capital industry did not exist, it's possible, even likely, that none of these businesses would be around today.

Of course, venture capital is much more than money. It's the passion and intelligence that links an enthusiastic entrepreneur's groundbreaking vision with the successful execution of that vision. It is what can transform a dorm-room startup into a global powerhouse.

Venture capital runs deep in the Draper blood. General William Draper was a pioneering American venture capitalist who started the world's first limited partnership. His son Bill (the author of this book), who now has several hundred investments to his name, got started in 1959, before the phrase "venture capital" was even understood. Bill's son Tim, founder of Draper Fisher Jurvetson and the DFJ Global Network, is among the most prominent venture capitalists working today. And all three Drapers have played an integral role in the unfolding of this fascinating venture capital–entrepreneurial ecosystem.

Whether you've experienced the joys and pains of Silicon Valley directly or just want to learn from those who have, you can't do better than this firsthand account of the storied three generations of Drapers. Bill has done a huge favor for those of us who are passionate about technology and innovation by chronicling their experiences. Theirs is a tale worth telling.

—Eric Schmidt
CEO and Chairman of Google

INTRODUCTION

Breakfast at Buck's

L ET'S BEGIN THIS unusual journey in a unique place that is not exactly what it seems: Buck's restaurant, pride of Woodside (population 5,352), on the well-manicured fringes of California's Silicon Valley. Yes, "unique" is an overused word, but let me persuade you that Buck's has earned that distinction many times over.

From the outside, Buck's doesn't give you much warning of what is to come. True, there is that twenty-foot-long, carved wooden fish— "Woody"—floating incongruously several feet off the ground at the far end of the parking lot against a stand of scruffy trees. The restaurant itself, however, looks as if it could be the modest anchor of any upscale retail strip in any small town west of the Rockies: a mix of dark-stained and pale wood trim, a street-long wooden overhang protecting the sidewalk against bad weather—a rare occurrence here—and the name of the restaurant itself spelled out in the same blocky typography that blankets the town. All that's missing are some hitching posts and a watering trough or two.

But walk inside Buck's, and all bets are off.

Most likely, your eyes are first drawn to a human-sized Statue of Liberty: pale green, with her requisite spiky green crown, but holding aloft a torch that doesn't look quite right. On closer examination, her torch turns out to be a very lifelike chocolate sundae, drowning in whipped cream and hot fudge. Today, she happens to be wearing a stethoscope and a Hawaiian lei, but these accessories tend to come and go. Sometimes people hang their coats on Lady Liberty's crown. (I'm one of them.)

Now your eyes begin to take in the rest of the place, which resembles what the Smithsonian's warehouse might look like in the wake of a tornado as straightened up by the Mad Hatter. Treasures, junk, not-quite-right murals, and bric-a-brac cover almost every square inch of wall and ceiling space. In the main room, a scaled-down biplane is frozen in mid-plunge from the ceiling. Also hanging from the ceiling, a six-foot-long tiger shark appears to be morphing into a dirigible. Two pairs of cowboy boots—painted in jarring combinations of green, red, pink, and yellow—hang above the bar.

If your brain seeks relief by focusing on the two shallow, wooden display cases next to the front door, it is not rewarded. One, crudely labeled "THANKS FOR THE MEMORIES," turns out to be a carefully mounted collection of silicon memory chips manufactured over the years by Advanced Micro Devices, a company founded in nearby Sunnyvale in 1969 with $100,000 in startup capital. The other display case contains a sample of twelve breakfast cereals—Corn Pops, Cheerios, Cookie Crisps, and so on—lovingly constructed to match the chip display.

Depending on the time of day, you may also encounter the proprietor of Buck's, Jamis MacNiven, who (with his ever-patient wife, Margaret) founded the restaurant in 1991 and has been decorating and redecorating it ever since. He is a large, amiable guy with shaggy, graying hair swept straight back from his forehead. Outgoing, eccentric, loquacious, and hyperkinetic, MacNiven is my perennial candidate for World's Most Creative Entrepreneur. In addition to being a restaurateur, he's an author and part-owner of a dirigible. It was MacNiven who dreamed up Silicon Valley's own soapbox derby, the Sand Hill Challenge, which played upon the competitive instincts of local entrepreneurs and venture capitalists to raise money for anti–drunk driving campaigns and other worthy causes. Some contestants took the Challenge—a run on fabled Sand Hill Road, which the authorities agreed to close down for the duration of the race—quite seriously. (The futuristic yellow vehicle hanging from the ceiling in Buck's was designed and raced by Mohr Davidow, one of the Valley's most successful venture capitalists. It took Davidow and his team 1,100 hours to build.) Others, as MacNiven records in his inimitable book (*Breakfast at Buck's*), aren't quite so serious:

> Draper Fisher Jurvetson could always be counted for a team of transcendent whimsy. DFJ invests in original sciences, including nanotechnology, the world of microscopic gears and such. One year they erected a press tent and they all dressed in lab coats and displayed electron microscope photos of their Nano Car. It was a vehicle that was supposedly about a millionth of an inch long and had a tiny mechanical driver who would pilot it down the course. Because it was actually a quantum-mechanical car it had a handicap assigned to it; it was so incredibly fast that it had to run the course 10,000 times, back and forth. The team came forward with a pair of tweezers and Tim Draper dropped the car down a plastic tube onto the roadway. The crowd loved it and so did the magazine called *Small Times*, an engineering magazine devoted to nanotech. They took the press release and ran it straight, as if it were actually a scientific first.[1]

I've been eating at Buck's for years. So has my son Tim—founder of Draper Fisher Jurvetson, proud sponsor of the Nano Car, and the third generation of venture capitalists in the Draper family. It would make my storytelling easier if I could claim that my venture-capitalist father, General William Draper Jr., also ate at Buck's, but that would be a stretch. (Dad died in 1974, seventeen years before Buck's opened.) But because my father helped plant the seeds of what would become Silicon Valley, and because Buck's is the distillation of much of what is so odd, special, and compelling about the Valley—a place where great ideas meet smart money—I think he's with us in spirit when we sit down to eat at Buck's.

One That Got Away

"Ideas meeting money" is the other thing that I meant when I said that Buck's is not exactly what it seems at first glance. Along with a few other watering holes in the Valley, Buck's is not just a restaurant with a wacky decor, an inventive proprietor, and oversized servings. It is also a place where people are sized up, plans are challenged and probed, and deals may well be closed on a handshake. Buck's is where would-be entrepreneurs meet with venture capitalists, "angels," and other people with deep pockets and broad networks. Or, going in the other direction, it is where would-be financial backers chase a good idea.

The latter case—money chasing a promising idea—is the circumstance in which Tim and I found ourselves during the late winter and early spring of 1995. In the spring of 1994, Jerry Yang, 25, and David Filo, 27—two Stanford electrical engineering students pursuing PhDs in computer-assisted integrated circuit design—found themselves with time on their hands. Their faculty adviser was on sabbatical that year, giving them more free hours than usual. As they later wrote about themselves (in the third person):

> To their credit, and unlike generations of students before them, David and Jerry avoided the obvious and classic time wasters. They did not engage in countless Frisbee contests, hone their rock-climbing skills on the rocky edifices of the Stanford campus, start a home-brew club, or attend horror-film marathons. Instead, they became interested in the World Wide Web, just as it was becoming the world's deepest bottomless pit.[2]

More specifically, Yang and Filo were compiling a list of their favorite websites. Today, of course, you can ask just about any elementary-school kid to explain what a website is, and he or she can give you some kind of answer. Back then things were different. Just a few years before—in 1990— there were only a dozen nodes on the nationwide computer network that had grown out of years of Department of Defense–funded research aimed at creating a catastrophe-proof communications network. Those nodes were all located in government agencies and universities and were accessible only to the highest-level sorts of nerds, but the development of the Mosaic "browser" in 1993 changed that. It provided non-technical people with a graphical user interface that they could utilize to navigate around in the new world of cyberspace. In that same year, with his PhD studies in a fallow phase, Filo discovered Mosaic and started finding and documenting interesting websites.

Beginning the following spring, Yang and Filo together took three more important steps. First, they wrote a software program designed to sniff out new sites. Second, they came up with an indexing scheme, which—as more and more sites came into their "fold"—they expanded into categories, subcategories, and sub-subcategories. Third, they decided to share their work freely with anyone who was interested, which they thought to be in the free-form, self-inventing spirit of the web. Because the database resided on Yang's computer, they called it "Jerry's Guide to the World Wide Web." Once people started taking notice of the new resource, Yang renamed it "David and Jerry's Guide to the World Wide Web" because he didn't think he deserved all the credit.

The unwieldy nine-word name didn't last long. Searching for a less cumbersome replacement, they came up with "Yahoo," based on the sub-human creatures in Jonathan Swift's *Gulliver's Travels*.[3] Gradually, their after-hours efforts in the electrical engineering department's central computer facility became space-intensive, so Stanford donated a trailer for their use, "legendarily littered with overheating terminals, pizza boxes, dirty clothing, and golf clubs."[4]

By April 1994, Yahoo was composed of a hundred sites and was getting a thousand hits a week. By September, those numbers were up to 2,000 sites and 50,000 hits a *day*. By January 1995, it was 10,000 sites and up to one million hits a day. Somewhere in this time frame, however, Stanford let it been known that this "Yahoo thing" was consuming too many resources to be sustained by the university as the hobby of two graduate students. Thus, Yang and Filo began looking for other ways to support their budding venture.

So in a very real sense, it was the need to move Yahoo off-campus that pushed Yang and Filo to commercialize their addictive habit. True, they had entrepreneurial aspirations for other web-based ventures—they were by no means immune to the lure of commerce—but their original plan was to keep Yahoo free and grassroots oriented. Neither was a business-man by training; in fact, up to that point, neither had ever held a day job. Somewhat reluctantly, they asked a friend named Tim Brady—a second-year Harvard MBA student—to write a business plan for Yahoo.

Their plan was finished in March 1995. It described a service that would be free to end users, with ads appearing only on the top-five most-accessed pages. The plan forecasted revenues of $4.15 million for 1996 (the real figure turned out to be closer to $20 million). It identified Filo as president and Yang as chairman and CFO—a bit of a fudge, because both knew that they were not prepared to run a business.

Yahoo was incorporated on March 5, 1995. One distinctive feature of the web portal—built into its core architecture—was the ability to track where users of the system went on the web. Although Filo and Yang origi-nally conceived of the tracking function as a way to improve their cat-egorizing and indexing capabilities, savvy observers realized that this key feature could also be used to sell targeted advertising.

As a result, potential buyers and investors were already circling. For example, Yang and Filo received a $2 million offer from America Online's Steve Case (who made it clear that if they *didn't* sell, AOL would develop a competing offering and bury Yahoo). Venture capitalists also began mak-ing the trek out to the Stanford trailer. Among them were Mike Moritz of Sequoia Capital, a representative from Draper International LLC (me), and a representative from our family fund, Draper Associates (my son Tim).

Actually, I had only an accidental involvement in the chase for Yahoo. Robin Richards, my partner in Draper International, knew of this emerg-ing internet phenomenon. She had attended Stanford at the same time as Yang, and she had a strong inkling that he was onto something big. Obviously, I trusted Robin's judgment—after all, we were then in the process of launching the first venture capital operation focused on India together—so I called up Tim and suggested that he take a look. Because I knew that I would be devoting all of my energy to India for the foreseeable future, I was simply pointing him toward an exciting new opportunity.

I introduced Tim to Jerry Yang over breakfast at Buck's on a Wednesday, and we were both intrigued by what we were hearing. Truth be told, although I had backed one of the world's first software companies years earlier—Activision, the game developer that my Sutter Hill Ventures partners and I helped bring into being in 1979—I had been away from the West Coast for a dozen years, so Tim was already more clued into the emerging world of the internet than I was. The following Saturday, Tim rode his bike over to the trailer to watch a demo, and he immediately realized that this could be a home run.

Tim invited the two brilliant and visionary PhD candidates to the offices of Draper Associates to make a pitch aimed at interesting his partner, John Fisher, in the potential investment. The "pitch" is nothing more (or less) than the sales presentation that the would-be entrepreneur makes to try and interest potential investors in a proposed deal. I'll have more to say about pitches—what works and what doesn't—in subsequent chapters.

On the chance that I could be of help to Tim, I sat in on that particular pitch. During the meeting, Yang and Filo came across as a bit nervous but highly confident in their technical skills. I also recall that Fisher expressed his polite skepticism about their ability to manage this enterprise, given their near-total lack of business experience. Yang and Filo readily agreed with this assessment, so they asked Tim and Fisher to come up with a CEO candidate for the fledgling business.

Perhaps this notion surprises you: that an individual with an idea might be willing—even eager—to turn over the day-to-day management of that brainchild to a CEO put forward by a group of investors. In fact, it happens all the time, although sometimes it's not until a later stage in the company's development.

Not that it's *easy*. It's almost never simple to find the right fit between a visionary and a potential manager of that vision. Tim mentally went through the names in his personal network. (Networks are critical to the successful venture capitalist.) He was trying to come up with someone who was ambitious enough to help transform Yahoo from an idea into a blockbuster and who was, at the same time, adventurous enough to take a flyer on an almost untested vision of the future.

Tim decided that the best candidate was his good friend Jay O'Connor. Jay, then in his mid-thirties, had a strong track record of helping growing businesses succeed. He and I visited the trailer together one sunny afternoon in late March and we were taken on our own guided tour of Yahoo, much as Tim had experienced a few days earlier. The setting in the trailer was not particularly encouraging—I remember that we had to step around Filo's bicycle and climb over his skis to get close enough to his small computer screen to see anything—but the demo was nothing short of astounding. Filo asked me to give him a question that I wanted answered, so I asked him to tell me the current tuition at Yale, where I was a trustee. He typed in a few keywords, and almost instantly, a virtual bookshelf appeared on the screen where a few fat books whose spines spelled out "Yale University" in blue and white letters. (This was Yale's earliest home page—in the spring of 1995.) After a few more keystrokes, up popped the figure: Yale's $21,000-per-year tuition. Amazing!

As it turned out, Jay couldn't quite pull the trigger to commit to joining Tim in his proposal to Yahoo. (Tim's prediction to Jay at the time—"I think if you go with this, you'll make $10 million"—turned out to be a substantial underestimate.) Jay went on to have a successful career at Intuit, where he helped build QuickBooks into a dominant small-business financial management system. If he ever looked back, I'm sure it was with a combination of chagrin and amusement.

For more than a month, Yang and Filo continued their discussions with the competing would-be investors, including Tim. They also kept talking with Steve Case at AOL. Finally, in April 1995, Yahoo announced that it had accepted an offer of $1 million in venture funding from Sequoia

Capital, in return for 25 percent of the company. As part of the package, Sequoia would also secure Tim Koogle as CEO. This was Sequoia's first investment in a dot-com, and it had been orchestrated by Mike Moritz, who—unbeknownst to us at the time—had also visited the trailer. Tim called up Sequoia and asked for the chance to get into the deal as a coinvestor, but Sequoia, not wanting to dilute their holding, turned Tim (and presumably other potential coinvestors) down.

Yahoo went public one year later on April 12, 1996. The stock closed that day at about $33, which put Yahoo's valuation at something like $850 million. That meant that at least on paper, Yang and Filo were each worth $130 million, and Sequoia's one-quarter position was worth something north of $212 million. Of course, none of them sold their stock at that time, and today the market capitalization is over $20 billion.

Why recount at some length the story of "one that got away"? After all, each of the three generations of Drapers has stories to tell about the ones that *didn't* get away. Why not focus on those? It's because I think the Yahoo story contains a lot of the elements of real-life venture capital, which is part of what this book is about. It conveys something of the love that great entrepreneurs put into their product or service. It captures a lot of the pain, joy, suspense, frustration, and elation that we venture capitalists feel as we're closing—or failing to close—a deal. It underscores the fundamental fact that in venture capital, you're going to win some, and you're going to lose some.

In short, it introduces some of the key elements that we'll return to in later chapters, as I develop a picture of what makes the world of venture capital tick, what motivates entrepreneurs, and how they both support and are supported by the great economic engine of our democracy.

CHAPTER 1

Three Generations

Tomorrow to fresh woods and pastures new.

—*John Milton*

L ET'S LOOK AT A few stories spanning three generations of Drapers, which add dimension to our emerging picture of venture capital and entrepreneurship. Let me first reassure you, however, that my goal in this opening chapter is not to present three Draper biographies. Instead, my goal is to help you place my stories and my advice in a larger context.

Lessons from the German Coffeemaker Machine

When people ask me whether venture capitalists are born or self-made, I tend to waffle. I suspect it's a little bit of both, with definite shading toward the self-made.

In the late 1920s, decades before my father, General William H. Draper Jr.,[1] founded his venture capital firm, he worked on Wall Street as an investment banker for Dillon, Read and Co. For most of that decade, since the end of the tough recession of 1920–1922, the stock market had been soaring. Business-minded Republicans had occupied the White House since 1921. Wallets and bellies were full. An unbridled optimism filled the air. Wise men were talking smugly about the "end of the business cycle"—meaning that from that point on, there would no longer be any economic downturns, and the economic escalator would only go up.

One day in 1929, before the crash, my father was bitten by an early version of what we would today call the venture capital bug. At the time, he had just received a huge bonus. As he saw it, he had two choices. He could use the money to pay off the mortgage on our family's new house and we would own it free and clear. Or, he could invest his entire bonus in a new business idea that he had recently come across: a German-made automatic coffeemaker.

This brings us to an important lesson about venture capital: *don't invest any money that you can't afford to lose.* After all, as the name implies, venture capital is a risky business.

I'm not exactly sure how my father made his decision, but he had other business in Germany and might have been intrigued by the famous German coffee klatches. The 1920s was the decade in which a whole new universe of consumer-oriented gadgets was introduced—partly because of the gradual electrification of America—and bringing on the next indispensable device must have seemed appealing. And there was the heady context of the summer of 1929—business was booming, and it simply seemed that one couldn't make a bad investment.

So he plunged. He put his entire bonus into the coffeemaker venture. That turned out to be a bad decision. Two months later, the stock market crashed, and the investment crashed with it. The mortgage on our house remained a burden, and for many years there wouldn't be any bonuses being handed out on Wall Street. My father had to work night and day for the next ten years to keep us afloat.

I was born in 1928, so I was only an infant when these fateful decisions were made. But I gradually became aware that in the Draper household, money was tight. I remember, for example, that throughout my childhood, my father would invariably return the Christmas gifts that my mother bought for him, because he felt that the family needed the cash more than he needed a present. My father was by nature a hard worker, but in those difficult years, he drove himself at a punishing pace as he struggled to hang on to his investment banking job, in the deepest and darkest economic depression that our country had ever faced. One of his jobs—surely an unpleasant one—was to close down several Dillon Read offices that were outside New York City. There were many periods, as I recall, when he worked all night at the office. I remember later visiting his office at 38 William Street and seeing the wooden rolltop desk that had served as his makeshift pillow. His hard work paid off. In 1937, he was promoted to vice president at Dillon Read, and the financial pressure eased somewhat.

There was a second thread that continued through my father's life in this period. He had served in World War I and had stayed in the Army Reserves after the war. (Every summer he took a short leave from Dillon Read to serve as a reserve officer at the Army base in Plattsburgh in upstate New York.) He eventually reached the rank of chief of staff of the 77th Division, a post that he held from 1936 through 1940. In 1940, he was called to Washington by General George Marshall to serve full time on President Roosevelt's Advisory Committee for Selective Service. He thereby began two decades in which he alternated between distinguished stints of public service and equally notable work in the private sector, both in the United States and abroad. (I'll return to my father's career occasionally in later chapters, because these stories help to make some of the larger points of this book.)

In 1959, my father made history in his business pursuits. With his friends Rowan Gaither and General Fred Anderson, he formed Draper Gaither & Anderson: the first venture capital firm on the West Coast and the first limited partnership in the venture world.

My father has had a significant influence on my life, my character, and my actions. Why is the coffeemaker story so vivid in my memory? Because he told it to me many times and drove the message home. He wanted me to take away lessons from this misadventure, including the need to spread the risk, to always save something for a rainy day, and to work hard enough to make good things happen.

Getting My Feet Wet

"Venture capital? Sounds risky. I wouldn't do it if I were you."

The man speaking to me, Clarence Randall, former chairman of Inland Steel, was sitting behind a huge, dark wooden desk on the top floor of the new Inland Steel building in the Loop, the heart of downtown Chicago's financial and retail district. I recall that the view was spectacular on that particular sunny afternoon in June 1959.

I knew that it would be difficult to convince Randall to agree with my decision to leave Inland. I had had great opportunities and had been happy at the company for the previous five years. The "Randall's Rangers" management training program, in which I participated, was what had initially drawn me to Inland. Each year, the company recruited five or six Rangers from the graduating classes of the nation's best schools, with the expectation that they would later go on to join the ranks of Inland's top management. Randall had invested his reputation and a good deal of Inland resources to make the program a success, and he kept a close eye on us, both during and after that first year. Doors were opened for us. After completing my year of training, I was assigned to the sales department and eventually given responsibility for all of South Chicago, arguably the most important district. I was one of just nine salesmen in the entire company and was proud to have a company car and my own territory.

It had been fun and a great learning experience. My wife, Phyllis, and I were living in Highland Park at the time, and two of our three children were born during those five happy years in the Chicago area. We came to treasure the solid values and strong work ethic that the Midwest is known for. I still love Chicago and the Midwest. We made many close friends, particularly Cathie and Pitch Johnson, who remain our best friends to this day.

I met Pitch on my first day at work at Inland Steel in East Chicago, Indiana—a rather grimy mill town—where we ended up spending several memorable years together raising our new families in a company housing project. Pitch had grown up in Palo Alto, California, and had attended Stanford for his undergraduate studies. We had both attended Harvard Business School, and like me, he had first worked at another steel company before starting at Inland. We both were enthusiastic about the challenges ahead—he as a foreman in the Open Hearth operations, and me as a Randall's Ranger. We bonded like glue.

So why was I leaving? My father had called to say that the money had been raised, the timing was right, and the documents had all been signed. Draper Gaither & Anderson—the first venture capital firm in the West—was about to become a reality.

Conspiratorially leaning forward across his desk, as if the KGB might be listening to our conversation, Randall dropped his voice to nearly a whisper. "I had a friend in the financial business who lived in Highland Park," he said, "and he went bankrupt because he gambled in the stock market. He and his family left town and never recovered. You have a secure job and are on your way to the top of a great company. Let your father do his thing, and you do yours. Stay with your business family here in Chicago, and avoid taking a risk on something as dangerous as venture capital."

But it was too late. My heart and mind were already in California. I thanked him for his generosity toward me and formally cut the cord.

Before leaving Randall's office, though, I decided that I had to ask him a question that had been on my mind for several months: why did Inland continue to manufacture rails for the railroad industry when everyone inside the company knew that the rail business was a loser for Inland? Randall, seemingly unsurprised by the question, explained to me how significant the railroad industry was to the security and economic health of the country and how important it was for Inland to continue to supply rails as needed regardless of their profitability.

"There's a shortage of rails," he concluded, gradually raising his voice to oratorical levels. "It is our patriotic duty. As long as I have any influence on Inland Steel, *we will remain in the rail business.*"

Clarence Randall was not only a civic-minded businessman; he was also a dominant leader of a core industry that was then at the zenith of its power. This was the decade after World War II, when the country was rebuilding its infrastructure and meeting the long-deferred needs of its citizens, many of whom had made huge sacrifices for the war effort. Randall's heart was in the right place, and I knew he believed every word of what he was telling me.

Even then, though, I could see the handwriting on the wall. The U.S. steel industry hadn't modernized itself and had been shielded from foreign competition by protective tariffs. Aluminum, plastics, and other substitutes were moving in on steel's turf. Inland Steel's stock in 1959—the year I left the company—was at an all-time high: $59 per share. It never reached that price again, and it declined enough in subsequent decades to turn the company into a ripe takeover target. In 1998, after over a hundred years in business, Inland was acquired by ArcelorMittal, the largest steel company in the world.[2]

On the way back to my office, I thought briefly about the perils and pitfalls that Randall had sketched out. But even then, I knew I didn't see the world the same way he did. Where he saw risk, I saw opportunity. To him, the private investment business—in fact, any investment business— was risky. To me, venture capital was fresh, new, and exciting, and the risk seemed to bring with it big rewards. I would be leaving a tired, stagnant, and bureaucratic industry to join a creative, fluid, and challenging one. From Randall's perspective, I was giving up the fast track to joining the leadership ranks—maybe even becoming CEO—of the best-managed steel company in the country. In my eyes, that opportunity was a long way off, and it seemed far more meaningful to help create a family of new companies than to manage one old one. I was still young, and I figured that if venture capital didn't work out, I could do something else.

Then there was the lure of San Francisco. As I said, I loved Chicago— its energy, architecture, friendly and open people, and no-nonsense atmosphere—but San Francisco was, in my eyes, the glamorous "city on the hill" (actually, seven hills). True, I had only been there once, back when I was twelve, and when I try to summon up memories of that long-ago trip, all that comes to mind is a Barbary Coast restaurant with what seemed like mountains of sawdust on the floor. But the city had captured my imagination, and even today it still exerts a magical hold on me.

The prospect of working with my father also had enormous appeal. Because of his involvement in World War II, his subsequent assignments in Paris and Berlin, and later his role as chairman of Mexican Light & Power in Mexico City, I hadn't had the chance to spend much time with him. If I joined Draper Gaither & Anderson we would be able to see each other every day, and I would have the unique opportunity to learn from a master.

Finally, and most importantly, there were my wife and children to consider. Phyllis was thrilled at the prospect of living near the Stanford campus. (To this day, she is an incorrigible, perennial student.) She wholeheartedly endorsed my proposal to live our lives and raise our children in a more temperate and snow-free climate. In short, she was eager to start a whole new life.

I left my office that afternoon feeling confident about my choice to move to Palo Alto and help get Draper Gaither & Anderson off the ground. But if I had pondered my decision for a year or a hundred years, I couldn't have begun to guess what was to come. I was about to witness the birth of Silicon Valley and participate in its dramatic and unprecedented growth. I would have a front-row seat as my adopted home transformed itself into the heartland of high technology, venture capital, and entrepreneurship. Silicon Valley would become synonymous with creativity, productivity, and economic growth—the birthplace of Apple, Hewlett-Packard, Google, Yahoo, Cisco Systems, Oracle, Genentech, OpenTable, Tesla, Facebook, Twitter, and literally thousands of other great companies.

The median, annual family income in Atherton, California—the little town twenty-eight miles south of San Francisco where we would eventually settle—was $3,857 in 1950. By the year 2000, it would exceed $200,000. By the beginning of the new millennium, Atherton was one of the most affluent locations on the planet.[3]

It was Silicon Valley that made that possible, and it was venture capital that helped make Silicon Valley possible.

Landing in the West

Of course, what the future held wasn't apparent to Phyllis and me as we drove into Palo Alto in our new Chevrolet convertible, which we had bought in anticipation of the bountiful California sunshine. Unfortunately, we broke the latching mechanism for the top even before we crossed the Mississippi. We somehow got it shut, but we didn't dare open it again until we had figured out the cost of housing in Palo Alto and were sure that we could afford to put our limited resources into the car.

We made the trip out from Chicago a leisurely one, taking five days to cross the western half of the country. We had three small children in the back seat, so we didn't want to push ourselves. Every day, we would leave our motel at 7 A.M., drive all morning, and by 2 P.M. find our next lodging, preferably with a pool. It was exciting: a family voyage of discovery in a vast and beautiful part of the country that none of us had seen before.

Once we reached our new hometown of Palo Alto—then a somewhat sleepy college town of about 25,000 residents—we drove the tree-lined streets until we found Rickey's, an upscale motel that some friends had recommended. It was where Stanford students housed their parents, where visiting business travelers stayed, and where the local Rotary Club met. Most important for our purposes, it had a pool. On that warm July afternoon, the Draper family felt that we had arrived in heaven.

At that time, Stanford University was already the heartbeat of Palo Alto. In the course of fifty years, it had become a first-class university, on par with those in the Ivy League. The University of California, Berkeley, was the other great university in Northern California, but it seemed far away—across the Bay Bridge east of San Francisco.

Stanford University, amidst a blur of bicycles, was unique in many ways. It boasted an 8,180-acre campus adorned with miles of palm trees, large, sand-colored buildings with Spanish-tiled roofs, and most importantly a stellar engineering school aggressively on the move. If one were to give credit to only one man for creating Silicon Valley, it would be to Fred Terman, Stanford's dean of engineering and, later, provost. Of course it would be foolish to think that Silicon Valley was built by any less than an army of creative, energetic, talented, and dedicated souls, but Terman seemed to be the one who got it all started. He was the one who convinced others at Stanford to focus on engineering and put all possible resources into making the Stanford School of Engineering number one in the world.

Parenthetically, at the same time, President Whit Griswold of Yale, who had previously been my undergraduate history professor, dismantled an equally fine engineering school on the grounds that engineering was like dentistry, and Yale was not a trade school. Would New Haven, Connecticut, have become the home of Silicon Valley if Griswold had remained as my history professor in 1950 instead of accepting the position of president halfway through the school year?

I doubt it. There was another important factor besides the Stanford School of Engineering that was magnetically pulling potential entrepreneurs to Palo Alto, California: the weather. The sun shone ten months out of the year, the sky was clear and blue, and the climate was dry, not humid, so even the hottest days were still pleasant. Today, more than fifty years later, Bay Area residents are just as enamored with the inimitable California weather.

Draper Gaither & Anderson had done its homework, and the decision to start up in Palo Alto was an easy one. Gaither's law firm was in San Francisco, General Anderson had been stationed at Travis Air Force base (north of San Francisco), and my father knew the area well because of his visits during his investment banking days, when Dillon Read financed the building of the San Francisco–Oakland Bay Bridge. All three partners were eager to help Dean Terman fulfill his dream of connecting Stanford's great engineering discoveries with the necessary money and resources to produce superior products and services, and to deliver them through young startup companies on or near the Stanford campus. Litton

Industries, Varian, and Hewlett-Packard were all supported by this early ecosystem.

A few nights after our arrival in Palo Alto, Cathie and Pitch Johnson flew into town from Chicago and threw us a wonderful "Welcome to Palo Alto" dinner party. Because Pitch had grown up in the area, he had many friends, and he kindly introduced Phyllis and me to many of them. The next morning, Phyllis and the children relaxed and explored downtown. Meanwhile, I set off for my new job—excited and eager.

General Fred Anderson and a few of the others had already settled into our temporary office on Addison Street. With his warm, optimistic, and bear-hugging personality, Fred Anderson was about as far removed from the conservative Clarence Randall as Palo Alto was from Chicago. Anderson had had a distinguished military career as commanding general of the Eighth Bomber Command during World War II and was portrayed by Clark Gable in the renowned war movie *Twelve O'Clock High* (1949). Despite that, he was down to earth and accessible. He immediately put me at ease as he told me the exciting plans he had for all of us, and then he called the others in to meet me. Eventually, a group of us moved out to the sunny courtyard and chatted the morning away. Anderson was nearly bubbling over with excitement as he regaled us with tales of high-risk, high-reward opportunities in the area. He told us, for example, about a company in which he had recently invested, Raychem, which had just started up two years before, in 1957. In Anderson's opinion, Raychem— with its new patented, heat-shrinkable insulation—suitable for a myriad of industrial applications for covering wire with plastic—was going to be enormously successful. But Anderson spent just as much time talking about Raychem's founder, Paul Cook, whom he believed to be a great leader. Cook, Anderson said with conviction, was one of the very few entrepreneurs who possessed the leadership qualities necessary to take a company from a great idea to an international powerhouse.

As Anderson predicted, Raychem did turn into a massive hit. For its first 25 years, the company grew at an average rate of 25 percent per year—an amazing record. Raychem Corporation became one of the world's largest producers of industrial electronics components, with manufacturing, sales, or R&D facilities in forty countries, and it generated annual sales in excess of $1 billion.[4]

Later on, I was able to participate in Raychem's success. An old friend of Pitch's and a new friend of mine, Bill Bowes, was a partner at Blyth & Co. at the time. Blyth led the Raychem underwriting, and Bill encouraged me to personally invest $1,000. For me, that was an extravagant amount to invest in those days, but I ended up making ten times that in the public market. It doesn't sound like a lot of money today, but it was equivalent to a full year's salary for me back then.

Including myself, there were five young associates at Draper Gaither & Anderson, and we all received the same salary: $10,000 per year. This was the same salary that I had made during my last year at Inland Steel. Anderson had asked me what my salary had been at Inland; I told him, and subsequently all five of us were paid the same amount. Again, those were different times, when the cost of living was no higher in Palo Alto than it was in Chicago, so there was no argument. After all, we would get a ticket to participate in the thrilling game of risk-taking, reward-making *venture capital* and get paid a decent salary for the privilege. That day after work, I went back to Rickey's and couldn't stop talking to my family about my new job, my new associates, and the vistas that seemed to be opening up before me. Phyllis was fascinated, and we were all thrilled to be together at the beginning of an exciting new era in our lives.

A few days later, we moved to a less-pricey motel—the Restwell, on El Camino Real, which is the main commercial strip in Palo Alto—and began looking for a house. Shortly thereafter, we found a handsome, two-story stucco house on the corner of Cowper and Embarcadero; despite the modest size of our property, what really impressed Phyllis and me were the lemon, avocado, and persimmon trees that surrounded our home—a luxury that we had not been accustomed to in the Windy City.

Friends and Deals

Two of the three partners at Draper Gaither & Anderson each brought in one limited partner who had agreed to invest $2 million. My father brought in Lazard Frères, and Gaither signed the Rockefellers. Anderson brought in a friend from New York, and together with a few other individuals the total came to $6 million. (The firm was going to use their money to invest in ventures and hopefully make some good returns for them.) In October 1960, we moved into our brand-new headquarters on Welch Road on the Stanford University campus, having signed one of Stanford's first ninety-nine-year leases for a commercial enterprise.

Leasing Stanford land has an interesting history. In 1885, Leland Stanford donated 8,180 acres of farmland in Palo Alto to serve as the campus of a university named in honor of his deceased son, Leland Stanford Jr. In making the gift, Stanford specified that the trustees could never sell even one acre of that land. Because the university uses only a small portion of the land—in the entire world, only Moscow State University has a larger campus—the trustees dreamed up the idea of a ninety-nine-year lease, whereby the university would retain ownership, but the tenants would gain effective control of their properties. One of the world's most successful shopping centers now sits on Stanford ground, as well as a new Rosewood Hotel, Stanford Medical Center, and the legendary Sand Hill Road—home to many of the most powerful venture capital firms in the country, including Draper Fisher Jurvetson, which my son founded. Despite all of this successful development, about 60 percent of the Stanford lands remain undeveloped to this day.[5]

BusinessWeek ran a two-page article on the formation of Draper Gaither & Anderson. We were literally the only venture capital game in town, and we were off to a great start. Our headquarters, in a contemporary one-story building, was uniquely designed, with a plastic outer shell through which light could pass so no lighting was needed in the outer hallway surrounding each office. Every office opened up to an airy inner courtyard. Life was near-perfect in what we hoped would become a hot-bed of financial energy for California's entrepreneurs.

Pretty quickly, though, we faced our first setback, and it was a big one. As my father and General Anderson were putting together their new firm, they had selected Rowan Gaither as their third senior partner because of his powerful intellect, extensive experience, and unimpeachable character. Gaither had been president of the Ford Foundation; a founder of the Rand Corporation; and senior partner of Cooley, Crowley & Gaither, a top law firm in San Francisco.

Shortly after the formation of Draper Gaither & Anderson, Gaither was diagnosed with cancer. He flew to Boston, where he began getting treatment at Massachusetts General Hospital. I once visited him in his hospital room while I was on a business trip to Boston. He pointed at his chest and said, "Bill, feel this."

I reached over, put my hand on his chest, and felt a lump as big and as hard as a coconut.

He smiled ruefully. "I bet that thing is going to put me in the history books."

He died a few months later, at the relatively young age of fifty. In my opinion, if Rowan Gaither had lived, Draper Gaither & Anderson would have developed into one of the great and most durable venture firms ever, instead of lasting for only seven years. Gaither was a thoughtful, well-organized, and farsighted lawyer. He had contagious warmth and sincerity. Gaither was the connective tissue that could have held the firm together.

With difficulty, all of us at the firm returned to work in the wake of Gaither's passing. The first entrepreneurs whom I funded at DGA were Thomas Corbin and Elliot Farnsworth, two intelligent young engineers with a bonanza idea. Reid Dennis—who later became one of the Valley's most prominent venture capitalists—had suggested that I look at this new startup. I already knew that Reid had a good eye. He had been investing in small, private companies for Fireman's Fund Insurance Company for a number of years. If Reid liked an idea, it was probably a good one.

The headquarters of Corbin Farnsworth were located right down the road in Palo Alto, so it didn't take me long to get in front of the two founders. Even in those early days, I had decided that the best place to hold a first meeting is in the entrepreneur's own place of business. You get to see how the entrepreneur operates in his own digs, with his team right there on-site. This way, you put the entrepreneur and his colleagues more at ease, and you are able to see how they interact. I've become a little lazier about this in recent years, and now I often hold first meetings in my office. It's more time-efficient, but it's probably not the best way to go.

"Lie down," said Farnsworth.

I stretched out on a table while he pretended to zap my chest with a big round paddle, all the while narrating the steps that he was simulating. At the time, I wasn't aware that I was looking at the very first heart defibrillator—a device that would save millions of lives in the ensuing decades. A couple of days later, I brought General Anderson over to meet Farnsworth, and he liked the entrepreneurs and the company as well. We quickly agreed to a deal, and I had my first venture capital investment under my belt. The company was extremely successful, and we later sold it to Smith, Kline & French for a large gain.

The other associates at DGA were fun to be with, and we all got along well. Crawford Cooley, the son of Rowan Gaither's partner at the law firm Cooley Godward Gaither, was a dignified and droll young man who was well connected in San Francisco society. He had worked on the development of the first color television set at RCA, even though he was not an engineer by training. The truth is, none of us knew very much about engineering, which in hindsight I can see was a mistake. Technology is the bedrock that underlies the venture capital industry, and I've come to understand that it's extremely beneficial to have some technical competence in-house.

Don Lucas was the only one of the young associates who had credible Wall Street credentials. He was twenty-nine years old and had been on the fast track at Smith Barney. I distinctly remember the first question he ever asked us: "So what do we do when the six million is gone?" The rest of us associates were all astonished at the question for at least two reasons. First, unlike Lucas, we weren't used to the magnitude of Wall Street figures, or to the concept of $6 million ever being "gone." Second, we were young and optimistic, we had faith in the firm's leadership, and we just figured that something good would happen.

After the dissolution of DGA, Lucas continued on his own as an investor, and he is best known for his big hit as an early backer of Larry Ellison, the founder of Oracle. Today, Oracle physically dominates Redwood Shores, an affluent neighborhood near San Francisco. Oracle's corporate headquarters is impossible to miss: a dozen huge, silo-like silver towers situated around a man-made lake. The company is a true Silicon Valley star and provides software systems to many of the world's industries.

Larry Duerig was another important DGA colleague. He and General Anderson had worked together for several years in San Francisco. Duerig was an older, experienced investor and was therefore given partnership status in DGA. He was street-smart and blessed with a simple kind of wisdom. He was our unofficial coach and cautioned the five of us young associates not to be "mesmerized by the gold watch as it swings back and forth in the hand of the hypnotic and captivating fast-talking magician"—in other words, the entrepreneur. Duerig also chain-smoked cigarettes. When he was excited, he would talk fast causing his cigarette to bounce in his mouth. Hot ashes would then fall onto his round belly and burn holes in his shirts. He never came unhinged when the news was bad, and he was always receptive to a new deal.

Tom Carey, an eccentric young man with high-button, kangaroo leather shoes and a good financial mind, had worked with Duerig as an analyst on both private and public deals. He had an odd mix of sardonic humor and a sensitive nature. Carey was plenty of fun to be with. Finally, there was Bill Symons, our chief financial officer—although this was an era before that term was in common use. Symons was a CPA by training, and one of his important jobs was to examine the books of every company into which we proposed to put our money. He had a placid and kind manner that was extremely appealing, and the entrepreneurs never resented his probes into their operations.

The deal flow at DGA was surprisingly plentiful, and our newly assembled team found itself scattered in all directions. Much of my action came from Pitch Johnson's friends and from his friends' friends. Other potential deals came in through the partners, associates, and "over the transom." One episode from that time especially stands out for me. It was General Anderson who suggested I investigate this novel opportunity.

"Bill, how would you like to go to Hawaii?" Anderson asked me. "A developer named Chin Ho has an opportunity, and he read about us in *BusinessWeek*. He's building an apartment house on Waikiki Beach."

"Actually, they're not apartments," Chin would later tell me, briefing me on the way in from the Honolulu airport. "They're *condominiums*."

I had just come over on one of the very first jet airplanes ever to fly to Hawaii. "What on earth is a condominium?" I asked.

"Well," he chuckled, "there aren't very many of them. In fact, this will be only the second condominium development in the world. The first one is already underway in Arizona, and all the necessary legal work here has been done, so we're sure that the idea is workable."

The new building would be called the Ilikai, and it was to be located right next to the Royal Hawaiian hotel on Waikiki Beach. The apartments would be 500 square feet each, and there would be several hundred of them. Each one would be privately owned, with a service charge imposed for shared management, entrances, hallways, and upkeep. The key difference was that people would *buy* these apartments rather than rent them. "You will get all of DGA's money out, *immediately*," Chin emphasized, "without having to wait for the rent."

I told him that it sounded like a winner. He then dropped me off at the Royal Hawaiian so that I could rest up for our meeting in his office the next morning. After a whirlwind tour of the idyllic island—including an excursion to the brand new Ala Moana, the first shopping center ever built in Hawaii—I rented a surfboard and attempted to ride it. No one had told me that you're supposed to put wax on the board to help your feet get traction, so I never actually succeeded in standing up, and I almost drowned trying.

I was then charmed by a visit with Lowell Dillingham, patriarch of one of the five families that "owned Hawaii." (One could only lease their land, not buy it.) He, Chin, and I sat on the beach at sunset and drank mai tais. After that, they took me to a luau. It all seemed like heaven, and I was totally sold. Soon after returning home, I went to Seattle to visit the project architect, John Graham Jr., who also showed me his newly finished design for the Seattle Space Needle. The design for the Ilikai had been drawn in the shape of a Y on its side, with its long leg skirting the edge of the beach, so that almost all views from the condominium would be of the ocean.

I presented the Ilikai project to the partners at DGA, and they liked it, too. Everything seemed to be falling into place. Then one morning I received an ominous phone call from New York City. The person on the other end of the line said, "Dick Dilworth would like to speak to you in person."

"Who?" I asked. I had never heard of Dick Dilworth.

"Mr. Dilworth is a Rockefeller partner," she answered, "and he wants you in New York as soon as possible."

I caught a plane the next day, and I was soon taking an elevator to the top floor of Rockefeller Center. Dilworth's office was even bigger than Clarence Randall's. The carpet and furnishings were elegant, and the view was breathtaking.

My host was livid. I don't believe he ever asked me to sit down. In my day, I have been glared at, scolded, even shot at, but never have I been so harshly hammered as I was that morning by J. Richardson Dilworth.

"We can buy property in Hawaii," he said. "We can build hotels and apartments anywhere in the world. We don't need *you*, a person who knows almost nothing about it, to put *our* money in real estate and then collect a fee and a carry, to add insult to injury. We became a limited partner in DGA because you told us you were going to invest in technology and honest-to-God entrepreneurs. We don't need you in Hawaii. We need you in Palo Alto—if we need you at all. Now, *get out,* and get to work on something you are paid to do."

I knew this was not an argument I was going to win. I was in and out of Rockefeller Center within fifteen minutes. In a general partnership like Draper Gaither & Anderson, the limited partners like the Rockefellers were not authorized to give directions to general partners regarding which investments to make and which ones to decline. This protects the limiteds from both tax and legal problems. It gives the general partners full control over the use of funds and overall management of the partnership. But this was not a time for a young associate like me to bring up the legalities of the situation, and I was happy to catch the next plane home and leave the decision to older, wiser heads.

Needless to say, we did not go ahead with the Ilikai investment. Advice from an important limited partner, particularly one of the Rockefellers' stature, outweighs ordinary business logic almost every time.

Chin Ho was not pleased, particularly after DGA's very positive reaction to the project. It turned out that the Ilikai would have been far and away the best investment DGA could have made in its seven-year history. In that sense, Dilworth was "wrong." Although, I can't disagree with his main point, which was that we should have been focusing on opportunities in our own neighborhood—one that turned out to be one of the most explosive growth areas in the entire country.

A postscript: The Ilikai was the first high-rise building near Waikiki, and in its early years, it dominated the Honolulu landscape. Today, for better or worse, the Ilikai is much humbled, surrounded on all sides by far taller and grander complexes.

The Next Phase: Draper & Johnson

In 1962, after three years of learning the trade, I decided to go off on my own. Yes, I had loved working with my father as well as the other partners and associates, and I had thoroughly enjoyed my first experience in venture capital. Our motto was "a deal a day at DGA," and although that was a joke, the truth was that we made a *lot* of investments in those three years, and the time passed quickly.

Despite numerous successful technology investments and a modest return on the $6 million fund, DGA unfortunately only lasted for a total of seven years. As I mentioned before, Rowan Gaither passed away within the first few years of the company's existence. In 1964, my father returned to Washington DC after five years in venture capital because he had become passionate about the problems of exponential population growth in developing countries. In Washington, he started the Population Crisis Committee (now called Population Action International), which has become the leading advocacy and research organization focused on the issue. With two of the three senior partners gone, DGA closed its doors just as the venture capital industry was about to flourish.

The scores of young entrepreneurs with whom I had interacted while at DGA had provided me with insight—that I hadn't developed at Inland Steel—into the tradeoff between risk and reward. It seemed like they were all having fun, and I figured that I could practice venture capital independently and have fun too.

By the time I left DGA in 1962, I had scraped together about $25,000 to invest in a new venture capital company. I had no other assets besides my $40,000 house, which had a $20,000 mortgage on it. Given that thin capital base, setting up my own venture firm seemed like little more than a pipe dream. But about that time, Al Pyott, a friend at Inland Steel, sent me a copy of President Eisenhower's "Small Business Investment Company Act of 1958." I read it carefully and learned that if I could come up with $150,000 and invest it in an "SBIC," the government would lend me up to $450,000 for ten years at five percent interest—in other words, three-to-one leverage. Bingo!

Okay, so I would need a partner—which I wanted, anyway—and he would put in half the money, $75,000. I would have to borrow $50,000 to add to the $25,000 that I had saved up. Although my father was skeptical of my plan and didn't want me to leave DGA, he offered to help.

In picking a partner for a venture capital company, it is important to find someone with skills complementary to your own. In general, I would recommend finding someone with good judgment, a record of success in another form of business, a warm and friendly personality, and an intuitive sense of where the world is going.

I called my old friend Pitch Johnson. I liked the fact that Pitch had the great benefit of a Stanford engineering degree. I was a history major, and if I was going to have only one partner, I felt that he should be a trained engineer. In addition, Pitch was from Palo Alto, and his friends—good people like Bill Edwards, John Bryan, Reid Dennis, and Bill Bowes—had already been extremely helpful to me. Most important, Pitch was very bright, extremely sensible, and a highly decent human being. He was fun to be with, and I knew his family well. He would make a perfect partner.

"Well, let me think about it," Pitch said, in response to my telephone call. "But it sounds good."

I hung up and blurted to Phyllis, "He is going to *do* it!" I was ecstatic.

We had agreed that he would come out from Chicago, and we would put the plan together to see how it looked. A few weeks later, we were huddled around my kitchen table, and as we were looking at the financial projections we became more and more excited. I asked Pitch if he thought he would have trouble getting $75,000 together for his half of the company.

"I've saved up $25,000 from my salary and an investment I made in Cessna Aircraft. I'll ask Mr. Holman if he'll lend me the other $50,000," he said.

Eugene Holman, Pitch's father-in-law, was the retired chairman of the board of Standard Oil Company (NJ), later renamed Exxon. Mr. Holman readily agreed, but became fatally ill shortly thereafter. Our company had not yet been formed, and the loan had not been formalized. Anxious and concerned about keeping his word, Mr. Holman summoned his executive assistant to the hospital and told her, "Draw up the papers for Pitch's loan, and be sure he gets the money when he needs it." Pitch was very moved by this consideration and still mentions it, with great affection for Mr. Holman for characteristically keeping his promise.

A week or two later, I flew out to Chicago, and Pitch and I met for dinner downtown to iron out the details of the new company. Although we were to be equal partners, one of us had to be president of the SBIC—which was a corporation, rather than a partnership—and the other vice president. Before I could even bring up the subject, Pitch said that he thought that I should be president because I was experienced in the business. We retained the fifty-fifty relationship and treated all decisions as if we were a pure and equal partnership throughout the existence of the firm. We never had a serious disagreement, and we made decisions easily from that point forward.

Pitch and I rented a one-room office from some friends in real estate development, on the top floor of a two-story office building on the Stanford campus, across the street from Draper Gaither & Anderson. Our address was 780 Welch Road. I was not fond of the street name because our business depended on developing a reputation for keeping our word and not "welching," or reneging. One wall of our second-floor office was all glass, and our wives would pull over to the curb, toot their horns, and wave whenever they came down Welch Road.

For a while, that was our only action. Whereas Draper Gaither & Anderson had good publicity, positive buzz, and a strong deal flow, we had very little.

So we decided to take our business on the road. We leased two Pontiacs from a dealer on Van Ness Avenue in San Francisco. With an exuberant and probably unfounded confidence, we headed out into the fruit orchards of Sunnyvale, Santa Clara, and San Jose. Every so often, we would come across a building with a name that sounded technology related, and we would pull into the parking lot—often unpaved—walk in the front door, and ask the receptionist if we could speak with the president of the company.

"I'll see if he's in," the receptionist would invariably respond. "What did you say your business was again? Venture capital?"

Soon a dynamic young man, usually close to our age, would be standing with us in the lobby.

"What did you say your business was again? Venture capital?"

"Yes. We make small minority investments in private companies, hoping to get a capital gain on the stock after helping the company in any way that we can."

"Well, why don't you step into my office, and I'll tell you what we do."

Morning and afternoon, day after day, Pitch and I did the same thing. Soon, we knew almost every small company in what would later be known as Silicon Valley. Before too long, our phone began to ring, and our callers were an interesting mix of promising entrepreneurs and bankers. Through our incessant touring and pitching, we had become known as the go-to guys for small technology companies on the peninsula, and the San Francisco investment banking community eventually figured out that they could save a trip by calling us. In fact, two of those investors, John Bryan and Bill Edwards, paid us $1,000 per month to include some of their money in our deals. They were good friends and were overly generous, but in the end it worked out well for them.

More and more, the entrepreneurs started to come to us directly. One day, a man walked into our office and showed us a fork-like plastic holder for a spool of dental floss. Neither of us flossed at that time, and we didn't know anyone who did, until our bookkeeper overheard us talking about it.

"Well, I use dental floss every night," she said.

"Every night?" We couldn't believe it. You learn interesting things as a venture capitalist.

She took home the little device, used it every night for a week, and reported back that she loved it. We called the inventor and agreed to put up $1,000 to fly him out to meet a friend of mine, Wally Abbott, at Procter & Gamble. Wally later became vice chairman of Procter & Gamble, and although he was a very smart man, he somehow concluded that P&G could manage to get along without licensing this miraculous device. We wrote off our $1,000, but Pitch and I both got in the habit of flossing every day.

Our first investment at Draper & Johnson was for only $60,000—a relatively small sum, but it was the maximum that we could invest in any one company under SBIC rules. We told Joe Giulie, the entrepreneur, that although we were limited to that amount, we wanted at least 25 percent of his company, Illumitronics, or we wouldn't do the deal. He liked us—just as we liked him and his product—so before long, we were in. Giulie was creative, mild-mannered, and serious: a productive combination in a small businessman. He had invented a device that checked the weight of any product—a can of soup, a box of soap, or a jar of jelly—as it was flying along an assembly line. If the container was underweight, it would automatically be taken off the line as a reject without slowing down the production line. He had several customers, but he needed money for more marketing in order to take full advantage of his first mover position in the fast-changing world of automation. We convinced Giulie to hire a CFO as well. (We were acting as business *builders*, not just investors. We could see that Giulie could go further if he added to his team.) We ended up hiring an unusually talented CFO, Hank Riggs, who went on to become a finance professor at Stanford University and the president of Harvey Mudd College.

Ultimately, Illumitronics turned out to be like many companies that pass through the venture capital universe. Its sales, profits, and management were all stable, but the company wasn't going anywhere. It was a good living for the entrepreneur, but it was a bad investment for the venture capitalists with a minority stake. Pitch and I eventually sold our stake privately for a modest return. On balance, though, we were glad to have invested in Illumitronics. We had helped Giulie with his company and had made a good friend in Hank. Most of all, we had broken the ice by making our first investment. You're not in the game until you make a bet.

Electroglas was another early Draper & Johnson investment. The company had been founded by Arthur Lasch, a bright and creative engineer who had spent his early years at Fairchild Semiconductor—a company already being recognized as a wellspring of brilliant innovation. Lasch's specialty was the design of diffusion furnaces used in the manufacturing of semiconductors, and he was extremely good at that. But like many good technical specialists, Lasch lacked serious management training and strong business acumen, so he needed a CEO to help him build a company.

Coincidentally, around the time we were asking Lasch about his plans for getting his first customer, keeping the books, reducing costs, and so on, I received an interesting phone call. "Hi, this is Chuck Gravelle," said the voice on the other end of the line, "and I would like to invest in one of your companies and help run it. Can we talk?"

Pitch and I agreed to meet with him, and soon he was sitting in our office chatting away as if we had all been friends for years. Chuck, handsome and lean, was about our age. Outgoing and confident, he was immediately likeable and was soon to become one of our closest friends.

"My story is a little different from most," he told us. "I'm from Minnesota, and I've just resigned as the VP of marketing for a motor boat manufacturer. It was a small company, owned and operated by one man, and sales were all local, to boaters on the lakes of Minnesota. The owner gave me an annual budget of $25,000 for marketing. I spent it all on one full-page advertisement in *Life* magazine."

I know that Pitch and I both thought exactly the same thing at that moment: *this guy has guts*. Our second thought was: *and he may be nuts*.

"How did it work out?" I inquired, trying to disguise my skepticism.

"Well," he replied, "the fact is, I made a lot of money off of that advertisement, and because of it, my wife and I felt uncomfortable in that little middle-class town in Minnesota. So we headed west, and here we are."

He had our attention at this point.

"Well, what did you put in the ad?" I asked.

He smiled serenely. "I put in a picture of the boat," he said, "and an application to be a company distributor, along with an order form for one boat at full price. We were deluged with orders, and overnight we had a national distribution network."

"Chuck," I said, laughing, "how would you like to run a diffusion furnace company?"

Starting Sutter Hill Ventures

Pitch Johnson and I probably made a dozen investments between 1962 and 1965. Our investments were small, as were the returns, but we were able to help most of our companies in one way or another. Pitch's operational experience was invaluable to most of our inexperienced entrepreneurs. After three years of working together, Pitch told me he was restless and wanted to find an operating company in which to invest and that he could run, saying he would rather be a player than a coach. I had to figure out what I was going to do next.

Sutter Hill was a shopping center development company, not far from us in Palo Alto. It had been started a few years earlier by Frank Lodato and his brother-in-law, Greg Peterson, both Stanford graduates and friends of ours. They had raised their capital through "Regulation A" underwriting, which restricted them to under a hundred stockholders, but it was a simple way to raise enough money—a few million dollars—to get their business off the ground. Their shopping centers were successful and had good reputations, but Frank and Greg were eager to diversify, and we knew that they had applied for and received an SBIC license to invest in small companies. They had just hired Paul Wythes, a classmate of Greg Peterson's from the Stanford Graduate School of Business, to help get it started.

I called Frank Lodato and said, "I understand you and Greg want to get into venture capital and have hired someone to help you."

"True," Frank responded, "and we've already made a deal or two."

"Well, then, let's get together," I suggested. "We have a bunch of good deals, but no Xerox machine and no receptionist. We have a lot of experience, and you have a lot of money." It was as simple as that. Within a few weeks, we had merged our operations.

Pitch and I paid off all of our debts and took some stock in the holding company. At that point, we went our separate ways professionally, but we have remained best friends ever since. Pitch never ended up buying and running a company, but he later started his own venture capital firm, Asset Management Company. He has made many stellar venture capital investments including a huge hit he financed with Bill Bowes—Amgen, the highly successful biopharmaceutical giant.

I became president of Sutter Hill Capital Company (the SBIC), Paul Wythes became vice president, and together we managed to build a strong brand around the Sutter Hill name. Both Frank Lodato and Greg Peterson had suggested the combined entity keep the Draper & Johnson name, but I preferred the name that they had come up with. In fact, when we later paid off the debt of the SBIC and started a new venture capital partnership, we decided to call it Sutter Hill Ventures. Frank had originated the name "Sutter Hill," and he told me the idea was to link the image of the gold from John Sutter's mine (site of the first major gold strike in California and the spark that set off the gold rush of 1849) with the beauty of the seven hills of San Francisco.

Sutter Hill did well, in part, because there was so little competition around. The inimitable Arthur Rock and his former associate Tommy Davis, who later founded Mayfield, were the only other venture capital stalwarts in the Bay Area at the time. As we became more and more active, however, the SBIC structure began to show its inherent limitations. By 1969, we had already started up some significant companies, including Diablo and Century Data—early disk drive companies—and Kasper Instruments, the first mask-aligner company to support the semiconductor industry. We soon realized that Sutter Hill's reputation was becoming bigger than our pocketbook and that we were in need of additional funds if we were to capitalize on that reputation.

"If you ever need more money, please give me a call," said my friend Charlie Mayer, as we were riding bikes one day in the tranquil confines of the Stanford University campus. "My company, Société Générale de Belgique, wants to get involved with technology investments, and I've told them about you," he said.

Charlie was staying with Phyllis and me on a visit to what was then becoming known as "Silicon Valley." He was feeling grandiose on that particular bike ride—at least until we got back to my unpaved driveway in Atherton, where his bike skidded as he attempted to make a ninety-degree turn in a fraction of a second. He went down in a cloud of dust, and I have never heard such language, before or since. Charlie was born in Austria, and having two languages to draw upon—as well as his Phi Beta Kappa brain—he generated an amazing torrent of invective, mostly on the related themes of my having put him on such a dangerous bike and for not having paved my driveway.

Thirty minutes later, his scratches were bandaged up, and we were calmly sipping iced tea in my living room. He picked up where he had left off, before the accident: "Don't forget to call me if you want to take in some new money."

Shortly thereafter, I *did* call Charlie. A month or so later, Max Nokin, the chairman of Société Générale de Belgique, was sitting across from me at a Stanford Research Institute dinner. He told me that after hearing Charlie's report, he was very interested in making an investment in Sutter Hill. The problem, he explained, was that Société was a holding company and that all of their investments in North America were made through Genstar, a Canadian holding of theirs. I would have to talk to Genstar.

So before long, I found myself at Genstar's offices, on the top floor at One Place Ville Marie in Montreal. As the owner of Canada's largest construction, cement, and home-building operations—and with an effective monopoly on Canadian tugboat operations on both coasts—Genstar surely had the resources to fund Sutter Hill Ventures. But did they have the vision, the gambling instinct, and the opportunistic spirit to plunge into venture capital in the San Francisco Bay area? I was both hopeful and skeptical.

The meeting went well. "We are very interested," said Angus MacNaughton, the young, brilliant, and energetic president of Genstar, as we sat in his office on the twenty-eighth floor of Montreal's most glamorous building. "When can I come out, visit, and kick the tires on some of your technology investments?"

I smiled and said, "Whenever you like. But they don't have tires. Some don't even have wires."

MacNaughton replied, "Well, I am a numbers guy, but I want to see what you've got, and I have never been to California. Let's go meet our chairman." After a pleasant and encouraging lunch with the chairman, I had a gut feeling that we were about to put Sutter Hill on the map. Both men were enthusiastic about moving forward. All we had to do was to convince MacNaughton that we were making sound and lucrative investments. That should be easy enough, I thought, assuming nothing goes wrong on his visit to California.

MacNaughton came out a few weeks later. After introducing him to some of our portfolio companies in the Bay Area, Paul Wythes and I decided to take him to Southern California to show him an investment that we were very excited about. Duplicon had been started by a British entrepreneur who had ambitious goals of putting his former employer, Xerox, out of business with an exciting new copy machine. His machine would be faster, cheaper, and more productive, and it also had a sleek new design.

Eager to show it off, the entrepreneur said, "Mr. MacNaughton, give me a dollar, and I'll copy it." To this day, MacNaughton claims that he handed over a one hundred dollar bill; I maintain that it was a one. We all watched with anticipation as the copy machine was switched on.

Without warning, the entire machine burst into flames with black smoke pouring out of both ends. Someone—certainly not I—had the presence of mind to grab a fire extinguisher and put out the fire. But the machine, the magic of the moment, and MacNaughton's bill were all destroyed—up in smoke!

I figured that we were done for. As we walked out to the car, I said, rather lamely, "Angus, I told you things don't always go as planned in venture capital. In fact, demos of new products almost never go as planned. I must admit, though, that I have never seen a demo go up in flames before." With his characteristic boyish grin, Paul joked that our quick exit from Duplicon would give us more time for lunch.

As it turned out, Duplicon's engineers made a few important changes in the design of the copier, and we were able to sell the company for a profit shortly thereafter.

MacNaughton was unfazed by our misadventure. A few months later, he personally signed a $10 million check—roughly $58 million in today's dollars—made out to Sutter Hill Ventures. All's well that ends well. We got our money. Genstar paid off our SBIC debt, we turned in the SBIC license, and Genstar took over ownership of the stocks in that portfolio, though we continued to manage the exits for them. We then started a new limited partnership, Sutter Hill Ventures, with the $10 million from Genstar.

Genstar would receive 80 percent of the profits as the only limited partner, and we would get the other 20 percent as general partners. The partnership has maintained a 35 percent internal rate of return (IRR) since it first began in 1965. According to Angus MacNaughton, Genstar's $10 million investment returned almost $1 billion before they sold their position. Today, with investors like Yale, Princeton, Stanford, and MIT, Sutter Hill continues to be one of the leading venture capital companies in Silicon Valley and has launched hundreds of successful companies and returned billions of dollars to its partners.

Tim Draper's First Six Investments

In 1981, I was appointed by President Ronald Reagan to be the chairman and president of the Export–Import Bank of the United States. I've skipped over my early forays into politics that had brought me into contact with Reagan and other prominent Republicans, but I'll return to those days in later chapters.

It was a whirlwind time for me. I hastily packed my bags, and I was just as quickly on my way. Phyllis would be coming along shortly, as we set up yet another new life—this time in the nation's capital. Sitting on the plane on my way to start this new chapter, I reflected with a good deal of nostalgia on the more than two decades that I had spent in the venture capital business. I was immensely proud of Sutter Hill, the success that we had achieved, and the great friends that I had made. I was fully confident that Paul Wythes, Len Baker, Dave Anderson, and Bill Younger would be able to carry on that tradition of success and maintain the good name of the firm.

Then my thoughts drifted to my son, Tim. I felt an immediate pang of guilt. *Oh, boy,* I said to myself, wincing mentally. *I've left poor Tim in charge of Draper Associates without giving him any kind of coaching or advice whatsoever.* Draper Associates was a small family fund with half a dozen of my personal venture investments. Up to that point, Tim had zero experience in venture capital, and I had abruptly left him in a sink-or-swim situation.

That was the bad news, and it definitely induced a powerful mixture of guilt and anxiety. I had had the benefit of my own father's support and counsel for several years before leaping out of the nest; now I felt almost as if I were abandoning my own son.

But the good news—I told myself—was that Tim was both very capable and exceptionally intelligent. He had a degree in electrical engineering from Stanford and an MBA from Harvard. He had spent several years at Hewlett-Packard and another two years at the investment banking firm Alex. Brown & Sons. So maybe I didn't have to be so worried. Maybe Tim would fare well in the uncharted waters of venture capital.

In any case, he was truly on his own. My schedule in Washington was incredibly demanding. So it wasn't until about a year and a half later— when Phyllis and I were visiting California for the holidays—that Tim and I finally got a chance to meet with our accountant, Morey Greenstein, to discuss the outcome of the various investments that Tim had made through Draper Associates. There were six at that point in time. Greenstein asked Tim to describe the status of each, one by one.

This was more than a quarter century ago, but in my mind's eye, I can still see Tim peering into the accountant's book with the name of each company neatly printed on each line. He slowly ran his index finger down the rows. As he went, Tim intoned the name and fate of each company. The first five, as I recall, were as follows: *dead, dying, bankrupt, probably won't make it,* and *not so good.*

Uh-oh, I said to myself.

"And what about that sixth investment, Tim?" I asked, trying to sound upbeat.

He looked up and paused. "Home run!" he exclaimed, flashing his trademark grin. He had spread the risk over several investments, and even though five of his six had flopped, the sixth—Parametric Technology— covered all the rest and then some. Parametric Technology now brings in about $1 billion in revenue each year.

In the venture business, one out of ten isn't bad—if that one is a bonanza. One out of six is better. Tim's experience shows that a young man can succeed in the venture capital business with a small amount of money, a willingness to sift through a lot of chaff to get to the wheat, a tolerance for risk, and a reasonably good calibration of the potential of various entrepreneurs. It is also evident that luck plays a part, but the old adage comes to mind: the harder one works, the luckier one gets.

I was lucky to have had a good education. I was lucky to have been in Silicon Valley in the early days of the venture capital industry. I was lucky to have been born to a great father. I was lucky to have matched myself up with superb partners, both general and limited. I was lucky that my network captured some astoundingly capable entrepreneurs and that we were all able to be helpful to each other.

Luck is clearly a big factor in life, but I would advise any young person interested in becoming a venture capitalist or an entrepreneur not to be overly fatalistic. Work hard, work smart, and luck happens. Each of us has unique qualities and characteristics, and the trick is to play to one's own strengths.

CHAPTER 2

How It Works

The big secret in life is that there is no big secret. Whatever your goal, you can get there if you're willing to work.

—Oprah Winfrey

AMILY HISTORIES CAN BE interesting, but it's probably time to reward those readers who have been patiently waiting for insights into the inner workings of today's world of venture capital. In this chapter, I look at the contemporary venture capital trade along what I consider to be its five key dimensions:

1. The *funders*
2. The *team*
3. The *pitch, the product, and the market*
4. The *deal*
5. The *relationship*

Observant readers will have already noted my casual approach to chronology, which continues in this chapter. I draw on my father's experiences and those of my own both before and after my "missing" decade of public service. I also call upon the experiences of my son, Tim, in part because he is probably more qualified than I to talk about the current state of venture capital. However, I'm convinced that the five topics listed above are pretty consistent from decade to decade.

You'll note that within this chapter, my perspective shifts from time to time. Sometimes the story is better told from the point of view of the venture capitalist; other times, it makes more sense to adopt the entrepreneur's perspective. I conclude this chapter with a summary of the top ten avoidable mistakes that entrepreneurs make, a list that attempts to bring together the world as seen by the venture capitalist and as lived by the entrepreneur.

The Funders

Let's assume that you're either an entrepreneur who wants to get a handle on this particular source of funds—venture capital—or you're a would-be venture capitalist yourself. How does the funding side of the equation work?

First, some ancient history. The first venture funds (at least in the contemporary sense of the term) were based in New York and were essentially vehicles whereby a single wealthy family—such as the Rockefellers or Whitneys—pooled its resources in pursuit of what it hoped would be an above-average financial gain. Early on, these families discovered that those kinds of gains were more likely to be made through early-stage investments in companies that had not yet gone public. When those startups *did* go public, or went through some other kind of successful liquidity event, the Rockefellers and Whitneys could make a small fortune—and thereby more than make up for losses from their other venturesome investments. Some of these investments (e.g., Minute Maid and Eastern Airlines) were big hits in those days.

Soon, variations on the family-dominated venture firm sprang up. General Doriot's Boston-based American Research & Development (ARD) was the first independent (i.e., non-family) venture capital company in the country. It was publicly traded: a strategic decision that eventually came to haunt Doriot and his colleagues, because it greatly restricted their strategic options. My father's firm—Draper Gaither & Anderson—was the very first venture capital company in the world that was founded as a partnership with limited and general partners. Setting the company up this way sidestepped the kinds of regulatory constraints that ARD faced and, more importantly, avoided the impossible problem of trying to value a passel of private stockholdings for public shareholders.

Today, there continue to be many family funds that use a portion of the family assets to invest in venture capital opportunities. But for a variety of reasons—by far the most important being the staggering growth of the venture capital industry—they make up only a miniscule portion of the money invested annually in venture capital. Today, virtually all of that money comes from venture capital partnerships, rather than corporations or families. In 1994, the floodgates opened when the law changed and allowed pension fund managers to invest in venture capital partnerships.

The venture capital partnership format is simple: The *limited* partners put in the money, and the *general* partners do the work. This is very similar to what happens when venture capital firms and entrepreneurs set up a new company. The firms put in all the money, and the entrepreneurs do (almost) all the work.

Draper Gaither & Anderson was a limited partnership, in which the limited partners—the Rockefellers, the then-private financial services firm Lazard Frères, and a few individuals—invested a total of $6 million in return for a 60 percent share of any profits. My father and the other general partners—Rowan Gaither, Fred Anderson, and Larry Duerig—split the other 40 percent, which is referred to in the trade as their "carry." The general partners earned an annual fee of 2.5 percent on that $6 million (i.e., $150,000) to cover their overhead.

This is the structure that is in place at most of the hundreds of venture capital companies in business today, large and small. The fees range between 1 and 2.5 percent, and the carry between 20 and 30 percent, but the principles are the same. It is hard to believe that today, even after the economic collapse of 2008, the venture capital industry still has $200 billion under management, and many venture capital firms have hundreds of millions and even billions of dollars to invest.[1]

For tax reasons, the general partners must invest as limited partners at least 1 percent of the total money raised for any given fund. Today, there is some question about whether the general partners should continue to receive capital gains tax treatment for their share of the profits, as opposed to the higher rates that would result if those profits were taxed as ordinary income. I believe that capital gains tax treatment has worked extremely well, resulting in a huge boost to the economy as well as giving incentives to the individuals involved. It's one of those "if it ain't broke, don't fix it" situations.

When we set up Sutter Hill Ventures in 1965, we adopted an 80-20 split and imposed a 2.5 percent fee—more or less the same structure that is still in place at Sutter Hill today. But there was and still is one major difference between the structure of Sutter Hill Ventures and that of the rest of the venture capital firms in the industry. Sutter Hill was set up, and today continues to operate, as an "evergreen partnership." What does that mean? Rather than asking the limited partners to invest in separate funds (e.g., Funds I, II, and III, each of which has a limited life of, say, ten years), Sutter Hill values the whole portfolio every four years and allows the limited partner to take its money out at that time—either in the form of cash or of its share of each stock in the portfolio.

When I left Sutter Hill in 1981 to join the Reagan administration, for example, I took my share of each stock and later became a limited partner. That turned out to be a very good decision because they continued to do very well. In fact, their 35 percent internal rate of return (IRR) attracted the attention of major institutional investors. You'll recall that the Canadian company Genstar provided all of Sutter Hill's early funding. When British Tobacco purchased Genstar in the mid-1980s, the tobacco giant decided that it was uncomfortable being in the venture game through its new subsidiary. Yale, MIT, Stanford, and Princeton stepped forward to purchase Genstar's Sutter Hill holdings. That was more than a quarter century ago, but all four institutions remain limited partners to this day and they are all very pleased with their investment.

The original evergreen structure is one reason why Sutter Hill keeps doing well: The interests of the general partners are totally aligned with those of the limiteds, and the interests of the younger partners are similarly aligned with those of the older ones. As noted, at most venture capital firms today, investments are made in a series of separate funds, with a stated termination date for each separate fund. This mainly reflects the preferences of limited partners, who don't like the idea of a simple valuation at the end of four years—as is done at Sutter Hill—because they're afraid it won't be fair. My response to that argument is that the exiting limited partner can always take its share of the stock and sell it over time. In other words, the limited partner doesn't *have* to accept the general partners' valuation if there is doubt about the fairness of that valuation.

So what's the downside to a partnership managing a series of funds (Fund I, Fund II, Fund III, etc.)? Simply stated, in that situation there is a tendency to put the money out too fast, mainly due to pressure from associates and younger partners who hope to get a bigger share of the next fund. In addition, just by the law of averages, the termination of a fund may hurt individual portfolio companies. In other words, just when a portfolio company needs funding the most in its own life cycle, the fund termination date may arrive and shut off the spigot.

The evergreen system, by contrast, never runs out of money. The new-capital requests of each company in the portfolio are considered on their own merits, when they come up on their own schedule. Stated a little differently, all portfolio companies are in the same funding pool, and *the pool never dries up*. Sutter Hill sells a stock when the firm feels it is overpriced on the public market or after a merger with a public company. That replenishes the pool, and everyone—limiteds and generals, old and young alike—all benefit proportionally. Here's one interesting measure of how well this model has worked for Sutter Hill: approximately half of the limited partnership position is now owned by the general partners, who over the years when a distribution was made, put their money back in alongside that of the limited partners rather than pulling it out. That's a vote of confidence!

As you can imagine, there are interesting generational possibilities in each venture capital firm. When we started Sutter Hill Ventures, I was thirty-seven and Paul Wythes was thirty-two, and therefore Paul socialized with an entirely different age group. It almost seemed like a different generation, and it certainly was an advantage. Paul had a mechanical engineering degree from Princeton and an MBA from Stanford. He was a perfect fit for me: easygoing as the day is long, but at the same time, extremely careful when it came to handling money. His engineering degree helped me better understand some of the products we were backing. His judgment on people seemed to complement mine, and our wives liked—and still like—each other.

When we went in search of additional investment capital, it was because we were inundated with opportunities. Paul and I needed more money, and we also needed more skilled hands in the office. We both understood that venture capital is geared toward young ideas, young markets, and young entrepreneurs, so we wanted to find competent partners who were younger than we were.

Our first two hires, Len Baker and Dave Anderson, both of whom are ten years younger than Paul, are still active partners at Sutter Hill Ventures to this day. Len, with a Yale mathematics degree and a Stanford MBA, has an extraordinary mind for crisp analysis, loves to be the devil's advocate, and is never in doubt. A very hard worker, he does the best due diligence of all of us. Coincidentally, he joined the nineteen-person Board of Trustees of Yale University when I retired from that board. Dave, with an electrical engineering degree from MIT and a Harvard MBA, has a good eye for innovative technologies, a friendly but reserved demeanor, and an open manner that spells trust and loyalty. Dave brings a warmth and kindliness that puts entrepreneurs at ease when they come to Sutter Hill.

The four of us worked together for over fifteen years, and we complemented each other well. The age mix was an important ingredient. It helped us attract the best entrepreneurial talent, get our arms around new markets, and keep day-to-day relationships smooth and productive. To this day, we still owe a lot to each other, and we all know it.

The original split of the carry between me and Paul was 12.5 percent for me and 7.5 percent for Paul. After a few years, I gave Dave and Len each a 2 percent carry, which still left me with a slightly larger ownership stake than Paul. In my opinion, though, there wasn't a hierarchy based on ownership positions. We treated each other as equals, and our decisions were made easily and collectively. Yes, Paul and I were "out front" more— mainly because we had both been salesmen and enjoyed that role—but every deal belonged to all of us. We would designate one partner to be on the board of each new investment, but it wasn't necessarily the part- ner who brought in the deal. More important, when a portfolio company needed help, we all pitched in. Len's analytical mind, Dave's engineering talent, Paul's overall savvy, and my people sense all combined in produc- tive ways. After I left Sutter Hill, more talent was brought in, and the firm pursued a greater degree of specialization—a changing trend in the devel- oping Silicon Valley venture capital industry. But on balance, Sutter Hill still works just about the way it did when I was there, and it is still in the top tier of all venture capital firms.

Most of the venture capital companies that were established in the 1960s and 1970s are still around. Kleiner Perkins and Sequoia are among the most successful—with huge hits like Yahoo and Google—but there are many other very solid venture capital companies such as Mayfield, Greylock, NEA, Charles River, and Menlo Ventures that continue to make good deals, solidify their reputations, and build the stature of our industry.

Reputation is a big, *big* deal. This is true in almost every form of busi- ness, but I believe it's particularly true in venture capital—both on the company and the industry levels. The reputation of a venture capital firm takes a long time to establish, requires a lot of ongoing attention and is very easily dented and damaged.

Wise venture capitalists—the ones who earn a solid reputation—are used to working on a handshake. They willingly share the ever-present risk of failure and are not in it for the quick gain through stock flipping. These individuals are careful, because each investment should have the poten- tial to lead to a long-term, successful relationship. They are also careful because their reputation is inextricably tied to each company they back. Any company may fail, and many do. In and of itself, that is not a big deal. But how should venture capitalists behave in the wake of that failure? Are they calm and consistent in good times and bad? Is their advice helpful?

Are their contacts useful? Do they follow through on their commitments? If they don't get consistently good grades in all of these areas, they won't last long in what is a surprisingly tight-knit community.

"Angels" and Their Money

There is another funding source that should be explored. Today, there are several thousand individuals in Silicon Valley who act as venture capitalists but who operate independently from any venture capital company. They are known as "angels."

When I first worked in the venture capital business, the only angel investors were found on the fringes of the theatrical world. An "angel investor" might help a new musical open on Broadway; angels were never involved in financing new companies. At that time, the new company was referred to as a "special situation," and the money came from friends and family, the partner of a small investment firm, or a wealthy individual who had an adventurous spirit. None were angels.

Some of today's angels are extraordinarily effective, and every so often, one of them makes an investment that launches a company into the stratosphere. Ron Conway, for example, is an angel investor who has a reputation for having a hard time saying "no" to a young, serious, and vigorous entrepreneur. He has a vast network of contacts, and he often hears about new opportunities long before other people do. One Conway deal seems to lead to the next one. (This is true for most of us, but somehow, it's more true for Conway.) He usually limits his investments to $100,000, but he makes plenty of them—maybe more than any other individual in Silicon Valley.[2] Last but not least, he *promotes* his investments aggressively, in most cases turning them from good to better.

Often angels form breakfast, lunch, or dinner clubs, and entrepreneurs are invited to come make a pitch to the group. That makes it more worthwhile for the entrepreneurs, because they have a larger audience. Of course, this format is also helpful to the angels, because they get the benefit of other opinions in real time before committing to an investment.

The internet has made angel investing more practical and has probably increased a competent angel's chances of success. Today's angels can sift through mountains of information without ever leaving their desks. They can check resumes of the founders and get background on the market. They can reach out to all of their contacts at once to solicit their opinions on a given opportunity.

Angel investing, once thought of as an exotic variation in the industry—the last gasp of the rugged individualist—is here to stay. In many cases, it can serve as the lifeline for a startup before that new business can command the attention of more professional venture capital. Not all angels have the energy and connections of a Ron Conway, but every rookie entrepreneur needs all the help she can get. Sometimes even a relatively ineffective angel is better than no angel. It should be said, however, that whether entrepreneurs work with venture capitalists or angels, the quality and reputation of the investors are sometimes even more important than the money that they provide.

Strategic Investments from Corporations

Many of the young companies that have raised one or two rounds of venture capital find that another source of funding—strategic investments from corporations—is less dilutive and often more helpful.

This form of financing is not usually available until the company is well on its road to success. The investing corporation is interested in getting a front-row seat to observe a new technology, service, or approach that may have an impact on its industry. Economic return on the investment is usually of secondary importance. For this reason, both the entrepreneur and the venture capitalist are happy to welcome strategic investors—unless, of course, divulging their company's secrets is too dangerous to the success and future health of the company.

Examples of Draper Richards portfolio companies that benefited from strategic investments along the way include Kyte (an online and mobile video platform) and Online Anywhere. Telefonica, the European telecom behemoth, invested in Kyte at a very early stage—in fact, within two years of our original startup funding. Kyte's new technology allowed video to go directly to the cloud and be instantaneously delivered anywhere, without even going through the internet.

Online Anywhere was a company started by three Indians and backed by Draper Richards and Motorola Ventures. Motorola was interested in staying at the forefront of the technological innovations in the telecom industry, and it set up a separate entity to invest in new companies alongside venture capitalists.

Online Anywhere makes me laugh whenever it comes to mind. My partner Robin Richards and I were in Mumbai, India, when we were approached by Sridhar Ranganathan, one of the company's founders. He wanted to demonstrate a brand new concept: he would run our computer on the local TV set and do it wirelessly. We sat down and waited and waited and waited. The power had gone out all over the city, which in those days—the mid-1990s—was commonplace. We were disappointed that we were going to be unable to see the demonstration, as Robin and I were leaving for America the following morning. Sridhar, however, assured me that his partner would come to my house in California the following week and that he would show it to me there.

Sure enough, my doorbell rang the following week, and in walked Sridhar's partner Anurag. The demonstration was very impressive, and even though this technology seems outdated today, I had never before seen computer output on a TV screen. I was excited and eager to make an investment. Anurag said goodbye, obviously pleased with my reaction to his demo. That night, however, when I tried to turn on the TV, there was no power. *Uh-oh! I'll never invest in this company,* I thought.

The next day, the TV repairman came to fix the problem, and after just a few minutes, he gave me a bill for $40. I asked him what Anurag's demo had done to the television and what he had done to fix it. He smiled and said that Anurag had simply pulled out the plug and that he had plugged it back in—another short-lived crisis in the life of a history major wrestling with today's complex world of technology.

Draper Richards invested in the company along with Motorola, and it turned out to be a financial success. In 1999, we sold the company to Yahoo for $80 million,[3] and they only made one change to the company: they changed the name from Online Anywhere to Online Everywhere.

Venture Debt

Another form of early-stage financing is venture debt. I find it very unattractive. It works like this: when venture capitalists have made an investment in a new company, and it is clear that more money will be needed down the road, they may line up venture debt from a commercial bank that offers it.

Venture debt is a commitment to lend money to the company when it has "burned through" (I don't like that expression) its venture capital. The venture debt carries high interest and warrants to buy stock later at the same price paid by the venture capitalists. It is very expensive for the company, and I never recommend it. If things go awry, as they often do in a company's early life, the venture debt will become a huge burden, and in my opinion, it is far better, less expensive, and less traumatic for the entrepreneur to bring in more venture capital than it is to take on venture debt. When the venture capital funds run out and other alternatives such as merger and acquisition are not realistic, it may be time to shut the company down. This requires careful planning and sensitive management, as discussed in Chapter 7.[4]

The Team

I don't usually attempt to speak for my father or my son, but I think all three generations of venture capitalists in my family would agree that when it comes to investing in a new business, you have to make sure that you have the right entrepreneurial team. Nothing is more important. In fact, nothing is even a close second.

Simply stated, does the leader have the characteristics needed to lead? Does he have brains, judgment, charisma, commitment, empathy, staying power, integrity, and optimism? Of course, no one has it all, but the best leaders are well endowed with most of these qualities.

How do venture capitalists figure out whether they've found the right leader? The fact is, they usually *don't* figure this out during the first meeting. I tend to spend a lot of time in that initial interview asking many personal questions. There's education to consider, of course. Why did you choose that school? There are the brothers, sisters, the spouse. What are they doing now? Hobbies or outside interests? Do you know so-and-so? Why did you come to see us rather than some other respected venture capitalist?

Sooner or later in the middle of one of these seemingly meandering sessions, my would-be entrepreneur starts pushing a thick packet of paper across the table. "Oh, yes," I reply cheerfully. "The business plan. Yes, we'll definitely have to take a look at *that* again. Meanwhile, tell me more about great teams you've been on, what made them great, and what you contributed to them."

Personal style certainly enters into this interview process. I always try to be hospitable and friendly on the first visit. Other venture capitalists, like Arthur Rock, take a different tack. He says, "Hello," and then does little more than listen closely as the entrepreneur tries to fill in the void created by Rock's silence from that point forward. If it's a strong idea, and if the entrepreneur is good on his feet, this isn't a problem. But if it's a weak presentation—bad content, bad delivery—it can be over within fifteen uncomfortable minutes. A glum-looking Rock says, "No," and it's all over.

Like me, Rock feels that the most important ingredient in any company is the brains, guts, and vision of the leader. If the product turns out to be wrong, the visionary leader will come up with a new one. If the market shrinks, the leader will steer the whole team toward another one. So it's not surprising that Rock and I are less interested in the details of the plan and more interested in appraising the talents of the leader.

Since I emphasize the importance of choosing exactly the right CEO, I always chuckle when I think of how we got "exactly the right leader" for Quantum Corporation, one of Sutter Hill Venture's biggest home runs—a company that became the largest hard-disk-drive manufacturer in the world before that part of the business was sold off to Maxtor.

Three or four talented engineers came in to the Sutter Hill offices and explained their strategy for a new startup. Before too long I asked who the CEO would be. They looked at each other sheepishly and admitted that they hadn't thought about it. Then one blurted out, "Jim, why don't you be the president?" Another said, "Yeah. Jim, you have the least work to do!" James L. Patterson led Quantum until its revenues crossed the billion-dollar mark. We had witnessed one method of selection for "exactly the right CEO." Quantum Corporation was fun and we laughed all the way to the bank.

If the first meeting between the venture capitalist and entrepreneur goes well, the work *really* begins for the skilled venture capitalist. Thorough testimonials for the whole team are essential. Those references generate more references. I always ask a person referred to me by the entrepreneur if I should talk to anyone else. Often that person relaxes when I ask that question. She might feel constrained from telling the whole truth about the entrepreneur but knows that I will get the whole story from Steve or Joe—and obviously feels that I need to hear that story. Loyalty challenged by integrity is a complicated subject.

The entrepreneurs with the lowest risk of failure are those who know their field intimately; have run another company (or division of a company) similar to the one they plan to launch; and have an idea for a new feature, market, or technology that will support an industry breakthrough.

Dave Bossen, who wanted to start a new company, comes to my mind immediately. I met him on the recommendation of a college friend, Bill Hodgson, a partner at the investment banking firm William Blair & Company, who had been following Bossen's career. I had dropped by Bill's Chicago office on the way back from a fishing trip in Wisconsin, and he had suggested that I get in touch with Bossen, who had just moved to California. In the venture capital industry, connections are very important. Staying in touch with contacts and friends (i.e., networking) has resulted in a large venture capital deal flow for me.

In the late 1970s, Bossen had run a division of Industrial Nucleonics in the Midwest that made specialized equipment for the paper industry—equipment that measured the thickness and moisture content of paper as it runs through the mill. Bossen had asked his management to invest in digital technology so that the company could improve its products. However, he couldn't persuade them to spend the money, so he left to do it on his own.

Bossen had a degree from MIT. He was a proven manager and knew the territory. He understood the manufacturing process, the needs of the marketplace, and most of the somewhat specialized customer base. Sutter Hill Ventures quickly agreed to back Bossen, and with our help, he found not only the money he needed but also the necessary talent with digital engineering expertise at Stanford. He named his company "Measurex." Because Bossen had all of the essential leadership characteristics, I was more confident that Measurex would be a winner than I was about any other of my hundreds of venture capital investments. My confidence turned out to be well placed: after successfully launching on the New York Stock Exchange, Measurex became the preeminent company in its field and was acquired by Honeywell in 1997 for nearly $600 million, a handsome price in those days.[5]

Another example of a lower-risk venture-capital investment is a new company started by one of the senior managers (not necessarily the CEO) of a successful company in which the venture capitalist had made an early investment. As long as there is no ethical issue and the manager is leaving with the blessing of everyone concerned, the odds for success in the new company are good.

While I was at Sutter Hill Ventures, we were lucky enough to have backed Prime Computer, a Boston-based company with a powerful team and a great line of products. I went to visit them, but the president was unexpectedly unavailable, so Bill Poduska, vice president of engineering, came out to the lobby to greet me. Before I left, he asked me to step outside. "I have an idea for a new startup, and it is going to knock your socks off. How do you like the name Apollo Computer?"

After making sure there was no conflict of interest, I asked him to fly out to Palo Alto and discuss it with my partners. He was in our office a week later, and he told us that the idea was a line of unique computer "work stations." After lunch at the Palo Alto Club—started in 1952 by David Packard and Bill Hewlett—we agreed to terms, and Sutter Hill would lead a venture investment that later included Greylock and the Rockefellers. Coincidentally, we eventually sold Apollo Computer to Hewlett Packard for a whopping gain.

It was all so easy because Bill Poduska was a known quantity and a brilliant, creative leader. The message is that one good deal often leads to another—primarily because the venture capitalist and the entrepreneur know each other well and trust each other implicitly.

Leadership is not necessarily a forever thing. I have backed many companies as startups despite knowing in my bones that the founding entrepreneur was only capable of leading the company through the startup phase. The result? Almost all of these have failed or at best have generated a meager return on the capital invested. But it's not necessarily a question of finding the Forever Leader, either. Some of the best venture capital results come when the entrepreneur knows that he is unqualified to manage a fast-moving, quickly changing young enterprise for very long, and immediately asks the venture capitalist to help find an experienced CEO (along with supplying the money). I talked about Yahoo in this regard in the Introduction; Google is also a good example. Sergey Brin and Larry Page, although extremely brilliant and creative, were also young and inexperienced. They needed the superb leadership skills, business acumen, and the strategic brainpower of Eric Schmidt to take Google to the top of the world and make it not only a household word, but also the most useful social and business tool since the telephone.

While I'm assessing the leader, I'm also looking at the rest of the team. Are they exceptionally strong, and will they work well together? Usually a solid leader picks a solid team, but not always—and the weakest link can sink the venture. In the late 1990s, I invested in a new company called Barter Trust, which was set up to barter over the internet (e.g., trading a block of hotel rooms for advertising space). The business had a very capable leader with serious marketing skills. The supposedly world-class trading system—the company's raison d'être—was up and running, and trades were being made. But our super-sophisticated technology kept breaking down, and as it turned out, our Chief Technology Officer (CTO) simply wasn't up to the task. I still think Barter Trust could have been a great company, had we taken the time to properly vet the credentials of our CTO.

Let me say it again, in slightly different language: *each member of a team of entrepreneurs is crucial to a company's success.* In the startup phase, that team is necessarily very interdependent, and each member must serve in multiple capacities. Cooperative and empathetic types are particularly useful in the beginning stages of a growing business. A venture capitalist should dig deep to find these characteristics—and conversely, try to spot signs of a disruptive personality. Sometimes it's hard to distinguish the disruptive individual from the merely socially inept—the geeky types who populate our fair Valley—but it's an effort worth making nonetheless.

If you (either in the role of venture capitalist or CEO) realize that there is a weak or disruptive member of the startup team, take action *sooner,* rather than later. Everyone involved in the effort has to be of the highest quality. There can be no compromise. Think of it this way: the odds are stacked against any new business, including venture-backed companies. A decisive, talented, and demanding CEO can improve those odds substantially, moving the needle in the right direction. A weak team member can push that needle back in the wrong direction. If the CEO seems to be postponing the inevitable, the venture capitalist should push hard for change. However, if the venture capitalist finds she is having to push too hard and no changes are being made, it may be time to change the CEO.

The focus on the team continues well after the initial investment decision. A good CEO discusses every important new hire with the venture capitalist—and other members of the board—prior to making an offer of employment. Over the years, I have been asked to interview dozens of candidates for various significant job openings, and I have always felt that it was a good use of my time. I think most of my CEOs wound up thinking so, too.

In summary, there are no strong companies with weak management. If you're a venture capitalist, you need to get the management right the first time. If you do, your job will be easy. The money will pile up while you are sleeping, you'll have fun with the entrepreneur inside and outside of board meetings, and you'll build a strong and enduring relationship.

The Pitch, the Product, and the Market

Now let's switch perspectives and look at the "pitch"—the effort to sell the venture capitalist on the proposed business—from the point of view of the entrepreneur.

The previous pages tell you the most important thing you need to know about your pitch: first and foremost, you have to sell your *leader* and your *team*. You have to give me—the venture capitalist—confidence that you can beat the odds and pull this thing off.

Here's an experiment you can (and should) run. When you hand over that business plan to a venture capitalist, and if he looks at it while you're in the room, watch where the eyes go first. Most venture capitalists will go to the part of your plan that describes the key people in the proposed venture.

What else? Obviously, the venture capitalist wants evidence that your *product line* is differentiated from the competition. We often hear that there is "nothing new under the sun." Nonsense! If that were true, Silicon Valley would be a myth. I would say something new is created here in the Valley every time the sun rises. No, not all new products are unique. But if you can show how competitors will have a hard time coming into the market behind you, that's helpful to your cause. Similarly, if you can point to a patent or other "strategic narrows" that will defend your market position, that's a good thing. Be sure that there is a large moat around your castle, or early success will be inundated by the competitive reaction of existing industry stalwarts.

The size and character of your *market* is obviously of great interest to potential funders. Bigger is not always the only right answer. A niche market is all right, but if you know that you're limited to a niche market, you'd better be prepared to argue that you will be in a position to own it all.

Draper Richards' investment in DivX in 2000 was an example of a successful company that put itself in a position to dominate a small market. The idea was to come up with software and hardware combinations that could compress high-quality video onto chips, which would enable users to see video on the "three screens" (TV, computers, handhelds) that dominate our information stream today.[6] The product worked beautifully—often a DVD I see now says DivX on it—but my point here is that DivX has a strong position in a niche market. Although there are millions of DVDs made every day, the pennies paid for each DivX product don't add up to enough money to allow more than one or two major companies to play in that space.

Wilf Corrigan, founder and longtime CEO of LSI Logic, had his eye on a huge market when he told me he wanted to start a company. I had just finished speaking at a conference in Los Angeles about the promise of venture capital, and Corrigan was in the audience. The year was 1980, and Corrigan was still running the legendary Fairchild Semiconductor. Knowing his track record, I said I would be *honored* to back this new company and that I would tell my partners at Sutter Hill Ventures about it as soon as I got back to Palo Alto. It took somewhat longer than I expected to convince them to go into this deal, in part because Corrigan had a reputation for being a very tough, almost ruthless, manager. We ultimately did the deal, and LSI Logic quickly took off, in part because the market for the "large-scale integration" (LSI) of computer chips was a huge and growing market—the kind that comes along once in a lifetime. Yes, there are other big players in that space, but the space is big enough for all of them.

Obviously, your pitch (and especially your business plan) has to give a clear sense of your *capital requirements*. How much do you need, and when? What are your fixed and variable expenses, and how will that ratio change when you start experiencing all that growth you've promised us? Understand that savvy venture capitalists will look at these numbers as more or less imaginary, especially the further out you go on the timeline. But the venture capitalist wants to know that you have good numbers sense, that you've wrestled with these issues, and that you've given them your best shot.

And of course, we want to see that you've got "skin in the game." Are you putting a substantial piece of your personal net worth at risk? If you're *not* betting on yourself, why should we?

One last word of advice in this realm: if you ever make a pitch to me, I'd prefer that you don't use the phrase "burn rate." I don't want to think that you will ever be burning my money. You may be investing my money faster than you are making a return on it. That's fine. Just don't burn it. Although, I do have to admit that the term has become so common these days that I've even caught myself asking, "What's the burn rate?"

I haven't talked about the *style* of your pitch. I don't have much advice on this score, other than to *be yourself.* Nothing is more awkward than watching a nerd attempt to be a smooth salesman. Speak from the heart. Use PowerPoint sparingly—as a tool for summarizing information instead of a crutch for struggling through a half-memorized speech. Rather than stare at a screen, I prefer to look people in the eye when they are making their pitch. If you already have an office or functioning plant, invite me over. Show me your confidence and enthusiasm. Make your world sound like the exciting place that it is.

Realistically speaking, many of the best venture capitalists are pressed for time, and therefore the entrepreneur may have to describe the opportunity in an unusually succinct and efficient manner. When this is the case, it is essential that the entrepreneur keep his cool. An extreme example of this was the pitch Daniel Graf, founder of Kyte—the online mobile and video platform mentioned earlier—made to Draper Fisher Jurvetson back in June 2006. I had met with Graf already and liked what I saw, so I asked Tim to set up a meeting with the partners.

Like most venture partnerships, DFJ has its partnership meeting every Monday morning, and Graf's meeting was scheduled just before that, at 9 A.M. He would have thirty minutes to make his pitch to all of the partners. Graf and I arrived on time, but because of various scheduling conflicts, most of the partners weren't in the room until 9:25 A.M. At that time, one of the partners turned to Graf and said, "You've got five minutes." Graf was taken aback. He probably had thought that they would have delayed their partner meeting, but he remained completely cool and confident. He whipped out his smartphone and took a photo of Tim—which immediately appeared on the large screen for all of us to see. The demonstration would not be impressive today, but in those days this type of technology was a novelty, and the partners were immediately sold on the potential of Kyte. In five minutes, Graf had made his case, and DFJ, after completing further investigation, became the lead investor in Kyte.

The Deal

So what kinds of deals get struck between the entrepreneur and the venture capital firm?

If you jumped to this section first, I'd recommend that you go back and read the previous sections. Believe me: they're more important. If you have a great idea and you execute brilliantly, you will be amply rewarded for those efforts. Do not, however, take the first offer on the table until you have compared it with a few more term sheets from competing venture capitalists. Also, remember that the highest dollar bid, although tempting, isn't necessarily the best bid, because it may not factor in the intellectual capital and reputation of the venture capitalists involved.

That said, there is an almost infinite number of variables that can affect the deal. Prices go up and down, whether you're dealing in tangibles (e.g., real estate) or intangibles (e.g., a potentially hot startup). The stock market, the price of gold, and the valuation of private companies all fluctuate. In this kind of turbulent context, what's "fair"? It all depends.

During my first twenty years in venture capital—that is, in the 1960s and 1970s—we had a rule of thumb that we used in order to measure the value of a private company with no earnings, but with good revenue and good prospects: we were willing to pay one times annual sales. The majority were technology-driven companies, and experience suggested that most were likely to double their revenue in a few years and become profitable. So our logic was as follows: if the company was profitable and selling "over the counter" on the stock exchange, it would be priced at about twenty times earnings and making 5 percent after taxes, which translates into one times sales. Of course today extraordinary new social markets demand a different kind of reasoning.

I've already introduced the subject of capital requirements. Most entrepreneurs are too optimistic. The majority of venture capitalists are *also* too optimistic. But that bright outlook is a prerequisite in most cases. Startups are fraught with unknowns, and it is almost impossible to get any of them off the ground without a big dose of optimism. We venture capitalists also have to be hard-nosed. Most of us assume that it will take two or three times the money in the plan, regardless of how "conservative" you, the entrepreneur, seem to be. Keep that in mind if and when your potential venture capitalist starts sounding "unreasonable" in their deal making.

Recently, some entrepreneurs have adopted an approach that starts out with a bridge loan. The idea is to get some early money—say, $1.5 million—without having to value the company. The bridge loan then gets the opportunity to convert into stock at the price established by the next venture capitalist when the $5 or $10 million round is needed, a few months down the road. The argument is that until the business has a product and a customer, no one can really know what it is worth.

This technique is usually most effective with angels. In fact, most established venture capital firms won't consider it. Why? Because the risk at the front end is the highest, and the investor or bridge lender has no idea what his money is buying. He must wait for someone else to set the value, and—although he usually gets about 25 percent warrants, in addition to conversion rights—that doesn't seem like a smart bet to me. Simply put, the warrants allow the investor to buy 25 percent more stock at the same price at a later date.

The indeterminate value of a startup reminds me of an episode that took place a few years back, in one of the cyclical peaks of over-the-top optimism in the entrepreneurial and venture capital communities. An unimpressive team of young entrepreneurs came into my San Francisco office and made their presentation for a company that needed $3.5 million to get started. When they finished, I asked what they thought was a fair deal. They said that the company was worth $7 million and that two-thirds for them and one-third for us sounded about right. I asked how they had arrived at the $7 million valuation. The answer, which the CEO delivered with a straight face: "There are seven of us, and we figure that we are worth $1 million each." I asked them why they didn't pick up three more employees on California Street before they came in the door, at which point they would have been worth $10 million. They left without our money and left us chuckling at their naïveté.

Typically the first round—the "A round"—of venture capital will take the company through one or two years, and this is followed by a "B round." Although I try to look at each opportunity as unique, I generally start with a fifty-fifty attitude; the venture capitalists put up all the money for the A round and the entrepreneurs put in all the blood, sweat, and tears. So unless the money needed is unusually large or small, a fifty-fifty split seems fair. When more stock options are needed for new employees or when more money is needed, both sides share the dilution equally.[7] In frothy times, entrepreneurs tend to want more, and every once in a while it is obvious to me that the entrepreneur deserves more, because of the especially exciting promise of their team and its project. If the entrepreneur is able to put money in alongside us in order to own more stock, and is willing to pay for that stock on our terms, I encourage it. In other words, if she puts in 10 percent of the money, and we have a fifty-fifty deal, the entrepreneur and team would own 55 percent of the company.

I always check how the entrepreneur plans to divide the stock and stock options that are available to the team. If it's 90 percent for one founder and 10 percent for the other six key team members, a yellow flag goes up in my mind. (Aren't all these team members highly competent and therefore valuable?) Again, though, as a venture capitalist, you have to look at opportunities on a case-by-case basis. Sometimes, even a seemingly unbalanced split of the stock and options can be the right one because of the extraordinary talent of one person or one individual's ownership of an essential patent.

Stock options are usually created for all employees on exactly the same basis. (In fact, to create a "qualified" stock option plan with its associated tax advantages, all employees *must* be treated alike.) The board approves all stock options, and in most venture capital–backed companies, 1/48th of the options vest every month, with a one-year "cliff."[8] In other words, the employees must stay at least one year before any of their options have value. After one year of employment, options continue to vest every month, until 100 percent are vested at the end of the forty-eighth month.

The B round of venture capital tends to involve some complicated calculations for both sides. Should management go outside for the B round, or should it be satisfied with a negotiated price and a certain amount of new money from the original venture capitalists and other original investors on an "inside round"? Sometimes the entrepreneurs' lawyers will recommend going with an outside investor, in part to help set a "market price" for the company and avoid problems down the road. That's fair enough, but those same lawyers should put a price on the distractions that an "outside round" will create for management. (Remember, we're still in the all-hands-to-the-pumps mode in this growing company.) Assuming that the two sides trust each other and are otherwise compatible, and also assuming that the venture capitalists are satisfied with the company's progress, I usually try to make the case that an inside round is better.

If the company is doing well and goodwill prevails, the B round is usually a piece of cake. On the other hand, if targets are being missed, management is panicked, and the venture capitalists are discouraged or "tapped out," things can get sticky. This is the juncture at which everyone involved may be eager to talk to new potential investors.

It's also a stage that tests the moral fiber of the venture capitalist. You're an optimist. You have put a ton of money into this struggling company. There's possibly a path through the woods to riches on the other side. But that path now looks like a hard one. How much of the disappointing news should be shared with a prospective investor who calls to ask your opinion on the company?

Honesty is the best policy. A straightforward discussion of the pros and cons is the only way to go. If the company is doomed, it is better to face up to that fact early. As the original venture capitalist, you will undoubtedly be asked to participate in the B round along with the new investor. If the money is dead on arrival, why do it? Why throw good money after bad?

In conclusion, the deal, or how the pie is divided, is important at each stage of financing but should always be put in perspective. Getting enough money in the company to keep operations running smoothly, and keeping the team well motivated and enthusiastic, are the main drivers in every deal. Loyalty, generosity, cooperation, and fair play are well remembered by all parties, and usually pay off big in the long run.

The Relationship

Does the relationship between the entrepreneur and the venture capitalist go beyond money? The answer is, it can, it does, and—in most cases—it *should*. Yes, venture capitalists have a particular point of view, and their vested interest has to be taken into account. At the same time, the venture capitalists probably have far more experience with the life cycles of companies than does the entrepreneur, so they can be sage counselors when key decision points arrive. They can provide financial expertise, help with hiring, make certain customer contacts, give endorsements for follow-on funding, and scout out potential buyers if acquisition is an appropriate option.

We should briefly examine the role of a board. The board is the ultimate decider on policy and strategy, but it can't run the company. The CEO is the commander-in-chief. She must lead the board, guide it, and use it to move the agenda forward—always with the stockholders and employees in mind as the most important stakeholders. Board meetings should be about 1) briefings from management, and 2) decision making. They should not be about insignificant minutiae of the business.

Typically, the venture capitalist is only one voice among many on the board, but as the representative of key investors in the company, he has to ask and answer a particular set of questions. For example, how is the CEO performing? Is she in command and comfortable in that role? A good listener? Leading or following? Done well, either is okay. Mahatma Gandhi once said, "There go my people. I must hurry to catch up with them, for I am their leader."

The quality of the CEO is crucial, but of course, from time to time other members of the team should attend and participate in board meetings. Is the team on top of the details? Do they all seem to be headed in the same direction? Do they know their role and know how important their part is in the success of the whole venture? Is the company strategy clear to all and does the team support it wholeheartedly?

In searching for answers to these questions, venture capitalists should be circumspect, collegial, and nondisruptive. At the same time, they can't be shy about digging deep and asking tough questions. They can't be afraid of asking follow-up questions when they don't understand the thread of logic as presented. Like every board member, they have a legal and moral responsibility to probe, challenge, and inquire. They should insist that board materials be emailed well before the board meeting and then study them carefully. Materials should include detailed financials, engineering, sales, marketing, and personnel reports, as well as a CEO summary of the current standing and strategy for the future. Customer penetration, status of the product or service, and competition, in particular, should be of substantial interest to the board.

Sometimes questions regarding strategy generate a difference of opinion between the venture capitalist and the entrepreneur. Unfettered honesty in presenting the logic behind each position and a healthy open discussion can lead to improvements or radical change in company strategy. Entrepreneurs, however, should be unwavering in their defense of a strategy that has been thoroughly vetted and has their total confidence.

One example of this from my experience is Thomas Layton, then-CEO of OpenTable, and his defense of the company's strategy. While I was not on the board of OpenTable, Draper Richards supplied the startup with seed capital, and so Thomas and I met often. He was a strong strategic thinker and a good operator. My role, as I saw it, was to stay informed of the company's progress and to challenge him every once in a while.

My wife and I enjoy dining out at restaurants, and there are plenty of them in San Francisco. After making the investment in OpenTable, I would ask the hostess how she liked OpenTable whenever I saw the computerized reservation station near the entrance of the restaurant. She would always reply something along the lines of, "We love it. We can't live without it. It has made making reservations and our lives so much easier."

Now, each restaurant pays $1.00 per person in any party when the reservation is made through OpenTable. During one of my discussions with Thomas, I asked, "Why don't we charge $2 per person, and why don't we have the restaurant pay up front for the computerized reservation system instead of leasing it to them? Or why don't we just sell them our software and get out of the hardware business entirely? They all love us, and right now we are too capital intensive."

Thomas had good answers to every one of my questions, and most of them revolved around having control over the restaurant's entire reservation system, reducing its costs, improving its service, and never letting others even think about competing with OpenTable.

He wanted to own the territory and was willing to sacrifice short-term profits for long-term sustainability and dominance. In the end, he and his team built a great company that is now deeply embedded in the vast majority of quality restaurants in almost every U.S. state and many international cities. In 2009, the company had a successful public offering of its stock, and it is on very solid footing and has great potential to continue expanding.

My message here is to encourage openness, honesty, and clarity in the relationship between a venture capitalist and an entrepreneur. Neither of them is likely to be right all of the time. Both of them might be right in their logic, yet a decision has to be made, and in the end I think that it is really the entrepreneur and/or the CEO who must make that decision. The venture capitalist can only, and should only, advise the CEO and then support his decisions as aggressively as possible.

It is my opinion that a venture-backed company typically goes through three stages on its way to becoming a mature, healthy, and profitable entity. In each of these three stages, the board (including its venture-capitalist representatives) plays a somewhat different role, and therefore should change its methods (and perhaps its membership) accordingly.

The *trial and error* stage is where most startups with a new idea and unproven management begin. The board (and especially its venture capitalist members) can help by providing personnel contacts, customer references, and advice on strategy for the new management team. It is crucial to try to get it all right at this juncture in a company's history. Here is where an entrepreneur builds her reputation. At this point, the board— with calm, intelligent, and experienced support—can be most helpful.

The second stage, *reality*, comes a little further down the road. The management has hit some targets and probably missed some too. The board is either pleasantly surprised by the progress, or is pressing for good answers. Why are revenues so disappointing? Why doesn't the product work yet? Why are expenses so high? Sorting out the answers and deciding whether to put up more money comes next.

The third stage, *rev it up or close it down*, is full of choices, many of them difficult ones that the board has to confront. The perennial optimists never want to let go. The realists are losing confidence. The naysayers are holding their nose and saying, "I *told* you so. If only you had changed direction, or management, or strategy as I had recommended months ago, we wouldn't be in these dire straits."

If the decision *is* to close down the company, the board has a fiduciary responsibility to see that there is enough money at the end to manage the process in a businesslike manner. Yes, banks and secured lenders come first, but management and employee commitments also must be honored, suppliers have to get paid, the landlord has to be satisfied, and so on. Again, think *reputation*. It's a small world, and you most likely will want to do business in it again.

Every case is different, and yet—as suggested above—there *are* some patterns in manager-board relationships. To illustrate both of these points, let's analyze in depth a relationship between a real-world company and its board.

Steve Wyle and Elena Medo were trying to convince me that their new startup, Prolacta Bioscience, would become as successful as Baxter Bioscience. They would use the same model but would substitute milk for blood plasma.

What exactly did this mean? Baxter gathers blood from donors and the Red Cross at very little cost, processes it, and sells blood products at a very high price. The company is very successful. The plan for Prolacta was to replace infant formula with mother's milk for premature babies in hospital neonatal intensive care units (NICUs) across the country. The new company would collect the milk, pasteurize it, and sell it.

Intuitively, I thought that mother's milk would be more nutritious and generally better for babies than formula or any other substitute, so I figured that it would be an easy sell. "But wait a minute," I said to Medo, the company's founder and chairman. "Why don't the hospitals use mother's milk *now*?" In response, Medo related the history of milk banks. They were plentiful throughout most of the twentieth century. In fact, until the early 1980s, milk banks were the food source used for most babies when their own mothers could not lactate, which is often the case with mothers who give birth prematurely.

Then came the HIV/AIDS epidemic, and instead of fifty or sixty milk banks in the United States, the number shrank to eight or nine. Mothers and hospitals alike were fearful that another woman's milk might be contaminated, and they switched to infant formulas. Nestlé donates their formula to the hospitals in the hope that mothers would buy it from the store once they were able to bring their babies home. "Oops. *Free?* Everybody likes free," I said to Medo. "How are we going to sell Prolacta milk when the competition is giving their product away free?"

"Because we have a better product," she responded. "It's the *real thing.*" This was true. Studies show that human milk provides nutrients that are not fully replicated in artificial milk products.

I set up a meeting with Lucille Packard Children's Hospital at Stanford in order to gauge the reaction of one of Prolacta's potential customers. The five or six staff members in the meeting at Lucille Packard included the operations manager, the nurse in charge of feeding, and the MD responsible for the NICU. All were ecstatic about the idea of starting a new company that would process mother's milk, guarantee that it is free of any contaminants, including HIV, and deliver it for as little as $6 per ounce.

I was still uncertain about the supply, so I conducted an informal "mother-in-law survey" and checked with a few young mothers about their willingness to give extra milk if it were to be frozen, processed, and sold to NICUs. One of these young mothers was my wife Phyllis's niece, who had delivered twins; each had weighed only one and a half pounds at birth. The mostly affirmative responses that I received gave me confidence that milk donations would be plentiful. (In reality, this proved to be inaccurate, and we had serious supply problems later on but eventually managed to overcome them.) Mother-in-law surveys are quick and easy, but in hind-sight, I would definitely recommend spending a little extra money and time on more sophisticated research.

In any event, I was ready to go. In Elena Medo, we had a talented and creative president who had come up with the idea after starting another company that produced a novel breast pump—a company that her husband was running at the time. In Steve Wyle, we had a solid businessman whose father had started Wyle Labs (an aerospace contractor), and whose own experience seemed to have equipped him for managing a small startup. We had a product that would be donated to us and that would be sold at $6 per ounce. We had a few PhDs who would oversee what seemed to me to be a simple dairy. In addition, we lined up a national distributor who sold other products to hospitals. We only needed to invest a few million dollars and would own about half the company, though we expected to raise more money shortly after getting started. Best of all, this company would save lives.

What could go wrong? Soon after our money was in, Medo called me with some disturbing news. "What do you mean, you *fired* Wyle?" I asked incredulously. "He is the business brains in the company."

She replied, "Well it seems on Saturday, Wyle was at our brand-new plant, and the telephone guys couldn't install our phones without going through our neighbor's office with a master key he had obtained some-where along the way. The neighbor is pressing charges. Wyle is still in police custody, and I fired him."

The ethics of the "crime" itself are clear. Wyle should not have entered the adjacent office without permission. But how should one react to Medo's decision to fire him? That was my dilemma. Should I be loyal to Wyle, whom I didn't know too well, but I certainly had no thought that he had a dishonest bone in his body? Moreover, his business sense was needed. Should I back up Medo in her decision? After all, she was the founder, and she had made a firm decision with a reasonable rationale. I suspected that this incident was the culmination of other problems between them that I had not yet uncovered. I later talked to Wyle, who was contrite but felt unfairly injured. It was true that they had had other problems, and I probably did the right thing to tell Medo that we should move on and that I would help her to find another general manager.

In the interim, we needed someone to hold things together, so I sent in Jim Simmons—a good friend and an experienced executive—to take on the role of general manager on a temporary basis. About three weeks later, I got a call from Simmons. "She fired me, too!" he said.

I went down to Monrovia, where Prolacta Bioscience is headquartered, to investigate. Medo told me Simmons had made a forecast miscalculation, and she thought that with the office manager, plant manager, and others she had on board, they didn't need Simmons. The company was just getting started, and I was not ready to draw a line in the sand, so again I gave Medo the benefit of the doubt. She was key to the success of this venture, and I couldn't afford to lose her. She had the motivation because it was her idea. Medo also had the contacts with the few remaining milk banks and a plan to expand their number. She also maintained the connections with the hospitals, and she was the creative force in the company.

The milk supply problem was getting worse, but Medo reported that Pauline Sakamoto, the president of Human Milk Banking Association of North America, would expand the number of milk banks in cooperation with Medo and her new system for cleaning the milk. Sakamoto had been one of our contacts when we were doing our diligence to decide whether or not to invest in Prolacta. She had been very encouraging and this had been a factor in our decision to back the startup. Imagine my surprise when at the next board meeting, as nervous questions arose about the dwindling milk supply, Medo casually said that she was no longer speaking to Sakamoto.

Things were not going well, and we all knew it. I also found out that Prolacta had given $400,000 in advance to another entity that was going to open milk banks and deliver processed milk. Nothing had been delivered. On the other hand, we *were* processing milk, and the end product was good. Some babies with serious health issues were still alive because of Prolacta.

Later, we found out that we no longer had supply problems. "Two Maids a Milking," an affiliate that works exclusively with Prolacta, had collected huge supplies of milk through an appropriate incentive program conducted over the internet. The problem then became sales—and, unfortunately, another ethics problem.

The board gathered in good spirits and had just had a tour of the newest changes in the plant. The very capable operations manager, whom we had hired from Baxter, had directed the tour. The coffee was served, the slideshow was over, and then Medo dropped the bomb. The head of our national sales distributor, who was then sitting as a board member next to me, had just been indicted for grand theft. He was a handsome, suave, and well-dressed thief. He had moved the cash he made in his company offshore through a complicated credit card scheme in order to avoid U.S. taxes.

Wow! This was a first for me. My initial reaction was to move my chair slightly away from him. Needless to say, he resigned from the board that day, and we fired his firm. It was an easy decision for all of us, but we knew it meant a lot of work to rebuild our distribution network. Good ethics comes first every time.

With disappointing initial sales, Medo explained her idea for an additional product. During one of the board meetings, Medo mentioned that we could produce "fortifier," concentrated human milk with essential minerals and proteins, which would be added to regular mother's milk to help babies grow. (The standard of care at the time was to add cow-based protein, and it was suspected that this caused irritation and intolerance in some babies.) This product had never been made on a mass scale, and Medo felt it would be a good product. Then she let us know that we needed at least $250,000 to purchase the equipment and that she would like to do so in the next few months. The problem was that the cash on hand at the time was $300,000, and the company was spending $200,000 per month. There was no reason to spend the money when we were still trying to prove we could sell the first product.

Michael Labadie was our general contractor and was in and out of the facility more often once the operations manager left. He knew we were thinking about the equipment needed to make fortifier. He also performed work at other local biotech companies, including Baxter. As luck would have it, one day a Baxter employee asked Labadie if he would help dispose of a piece of equipment. Turns out, it was a miniature version of what we needed—perfect to develop proof of concept—and after thorough cleaning, sterilization, validation, and testing, it worked. It allowed us to prove we could make what is now the flagship product of the company.

It was time for a new CEO. We had a good, cooperative venture capital team. DFJ Frontier had brought me in, and I had brought in John Bryan, Bill Bowes, and Prabhu Goel—all highly experienced individual investors. In fact, Bowes is a founding partner of U.S. Venture Partners and is one of Silicon Valley's most successful venture capitalists. At first, we put a lot of effort into interviewing and making an offer to a prospective CEO candidate, "Donna," who seemed to be incredibly qualified based on her background and accomplishments. However, during the normal background check, things started not matching up: her employer did not verify her stated income, and the dean of her MBA program who had signed the glowing reference letter about "Donna" had never heard of her.

Ultimately, venture capitalist Frank Foster of DFJ Frontier took the reins as interim CEO and did a superb job of stabilizing the company while we brought in new investors. Medo stepped aside to become the company's chief evangelist—which was really her role all along—and seemed happy to be out of the day-to-day line of fire. Alta and Arcturus, the new investors, were knowledgeable in the health care field, and the price they paid for Prolacta stock was substantially more than our cost. Finally, we brought in a fine and experienced CEO, Scott Elster, from Baxter, who was particularly strong on operations. Sales are still a problem today, but we have paid for extensive clinical studies, which are a necessary element in the sales effort as caution and safety are naturally so important to all hospitals. We have now agreed to have Prolacta products, regular and fortifier, distributed by Abbott Labs, and sales have begun to accelerate rapidly.

The point of this long Prolacta saga? It's simply that a board can and should be an active player in a company's fortunes *when it is a necessity*. It proved a necessity at Prolacta far more often than I had ever expected.

But when the moment of crisis passes, the board should go back to a more passive and supportive role.

The Top Ten Avoidable Mistakes of Entrepreneurs

Over the last fifty years, I have come across and worked with an array of entrepreneurs from a variety of industries, and I have noticed that there are certain preventable blunders that seem to crop up repeatedly. To an extent, everybody has to reinvent the wheel and make his own mistakes, but I offer the following in the hope that at least *some* entrepreneurs will take *some* of these prescriptions to heart and maybe make their avoidable mistakes less costly.

1. **Creating overly optimistic projections about market size and customer acquisitions**.
   My advice: Do your homework in terms of market research. Don't blur the line between the number of potential customers who *might possibly* buy your product and the number who actually will. Don't overlay an arbitrary percentage on the largest possible customer base when estimating potential market share. In three words: *know your customer.*
2. **Underestimating timelines**.
   My advice: Remember the sage advice offered by Douglas Hofstadter, in a maxim he named after himself: "It always takes longer than you think, even when you take into account Hofstadter's Law." Wrap your mind around that one.
3. **Trying to do everything yourself**.
   My advice: There are only twenty-four hours in a day, and you generally can't get by on less than seven hours of sleep—maybe six. Nor can you be an expert at everything. Surround yourself with an experienced team, all of whom are smarter than you.
4. **Failing to master the elevator pitch**.
   My advice: Develop, practice, and memorize an accurate and concise message about your company's value proposition. Then get everybody else in the company to do the same, with *consistency* as a paramount goal.

5. **Not downsizing when necessary**.

   My advice: Don't be afraid to cut back. You may lose a little face but not as much as you think. You'll lose a whole lot more face if you go out of business as a result of not having made timely cuts.

6. **Being inflexible**.

   My advice: Deal with your changing reality. The market shifts. New competition arises. You have no choice but to be flexible enough to deal with the inevitable twists and turns.

7. **Not developing a clear marketing plan**.

   My advice: It's not enough to have an amazing idea, or even an amazing product. How is the world going to find out about it? Startups often fail to put sufficient resources behind sales and marketing. Don't be one of them.

8. **Building a board that consists only of friends**.

   My advice: Go for every kind of diversity. Find people with industry knowledge, contacts, operational experience, and enough time to be helpful. Beware of out-of-towners; telephonic board attendance is not optimum.

9. **Not taking action in a recession**.

   My advice: This is a corollary to number 5. Make cuts in human resources as necessary, but also: get suppliers to reduce prices and give better service, improve efficiency, and turn up the heat on your competition.

10. **Not knowing the right way to approach venture capitalists**.

   My advice: Be prepared. Read this chapter and this entire book. Be very clear about the problem that your company proposes to solve and who your customers will be. Provide detailed information about yourself and your key associates. After your first meeting, follow up, and don't be shy. After all, you will have the best product or service in the world. Right?

CHAPTER 3

What It Takes

No pessimist ever discovered the secret of the stars or sailed an uncharted land, or opened a new doorway for the human spirit.

—*Helen Keller*

THROUGHOUT MY MANY YEARS in the industry, young people have often asked me how to become a successful entrepreneur. In this chapter, I'm going to lay out the characteristics that I think help entrepreneurs succeed—*what it takes*. By the same token, I believe that these qualities are also possessed by top-tier venture capitalists. In fact, I would argue that the same characteristics help people thrive in almost any human activity. No, not every attribute applies equally to all, but I believe that the ideas in the following pages should have relevance for all professionals.

To avoid the monotonous tone of most similar lists and also to hold your attention, I'll illustrate these characteristics with stories that come from a diverse range of contexts and time periods.

Brains and Education

People who set out to make a difference need to be smart enough to understand how the world works today and be able to envision a range of better
outcomes for the future. I'm not saying that you have to be the "smartest
person in the room," but this does require a certain level of candlepower.

Another part of the equation is *disciplining* your natural gifts through
education. Go to the best schools you can get into, and then figure out how
to pay for them. If you go on to business school, at least three great things
will happen to you there. First, you will learn the ins and outs of how business works. Second, you are sure to make friends who will serve as the core
of your network for the rest of your life. And finally, if you're diligent and
open to new experiences, doors will open for you that would otherwise
have remained shut. Knowing how the world of business actually works is
a prerequisite to changing that world for the better and making money in
the process. If attending business school is not an option, then you have to
work hard to create as many connections and networks as possible so that
you will be able to draw upon them throughout your career.

I hope an example from my own student days and early career will
help make the point. (Antiquated though my story may seem, the same
kinds of things go on today.) While I was attending business school in the
early 1950s, I met and studied under a unique character—General Georges
Doriot—who was both an outstanding professor and the first independent
venture capitalist in the country. From this experience, I learned the profound impact that a professor can have on shaping the lives of his students
and, in turn, shaping the world.

Doriot had known my father when they were both in the Army in
Washington DC during World War II, where Doriot—on leave from his
Harvard teaching post—was serving as chief of military planning for the
Quartermaster Corps. Doriot had been born in France, and although he
had been in the United States since 1921, he retained a strong French
accent. (Indeed, some said that his accent actually grew thicker over the
years.) At business school, both before and after the war, he taught a second-year course called "Manufacturing." In fact, the course had very little

to do with manufacturing, a subject taught by other faculty members. Instead, Manufacturing was how Doriot presented his personal code of life—his philosophy on how a young businessman should conduct himself and succeed in a world full of potential pitfalls.

I took Manufacturing as one of my second-year electives, and I ended up enjoying it more than any other course I took at business school. Doriot was spellbinding as a lecturer—an absolute genius at mesmerizing a class of young, eager business wannabes. He focused almost entirely on teaching a particular way of looking at the world. *Keep your antenna up. When you go to the boss's house for dinner and he offers you his favorite alcoholic concoction, don't refuse it, but find a potted plant and water it with the drink. Fuzzy heads can't keep their antenna up. Always stay alert, mes amis, particularly around the boss.*

As I understand it, Doriot was the first professor at Harvard Business School to ask his students to divide into teams of four or five for various projects. (This is standard operating procedure at business schools today—sometimes called "team building"—but back then, it was seen as a truly strange way to teach.) My team focused on "metalworking tomorrow," which was natural for me because I had spent one summer working the night shift at Jones & Laughlin Steel in Pittsburgh. Doriot was very enthusiastic when I told him, toward the end of my business school days, that I had a job offer from Inland Steel. "Good," he said emphatically. "Chicago is a *man's* town. Steel is a *man's* work." Looking back, I can see that he had a significant influence on my decision to take the offer. I should admit, however, that I did not have a smorgasbord of choices because it was 1954, a recession was underway, and I had a young wife and baby to support.

Coincidentally, there's a second whole subplot to the Doriot story, which also intersects with my life. In the years immediately following World War II, a group of influential people in the Boston area—Doriot, MIT President Karl Compton, Boston Federal Reserve Bank President Ralph Flanders, and others—began worrying about the economic prospects of New England, which appeared to be turning into a commercial backwater. In part to combat this trend, they founded a pioneering firm called "American Research & Development": the first independent (i.e., nonfamily) venture capital firm in the country. Doriot agreed to serve as ARD's president starting in 1946, and for the next several decades—including the years that I was at business school—he had one foot in academia and the other in venture capital.

I confess that I knew almost nothing about this at the time, even though the launch of ARD had attracted a great deal of public notice. With the exception of occasionally hiring a graduating MBA student, Doriot kept his two worlds mostly separate. An interesting side note is that two decades later, General Doriot and I met to discuss the possibility of merging Boston-based ARD with my firm, Sutter Hill Ventures. He spoke of the synergy from which we would both benefit, should our two firms merge. He had MIT and Harvard Business School in his backyard; we had Stanford engineers and MBAs in ours. He had a more experienced team; we had experimented with some of the newest technology. The deal, however, fell apart when it became apparent that he was adamant about all of the decision making being done solely in Boston.

I saw Doriot once more after that. He was in the front row when I received my business school's Alumni Achievement Award in 1982. I suspected that he had had something to do with my being chosen for the award, and I was truly touched that he came to the ceremony, smiling and enthusiastically applauding his former student. It wasn't a moment for major speechifying on my part, but even so, I have always regretted saying so little of consequence in my acceptance speech that night. I especially regret my failure to mention how much I owed General Georges Doriot.

My point in relating my experience with General Doriot is to reinforce that I honestly believe that if you find professors who are intrigued with the real world, you will learn things from them that you simply can't learn in other ways. They may give you unique opportunities—or they may help you make your own.

Energy and Passion

These are two closely linked characteristics that seem to fuel one another in the great entrepreneurs and venture capitalists that I've met. Energy helps you discover and pursue your passion. Passion gives you more energy, which leads to more discoveries and pursuits.

Let me tell you about a person who comes to mind when I hear the word "energy": a young man named Jonathan Bush, one of former President George H. W. Bush's nephews. I first encountered Jonathan in 1988, when he was eighteen years old. I was in New Hampshire to support George H. W. Bush's campaign. A few nights before the state's presidential primary, I noticed that there was this high-school kid standing on the back of a pickup truck with a megaphone in his hand. It was dusk, and it was windy and *cold*. But there he was, full of enthusiasm—charming, witty, and even inspiring. I was absolutely struck by his obvious passion as he extolled the virtues of his uncle, the then–vice president and future president of the United States.

That impression grew stronger as I watched Jonathan operate over the next thirty-six hours, as we both went about our respective jobs. He seemed to be *everywhere*—calling on the phone bank, handing out "Bush for President" signs, going door to door, and hamming it up with friends and family. I remember thinking to myself, *This kid is going places.*

Jonathan's father and I had been vice chairmen of the first Bush for President campaign, and we had developed a strong and enduring friendship. So when he called me one day in 1997 to say that his son—now in his late twenties and armed with a Harvard Business School degree—was trying to make it as an entrepreneur and would welcome any suggestions I might have, I was delighted.

So much so, in fact, that I didn't wait for Jonathan to come to San Francisco. Instead, I flew right out to Massachusetts to get reacquainted with him and learn about his company. As soon as I arrived in his new office in Watertown and met a few of his teammates, I knew that the trip had been worthwhile. Jonathan still had that boyish charm and—most of all—the *energy*. He was so excited about his plans that he could barely hold still in his seat as he was explaining them to me with rapid-fire delivery. His passion was contagious, and I knew that it could not be stifled. Jonathan was a rainmaker; he would make things happen.

The company was athenahealth, and according to Jonathan, its mission was "to become medical groups' most trusted business service." In doing so, it would replace Gladys in the small office in the back of every medical clinic in the country. The mythical Gladys was the beleaguered office assistant who managed insurance claims, billing, and all other non-medical records. The service, athenahealth, would deliver all of that, and more, over the internet. My partner, Robin Richards, and I decided that we would bet on Jonathan and his team. Draper Fisher Jurvetson and Venrock joined us in the investment.

Fast-forward to 2007. The company went public, and Draper Richards got a return of ten times our investment in the company. Our faith in Jonathan's energy and passion was justified. In 2008, athenahealth posted client collections of $3.7 billion, which earned the company just under $140 million in revenue. By that point, nearly 1,000 people were working for Jonathan and his cofounder, Todd Park, and more than 22,000 medical providers subscribed to the company's web services.[1]

I shouldn't make this sound easy or inevitable. Doctors working in small clinics used their Gladyses to protect them from salesmen—and getting in the door wasn't easy for athenahealth. This was only one of the challenges that the company faced in those early years. In my opinion, the huge success of this startup, which has had an enormous impact on the medical industry, would never have occurred were it not for Jonathan Bush's energy and passion.

Another leader with energy and passion who undertook a very different challenge in a very different way was Narayana Murthy, founder of Infosys, the foremost computer software outsourcing company in the world. I call him the David Packard of India.

In 1994, I established Draper International, the first U.S. venture capital firm to focus on India (I will tell you more about the firm in subsequent chapters). My two new partners and I first met Murthy at his newly built Infosys campus, about thirty miles from our office in Bangalore. A company campus was a new concept in India—plenty of land, every possible accommodation for employees, and a very modern look that was startling against the backdrop of India at that time.

Murthy, a short, slight man with thick glasses and a confident persona, greeted me with a strong handshake and a warm smile. I complimented him on his futuristic campus, and he immediately got to the point.

"I am passionate about my employees, and I want them to have the very best working conditions possible," he said. He went on to tell me that he was also insistent that all of his employees own stock or stock options. And finally, he said that he was passionate about wanting all of them to know how essential they were to the company, and also to realize that the company relied on them to reach the highest level of excellence in doing their jobs.

To underline his point, Murthy called in an elderly man who was working in the kitchen adjacent to his office. Murthy picked up one of the water glasses on the table in front of us and held it to the light, turned it around, and squinted while he surveyed it closely for what seemed an eternity. To the great relief of the elderly employee, who had washed the glass, Murthy smiled and politely said, "You are obviously doing a good job," as he set the glass down. When we were alone again, he said, "I want every single employee to be as passionate about his or her job as I am about mine. We are all owners of Infosys, and if every one of us does an excellent job, we will own an excellent company." Unfortunately, Infosys was not looking for venture capital at the time, or I would have pulled out my checkbook right then.

I should point out that Murthy even helped Draper International directly by taking advantage of our short visit and suggesting we talk to Devdutt Yellurkar in Boston. Yellurkar led a small group of Infosys employees in building supply and inventory management software. Because they were employees of the company, Infosys owned the technology, but Murthy felt that this technology was not in line with company strategy, which was only focused on selling outsourcing services to others.

Murthy wanted them to spin off from Infosys and form an independent company. Yellurkar and his team were looking forward to the challenge of the startup game. We at Draper International wanted to use our venture capital funds to help Indian-led startups. The result: a three-way deal and the founding of Yantra. Of course, it took a good bit of due diligence on our part before we finally closed the deal with some negotiation and a three-way virtual handshake over the Infosys videoconferencing system, which was a novel technology at the time.

As a board member of Yantra, I learned that Yellurkar had extraordinary passion and energy, too, as he struggled to compete against the steamroller impact of much larger companies—for example, Oracle—that were already embedded in the marketplace. The company eventually became a successful leader in the supply management industry, and we all cashed out for a big gain when it merged with a division of AT&T in 2004.

I should point out that we had brought in Don Feddersen and Ezar Armony, partners of Charles River Ventures in Boston, and both were extremely helpful in guiding the management strategy. Being that I was based in San Francisco, if I hadn't shared the deal with Charles River Ventures, my investment likely would not have been nearly as lucrative.

Passion and energy are critical and present in the leadership of every great company, large or small. There are entrepreneurs, however, who are fully as passionate and energetic as the successful ones, but something else was missing, and all their efforts end up in the dustbin; they are left with nothing to show for their work. Why? In many cases, the cause is just plain bad luck or unfortunate timing. These are truly sad stories, and my heart goes out to them and their families, who have both sacrificed so much for so long. Remember that on average, entrepreneurs in startups put in fourteen-hour days, and their divorce rates are the highest in the country. I always try my best to help them in getting to their next gig. I also try to point out that they have matured and gained important experience, so they will have more to offer their future colleagues.

Expertise

I won't spend as much time on this subject, which is pretty much self-explanatory. You take your smarts, education, energy, and passion, put them all together, and then you go out and get *really good* at something.

Why did Jonathan Bush and Todd Park succeed with athenahealth? Yes, they had smarts, energy, passion, and enough money from us and others to get going. But the company originally grew out of Bush and Park's personal experiences. Before starting athenahealth, they had purchased a birthing practice in California and found that they were almost immediately "buried in paper." They provided quality services to their clients, which is what they wanted to do in the first place, but they found that they were spending most of their time and energy trying to get paid. They "looked for a solution but couldn't find one."[2]

This is an absolutely classic, typical scenario: those with a personal interest in something hit a snag, go looking for someone else's existing solution to the problem, and discover to their astonishment that there *isn't* a solution yet. Then they go to work solving the problem. Don Fisher, founder of The Gap, once told me that he could not find Levi's blue jeans in stock that were cut appropriately to his pant length—only to his waist size. He therefore started up what became a behemoth retail enterprise "to do it right." In Don's case, he saw the need but lacked the experience, so he hired the best retail brains he could find, and the rest is history. You can also think back to the example in the Introduction of Yahoo founders Jerry Yang and David Filo: the internet is a cool place, and we need to be able to navigate around it. So why hasn't anybody come up with a directory of cyberspace? What would such a directory look like, and how would it get built? Without a base of sectoral expertise, you can't begin to answer those kinds of questions, regardless of your passion for the subject.

There's another by-product of expertise that is invaluable to the entrepreneur: *self-confidence.* If you believe that you've come up with an elegant, economical, and unique solution to a pressing problem, it shows. It's apparent on your face and in the way you carry yourself. When the venture capitalists walk in the room, they are looking for signs of that calm self-assurance: *these people are onto something.*

And finally, expertise and self-confidence lead to yet another desirable attribute in an entrepreneur—*decisiveness.* You can never have all the information you need in order to act. It's impossible to research away all the variables and unknowns. There's no way to take all of the uncertainty and risk out of any significant decision. All you can do is do your homework as best you can and then act decisively. That's another thing that venture capitalists are looking for: the ability and willingness to make the tough call without hedging. Being confident about your skill set makes that possible.

Here's a helpful illustration of how far expertise can carry you. The year was 1979. On the same side of the conference table with me in my Sutter Hill Ventures office were my partners Paul Wythes, Dave Anderson, and Len Baker. On the other side were David Crane, Larry Kaplan, Alan Miller, and Bob Whitehead: four Atari game designers who wanted to start their own game company, which they proposed to call "Activision."

Why were these four talented programmers—known as the "Gang of Four" at Atari—so eager to leave the gaming company at the height of its success? Looking back, Crane remembers it as a decision that hinged on *equity*, in both senses of the word:

> We saw that as a group, we were responsible for 60 percent of [Atari's] $100 million in cartridge sales for a single year. With concrete evidence that our contribution to the company was of great value, we went to the president of Atari to ask for a little recognition and fair compensation. [Atari President] Ray Kassar looked us in the eye and said, "You are no more important to Atari than the person on the assembly line who puts the cartridges in the box." After that, it was a pretty easy decision to leave.[3]

I asked Crane what he wanted to do in the long run, assuming that their new startup idea proved a success.

"All I want to do for the rest of my life is to design games," he replied. "Me too," seconded Miller. Kaplan admitted that he would probably want to try something else after another ten or fifteen years, but for the time being, game design was his only interest, too.

I asked if we could see a sample of their work. The proposed new company's games had to be played on an Atari console complete with joysticks. Each of the programmers in my office was then working on a different game.

"Do you play bridge?" asked Kaplan.

"Sure. I love bridge."

"Well, take this home," he said.

Of course when I got home, I immediately set up the game on my new RadioShack "computer" and was instantly hooked when I was able to play bridge—complete with black spades and clubs, red hearts and diamonds—all by myself. The game had color graphics! Today, this game would be lucky if it drew a long yawn out of a gamer, but thirty-odd years ago, the experience struck me as magical.

We liked these four ambitious programmers, who so clearly had attained a rare level of expertise in their field. I liked the first product that I tested, and my colleagues at Sutter Hill Ventures and I liked the fast-growing game sector a lot. But we knew for sure that we would need some seasoned managers if this were going to fly. About that time, a young-ish entrepreneur named Jim Levy, then working at GRT Records, was attempting to raise venture capital so that he could go into business making cassette tape software for early computers. He was also interested in managing a Silicon Valley startup, so we introduced him to Activision. It proved to be a great fit.

Each of the founders wanted 10 percent. We gave them that, and we gave Levy a little more. Sutter Hill got the balance, and we agreed to put in all the money: something just south of a million dollars.

Activision was formally founded on October 1, 1979. It grew rapidly—in part owing to Jim Levy's savvy decision to *celebrate* (and appropriately compensate) the designer of each game—reaching $300 million in sales within three years. The company's board meetings were great fun for me, mainly because the last item on the agenda was always "Game Time." I hated to give up that board seat when I went to Washington in 1981 to work for President Reagan, but Dave Anderson filled in capably in my absence (and got to enjoy Game Time).

Not long afterward, I came back to California for a Stanford Graduate School of Business Advisory Council meeting, which H. Brewster Atwater Jr., president of General Mills, also attended. To my surprise, he told me that he wanted to buy Activision. The General Mills game division, Parker Brothers, then featured only board games like *Monopoly, Clue,* and *Risk* (which happens to be one of my son Tim's favorite games). Atwater explained that he was interested in expanding the division into electronic games.

I asked Jim Levy to join me for lunch, and he introduced me to Cook's Seafood Restaurant—a new addition since I had gone to Washington. After we ordered, I told him that General Mills was interested in purchasing Activision. He weighed his response carefully. "I am not against selling the company," he finally replied, "but I want one billion dollars, and not a penny less." Activision was then valued on the public market at around $500 million. I knew that General Mills would pay a slight premium over market but not *double.* I briefly tried to make the argument that the market (and, by extension, Activision) was overpriced. But when I saw his jaw starting to set, I dropped the subject.

Some time later, however, I found cause to wish I had been a little more insistent. Almost overnight, it seemed, every child in the country put his Atari joysticks in the closet. Why? Because rather than paying $1,000 for an Atari system, parents across the country spent roughly that same $1,000 on a home computer, which of course offered a whole lot more than just games. Activision's stock plummeted, beginning several years of financial and emotional drama for the company.

The Activision story illustrates the value of having team members who have had significant experience in the same field as their entrepreneurial venture. The Activision team, with its Atari experience, was able to benefit from a jump start into the rapidly blossoming game industry. I have already pointed out that the quality of the founding team is the most important factor when one is trying to assess the chances of success in any given startup, and I think that the most important element to analyze when appraising the team is its expertise.

Vision

Leaders lead, in part, by painting a compelling vision of the future. "A rock pile ceases to be a rock pile the moment a single man contemplates it, bearing within him the image of a cathedral," wrote Antoine de Saint-Exupéry, the author of *The Little Prince.*

Let me cite two examples of vision that have an odd, tangential link in history: my father's efforts during the Berlin Airlift, and Freddie Laker's transatlantic, low-cost airline. They help make what I think is an important point.

At the age of twenty as a college sophomore, I went on a military mission with my father. By accident, I happened to witness the birth of the Berlin Airlift, which turned out to be an extraordinary vision, brilliantly executed.

My father was then U.S. undersecretary of war, and for the previous three years had been stationed in Berlin, where he supervised the economic side of the U.S. occupation of Germany under General Lucius Clay. As undersecretary of war, he had the responsibility of overseeing the U.S. occupation of Germany, Japan, and Austria. My father called me from Washington DC, while I was in the middle of exam week, and asked if I wanted to go back on active duty. I had previously served eighteen months in the Army and had ended up a second lieutenant in the 82nd Airborne Division. Although it had been a wonderful experience, I knew, *for sure*, that the military was not going to be a career for me. I had no intention of returning.

"No, thank you, Dad," I said. "I like civilian life."

But then he told me that it would only be a thirty-day stint and that I would be the aide-de-camp for a group of senior military officers and civilians whom he was taking to Berlin and other European locales to appraise the economic and military situation. These were fascinating and influential people, he continued, who would be doing important things. I agreed that the opportunity was too good to pass up.

On June 24, 1948, a few weeks after that initial conversation, our flight departed Washington. Flying was still a novelty to me in those days. My eyes were glued to the window as our DC-3 gained altitude. I watched the Washington Monument and the Lincoln Memorial shrink into the distance.

After a long and bumpy night, I surveyed the group on board. They were individuals who turned out to be every bit as impressive as my father had promised—including generals with several stars on their shoulders, and civilians like Paul Hoffman, then president of Studebaker Corporation and later the first administrator of the United Nations Development Program (a position to which, coincidentally, I would be elected some forty years later). I could see why my father was so insistent that I come along for the ride.

What I didn't know was that at precisely the same moment that I began eating my breakfast, my father's chief planning officer, General Albert Wedemeyer, opened a cable that had just come in. He immediately passed it on to my father. It read: "All roads and rail lines into Berlin have been blockaded by the Russians." Drew Middleton of the *New York Times* would report two days later that "storm signals [were] flying in Berlin." We were headed right into the center of the storm.

Of course, my father had known for weeks that trouble was brewing. The four-nation council that ruled the city of Berlin—divided into four sectors in the wake of the Allied victory in World War II—had recently been engaged in near-constant disputes. At one point, the Russians walked out of the council chamber after a bitter disagreement over a proposed revaluation of the highly inflated German mark. "We watched the rising emotion and the rising level of argument," my father later told an interviewer, "with the realization that we were perhaps moving even toward war with Russia."[4] If anything, my father's understated speaking style downplayed the drama and danger of that moment. As historians D. M. Giangreco and Robert E. Griffin later put it: "Probably at no time in post–World War II history, with the exception of the Cuban Missile crisis of 1962, has the world ever been closer to World War III than it was during the period from June 25 through late July 1948."[5]

My father knew he needed to devise an immediate action plan to recommend to the White House as soon as he landed in London, which was our first stop. He and his aides reviewed their limited options. Should they attempt to ram through the blockade on the ground and risk setting off a new global conflagration? Gradually, one less confrontational option gained momentum: an airlift of food, coal, and supplies into beleaguered Berlin.

During WWII, General Wedemeyer had been in charge of the airlift from India to China over the "hump" of the Himalayas. He had a good idea of the tonnage that various planes could carry if they were called upon to save Berlin from starvation. For his part, my father had previously negotiated with the Russians in Berlin for the feeding of the American, British, and French sectors they surrounded, so he knew the minimal tonnage of food necessary to feed the 3 million people on a ration level in those areas of the city. Both men knew how many planes then stationed in Europe were capable of supplying such a tremendous amount of cargo. General Wedemeyer estimated that a minimum of two minutes was required between each landing in order to deliver the food safely. After a few hours of pencil pushing and calculating, they had devised a plan. The Berlin Airlift—an amazing vision that wound up keeping Berlin alive for more than a year—was born on that flight.

In London, my father and General Wedemeyer met with British Foreign Minister Ernest Bevin, who offered twenty-five planes—all the United Kingdom had in those lean postwar years. "We're all for it," Bevin told them. "You can never make it work, though. You can never feed 3 million people from the air. But it'll make a great psychological impression. The Russians are trying to starve the Germans, and we're trying to feed them."

Our next stop was Paris, where officials in the French government offered support—and, significantly, an airfield for our use in the French sector of Berlin—but no planes. Then we were off to Berlin. We had loaded two tons of food on the plane in London, so one might say that we were the first plane of the Berlin Airlift when we landed at Tempelhof Airport.

I watched both my father and General Clay in action during the next few tense weeks—in a series of secret meetings that I was permitted to attend. Perhaps most daunting, there was a wide divergence of opinion among the U.S., British, and French officials about the feasibility and desirability of remaining in Berlin. Almost none of those officials believed that the city could be supplied completely by air over an extended period of time. What Berlin needed was a vision.

General Clay combined a take-charge manner, a brilliant mind, and a deceptively soft Southern charm. He was more accustomed than most to dealing with the Russians, and he was calmly confident that they would fold under pressure. Even though I wasn't then thinking in terms of "vision," nor yet seen much of the world, I could see the powerful impact that Clay was exerting on his colleagues.

My father played a complementary role in those difficult days, with the world on the brink of another war. He was the ultimate planner: conservative, thoughtful, and methodical. He was always empathetic—a skilled listener. At the same time, he was a powerful and articulate advocate once he had decided on a plan of action. Though many around them thought it couldn't be done, General Clay and my father shaped a vision. They were able to convey the power of that vision and convince the majority of disbelievers to share it. Then they helped to construct and carry out a plan that worked.

Nothing about the Berlin Airlift was easy. My father later recalled that the city nearly ran out of food about three months into the effort.[6] His team made a strategic decision to replace the smaller DC-3s they had been using with DC-4s, which could carry about five times as much cargo. The effort would require all the DC-4s that the United States had in Japan, Europe, and at home—every single one. These were the same planes that we would need to ferry troops in the event that a war broke out, so it was a big gamble. Food levels in the city began to rise again.

Next, when cold weather set in and Berlin started to run out of coal, the Army Air Corps (the predecessor of the Air Force) turned the DC-4s into what my father later called "the most expensive coal wagons the world ever saw." They even tried dropping the coal from the air, but it turned into powder and blew away even before it hit the ground. Ultimately, they had to land the coal planes and unload them just like the food planes. Slowly, the coal stocks built up.

The problems kept coming. As my father recalled:

In November we had an early winter, and early fog. The fog's bad in Berlin, anyway, but this year it was worse than they had ever seen, and it came down about the first of November and it just stuck. It meant that you had to [fly] on instruments entirely. In the meantime, the Russians were buzzing the planes. They didn't shoot any down, but they came right near us. It's a wonder there weren't any accidents, starting a war, because that would have probably done it.

It looked like curtains. If that fog had stayed another three weeks we probably would have had to run up the white flag. We probably couldn't have gone on. You can't have people starving, and keep on with the occupation. But the weather lifted about January 5, and immediately we restored the situation. The Russians knew they were licked right away, but it was May before they finally gave up.[7]

In the end, Generals Draper, Clay, and their team of pilots wound up flying more than *1,500 flights a day*—an astonishing number, in light of the fairly crude airplanes and airport involved. (By way of comparison, Chicago's O'Hare Airport, one of the busiest in the world, handled an average of 2,409 planes per day in 2008.[8]) At the height of the airlift, a plane touched down in Berlin every thirty seconds. Yes, a number of crashes, due to heavy fog and other factors, cost the lives of 101 people. But their sacrifices saved innumerable lives in Berlin and probably helped avoid an unimaginably terrible war. To this day, the Berlin Airlift remains a shining example of American leadership—imaginative, courageous, and competent—and of the power of *vision*.

Beware of Vision with Bad Execution

Between 1966 and 1977, Freddie Laker transformed the UK-based Laker Airways from a charter airline into the first long-haul, "no frills" airline.

He operated low-fare scheduled services between London's Gatwick and New York's John F. Kennedy Airports. Laker Airways was the forerunner to Virgin Atlantic Airlines—which the chief pilot of Laker Airways later helped form—and served as the model that many other airlines, like Southwest, JetBlue, and Ryanair, would later use as a template.

Here's the odd historical connection to which I referred earlier: Freddie Laker coincidentally made his name in aviation, as a pilot, during the Berlin Airlift. His planes successfully completed 4,700 flights in and out of Berlin and reportedly carried 10 percent of the total food and supplies that went into the city.

In 1982, when Freddie Laker walked into my office in Washington, his luck was about to run out. I was then president and chairman of the Export–Import Bank of the United States (Ex–Im). Laker was truly a risk-taking pioneer. He had revolutionized air travel with Laker Airways' Skytrain, the first affordable, no-frills transatlantic airline. Laker Airways operated according to the model for train travel: passengers could turn up on their desired date of travel, purchase tickets for as little as £32.50 one-way in winter, and be on their way. The airline also pioneered cost-saving ways to reduce its planes' fuel consumption and wear and tear by lowering its baggage weight limit and adopting innovative takeoff techniques. Laker could break even on his new planes with only half-full flights—a far lower break-even point than his competitors could achieve with their aging aircraft.[9]

Skytrain enjoyed immense success in the late 1970s and expanded rapidly around the world. By 1981, it was the fourth-largest transatlantic scheduled airline between the United Kingdom and the United States, behind British Airways, Pan Am, and TWA, as well as the fifth-largest overall. By that time, the airline had carried over 2 million Skytrain passengers.[10] Freddie Laker was a public hero in England—even something of a cult figure—because he had made it possible for the average person to travel abroad, which was a luxury previously reserved exclusively for the well-to-do. British Prime Minister Margaret Thatcher heralded him as an icon of free enterprise.

A few years prior to my taking over as head of the Export–Import Bank, the bank had financed five DC-10s that Laker was to use for his transatlantic service. Laker was a fun guy, a genuine entrepreneur, and a man of vision, but his business model had some fatal flaws. He was paying for his airplane fuel, leasing costs, and growing debt in dollars, but he was selling the majority of tickets in British pounds. When I met with him soon after I took over Ex–Im I asked what seemed to me to be an obvious question: "How will this work? If the pound drops, you're going to have a difficult time."

He flashed his classic salesman smile. "Bill, you don't understand the business. The whole business is about filling the seats with more bloody arses!"

It was true that I didn't know much about the aviation business, but I did know finance. I wasn't surprised when just half a year later, when the world was hit with the severe recession of the early 1980s, all of the markets turned against Laker. Oil prices went up, and the British currency went down. Laker was whipsawed by a major exchange-rate shift, a spike in the price of his biggest expense—oil—and overwhelming competition from the more established airlines, which cut fares at the same time. And although Laker Airways had lower costs and a rather simple organization, it needed high year-round passenger loads to make money at discount prices. Most of its discount-seeking passengers were likely to travel during the summer peak period, which made it challenging to achieve high loads during the winter.

It was a perfect storm. It wasn't long before Laker showed up in my office again, this time seeking relief for his Ex–Im credits. At one point during our discussion, I asked him about his management style, and he said, "I come in on the first floor—that's where operations are being discussed—and I ask, 'How are things operating today?' Then I go to the second floor, and I ask people how sales are today, and then I go to the third floor and we talk about marketing. Finally, I go to the fourth floor, and we talk about finance." *He ought to spend more time on the fourth floor,* I thought to myself. I said, "Freddie, we'll see what we can do about your situation."

We tried to get key-man insurance on Laker, because he was so impor-tant to the company, but the insurance company required him to take a stress test. His doctor advised him not to take it, saying that it might be bad for his health. On top of the credit risk, we now had a health con-cern. Then we asked for his financials. We couldn't understand anything from the jumbled presentation he gave us, so we had to send one of our employees to Laker's offices to restructure it in a way that Ex–Im could understand and analyze the numbers. Then we spoke with Laker's suppli-ers of aircraft and engines—McDonnell Douglas and GE, respectively—because they had both made loans as part of the credit package to finance the five aircraft with which we were involved. At one point, they were even thinking of injecting an additional £5 million to keep Laker afloat but later decided against it. In talking with them, we also discovered that the airline had debts to the Japanese as well. We were all in the same boat, and it was sinking fast.

Later, the British government stepped in. Prime Minister Thatcher was trying to promote the private sector and privatize public companies, so she asked the Bank of England to intervene. The bank called a meet-ing, so my colleagues flew over to London to see if it would be able to refinance Laker and keep him flying. Soon after, that fell apart too, and by that time, every option had been exhausted.

Laker Airways collapsed on February 5, 1982, with debts of £270 mil-lion. It was the biggest corporate failure in the United Kingdom up to that time.

Virgin Atlantic Airlines, meanwhile, benefited from the hard les-sons of Laker Airways. Richard Branson, owner of Virgin, knew Freddie Laker well and found him charming and courageous. He said that he wanted to name Virgin's first plane after him, but Laker thought that he would be a less-than-auspicious symbol for a new startup airline. It would be years before he let Branson christen an airplane as the "Spirit of Sir Freddie."

Branson well remembers some sage and prescient advice that Laker gave him:

He warned me I would have to defend my business against monopolist and protectionist governments, and also explained why we needed to beat competitors on quality of service as well as price. He concluded his advice with the immortal words: "When [British Airways] comes after you, which they inevitably will, shout long, shout hard, and then sue the bastards!" Within six years everything he had predicted in that one sentence came true, but—partly thanks to his advice—we won. I will never forget him.[11]

How do the Berlin Airlift and Laker Airways fit together? My argument is that vision is the indispensable prerequisite to moving mountains, but in and of itself, it's not enough. It's one part vision, and one part execution. Without exceptional execution—the successful implementation of an effective strategy for getting from here to there—a vision of the future remains an illusion. As a Japanese proverb says, "Vision without action is a daydream. Action without vision is a nightmare."

Henry Ford—one of the greatest entrepreneurs of all time and one who certainly excelled at the startup game—put it another way: "Vision without execution is just hallucination."

It Takes Integrity

I've already introduced this topic, but let me pick it up again by stating my position, first, in black-and-white terms: *Integrity can't be parsed. Either you have it, or you don't.*

Now let me dig a little deeper, first by calling on an episode from my childhood that I can recall almost as vividly as the day it happened. I was only a young witness to the circumstance that unfolded, and yet, it has remained ingrained in my memory for more than seventy-five years.

In the summer of 1934, my parents took my two older sisters and me to Lake Champlain in Quebec, where we went fishing and enjoyed the outdoors. The vacation was fun and exhilarating, to be sure, but what really stands out in my mind is what happened on the car ride home. Those were different days—when cars were much less dependable, and breakdowns were commonplace—so setting out on this long drive was an adventure in itself. Two hours had passed since we had begun the long, eight-hour journey back to Scarsdale, New York. At that point, my mother casually remarked that she had a little souvenir of our trip.

"Look at this pretty green ashtray that I took from our hotel room," she said.

My father kept looking at the road ahead. Then he abruptly asked, "You did what?" I had been half-dozing off in the backseat, but upon hearing this first exchange, I sat up and listened more closely.

Her finger traced out the name of the hotel, "Le Chateau Frontenac," which had been carefully painted on the surface of the ashtray. "I liked it," she said, "and I figured that it would be a good advertisement for the hotel. I'm sure they won't mind."

"We'll see about that," my father replied in a steely tone. "We are going back to return that ashtray." A heated argument ensued between my mother and father, but there was no way around it: My father had made up his mind. He abruptly turned the car around and began the long drive back to the hotel—which meant four extra hours in the car, two each way.

Arriving at Le Chateau Frontenac, we all trouped back inside. My father presented the ashtray to the concierge, who said, "Well, you can certainly take that home with you as a souvenir of our hotel, Mr. Draper, but we must charge you five dollars for it." Having driven hundreds of miles out of his way to make his point, my father was more than content to pay five dollars for the ashtray. My mother was livid—the angriest I ever saw her, before or afterward. In retrospect, I'm sure that she was more than a little embarrassed by the whole episode. That green ashtray was a fixture in our living room for years to come—a mute but telling reminder of my father's principled stand.

Obviously, my father lived a life of strict morality. Couldn't he have just mailed the thing back to Quebec or sent them a check? Yes. But that wouldn't have made the same unyielding statement to his family. I watched him throughout his life, and I never witnessed a single tear in his moral fiber—not one.

I was with my wife, Phyllis, one evening in New York several years ago. It was early evening, but it was already dark, and it was pouring rain as we stepped out of our taxi on our way into the theater. I happened to look down at the rain-soaked pavement, and there I spied a plump black wallet. I picked it up and flipped it open. Inside were tiered rows of credit cards and several hundred dollars in cash.

My father's example immediately popped into my head. I reacted automatically. As quickly as was reasonably possible, I dug out the owner's driver's license, found his address—in Connecticut, somewhere—got his telephone number through directory assistance, and called him to arrange a return of the wallet intact.

Entrepreneurship—and by extension, venture capital—is built on *trust.* They are built on the good reputations of the principals involved. More than most places in the world, Silicon Valley is the home of the handshake. Your word is your bond—or you're in trouble.

No, it's not always easy. I have seen many, many cases in the world of entrepreneurship and venture capital in which integrity has been tested. One recent example revolves around two entrepreneurs—John Pollard and Shree Madhavapeddi—and the company they started called "Jott," to which Draper Richards L.P. had supplied seed capital.

Jott provided a service that transcribed spoken messages to text and then emailed or inserted the text into a variety of web services used by the customer, such as to-do lists. The service was particularly helpful to salespeople on the road, and hundreds of thousands of people had gotten in the habit of using it—*when it was free.* In 2008, however, the company started charging users a small fee of a few dollars per month for the service, and the user base contracted sharply. Meanwhile, the nation was in the middle of an historic economic downturn. The company faced a very difficult cash situation.

We at Draper Richards began taking the necessary steps to put more money into Jott, simply because it was out of cash. We had also heard that despite the catastrophic housing market nationwide, a large real estate company with 8,000 reps had recommended the product to its agents.

In the end, fewer agents signed up than we had hoped. Pollard and Madhavapeddi immediately gave us the bad news, which prevented us from putting in good money after bad. The way the timing worked out, they could easily have taken our money and allowed us to discover the bad news on our own, somewhere down the road—but their personal integrity wouldn't let them do that.

Despite the discouraging news, Pollard and Madhavapeddi decided to make one last push to find a buyer for the business. Lacking a new cash infusion from us, they decided to fund Jott's payroll out of their own pockets—an honorable path that they didn't have to take. After several chaotic weeks, Pollard called to say that they had worked out an agreement to sell the business to Burlington, Massachusetts–based Nuance Communications, a very strong company that provides speech recognition and predictive text products. He also informed us that my partners and I would get back most of the money that we had put in. Needless to say, I was very happy to hear that we would not be taking a big hit. I told him and Madhavapeddi to deduct the cost of two bottles of champagne from our share and to celebrate their hard work and reasonably happy outcome with their wives.

But the more important point was that, once again, these two men had had the opportunity to show what they were made of, and they passed this new test with flying colors. How so? Nuance was interested in giving big incentives to the management team to make sure that it stayed in place after the merger. Under the circumstances, Nuance had absolutely *no* incentive to keep us—the investors—happy. A deal could easily have been struck providing less purchase money and more options for Pollard and Madhavapeddi. But again, their integrity would not allow it. They felt that they had an obligation to us, and they wanted to do their best to meet that obligation. Both ended up joining Nuance in senior roles, and as it turned out, most of the Jott team made the transition to Nuance as well.

Will Pollard and Madhavapeddi ever get "paid back" for acting honorably? Of course. Their reputation is intact, their conscience is clear, and their "luck" will be enhanced as more and more people want to do business with them. If someone were to call me looking for a character reference—and believe me, these kinds of conversations go on *all the time* in the venture community—I would jump at the chance to talk about them in glowing terms. They have a bit less money in the bank but infinitely more "capital" in their reputation than they would have had by taking a less honorable course.

Last but Not Least: A Sense of Humor

Although they often involve rewarding and exciting pursuits, entrepreneurship and venture capital can at times be extremely stressful and exhausting. For this reason, among others, it is important that all parties have a good sense of humor and expect the unexpected. Venture capitalists and entrepreneurs should be able to laugh at themselves and at the funny situations that will certainly arise along the way.

I remember one particularly hilarious incident from my early days at Draper Richards L.P. I had just come back from a board meeting and was headed into my office when I stopped to ask my partner Howard and my assistant Rhonda—who were laughing raucously in the lobby at the time— about the pitch meeting that they had just finished in our conference room. Blushing, Howard told me that the product idea was a luxury vibrator. They both seemed totally surprised and taken aback when I reported that my daughter Polly had bought one for my wife recently.

This was true: Polly had sent Phyllis a large blue massage chair—which in my head was a "vibrator"—with a complicated set of buttons to activate back vibrators, make lumbar adjustments, and otherwise create all sorts of bumps and grinds. I tried it once or twice, and it was quite enjoyable.

"So how does *this* one work?" I asked.

"Well, um, like every other vibrator but maybe a little more elegant," Howard cautiously replied.

"Oh," I said, "Phyllis *loves* hers. It's very elegant, very big, and has lots of different settings. It's good-looking, blue, and we could even use it in our living room. Our guests would love it, but Phyllis didn't think it appropriate, so we have it in Paulo's playroom." (Paulo is an extraordinarily talented and charming eight-year-old Filipino boy who, together with his mother, lives with us.)

After I noticed a few more nervous glances back and forth between Rhonda and Howard, I asked what the problem was. All of a sudden, the light went on for them. I was still in the dark. They both blurted out at once, "Are you talking about a vibrating *chair?*"

"Of course," I said. "What are *you* talking about?"

CHAPTER 4

My "Missing" Decade

*Seize the moment of excited curiosity on any subject to solve your doubts;
for if you let it pass, the desire may never return, and you may remain in
ignorance.*

—*William Wirt*

I 'M SURE THAT IT was the compelling example of my father that first
focused my attention on public service.

As explained in previous chapters, he seemed to move effortlessly
from the private sector to the public sector, and then back again. Perhaps
most important, from an impressionable son's point of view, was that he
didn't really draw sharp distinctions between the two. His goal in life—
almost never articulated in these kinds of words—was to *make a contribution* and to *make a difference.* My father believed he could work toward
that goal both in business and in government.

In this chapter, I recount the somewhat tangled tale of my own forays
into public service. I call it my "missing" decade, even though (1) the
story spans more than a decade, and (2) I wasn't really missing, except in
the sense of being out of the venture capital game. In some ways, during

my missing decade, I was more conspicuous and easier to find than ever before.

I hope these stories are interesting, entertaining, and have some historical value. But I also include them because they help make my case that both great entrepreneurs and great public servants draw upon some of the same personal attributes—especially vision—as they set out to make the world a better place. For example, what do aviation entrepreneur Freddie Laker's vision and China's former leader Deng Xiaoping's vision have in common? On the surface, almost nothing. But if you look further, I believe that you'll start to see how a vision, compellingly drawn, can help people from all walks of life to move mountains.

My Unimpressive Run for Congress

I try to give my all to everything I do. I make a plan, take my best shot, and hope that the wind is at my back. In general, this has worked well for me. In 1967, though, it wasn't enough. My one and only try for elected office—which I include here because it really was a sort of prelude and prerequisite to my missing decade—didn't go so well.

It began with a breakfast at Ricky's, the same hotel visited by the Draper family on its days in Palo Alto eight years before. My buddies Stuart Leeb and Bill Edwards had told me that they had something on their minds that they wanted to discuss with me. Stu is more than a real estate developer; he is also a political guru, a wizard. Bill was my next-door neighbor and one of my dearest friends.

In the car on the way over to Ricky's, I contemplated the likely purpose of our somewhat mysterious breakfast meeting. Several years earlier, Stu and Bill had introduced me to the California Republican Alliance, of which I subsequently became the president. The Alliance was an association of businessmen and lawyers who gathered every month or so with California politicians and would-be politicians who wanted to meet Bay Area professionals. I say "businessmen" purposely because I don't think there were any businesswomen in the Republican Alliance in 1967. At that time, professional women were still few and far between. I was pretty sure that Bill and Stu wanted to talk to me about the death of Congressman J. Arthur Younger from San Mateo, who had recently died of leukemia. Who would replace him? There would soon be a special election—rather than a primary—and it would be a free-for-all. We Republicans needed to get busy.

I apologized for being late, ordered my pancakes and crisp bacon, and asked what was on their minds. "Listen, Bill," said Stu. "We have a really great idea, and it involves you!"

"Okay," I said somewhat warily. By this time, I could spot a pitch coming my way. "What is it?"

They both started talking at once, but I extracted the gist of it: *You're the man! You're our guy! You are going to be our next congressman!*

This was one of those moments—perhaps you've experienced them—when your ego swells to a size where it fills the room, and in the process, squeezes out all logic. Already, I was saying to myself, "Well, these are two smart guys. If they *both* think it's me, could they be wrong?" I put on my poker face and said I would think about it and talk to my wife, Phyllis. Already, though, I was dipping my big toe into a tide of ambition, ego, and irrationality.

One obvious question—even for someone who was starting to be blinded by ambition—was, *Who else would be running?* The Democrats would almost certainly put up the popular and competent sheriff of San Mateo. The conservative Republicans were hoping Shirley Temple Black, former curly-haired child actress, would enter the race. Pete McCloskey, a liberal Republican from Woodside, had already announced. In the end, there were a dozen candidates, including a jockey from the Tanforan Racetrack in San Mateo.

I went to my office at Sutter Hill Ventures that day, but I found that I couldn't concentrate on business. I could hardly wait to go home and consult Phyllis. When six o'clock finally arrived, I went home as fast as traffic and the law allowed. Soon afterward, I was at the dining room table with my family. We started chatting as usual, and I didn't wait long to break the news that I might run for Congress. The kids were ecstatic; Phyllis was unenthusiastic. She didn't show it at the time, though, and just murmured some lukewarm encouragement: "Whatever you want to do, Bill." I missed the "lukewarm" part. My receptors were turned off. I had made my decision. I would run for Congress!

I called Shirley Temple Black, whom I knew fairly well. She, Pete McCloskey, and I were all thirty-nine years old, and we were all pretty good friends. I told her I was going to run for Younger's seat and wondered if she planned to do the same. "I am just looking out the window, Bill," she said vaguely. I knew then that she had made up her mind to run, and I confess that I was momentarily discouraged. Even though the movie *Bright Eyes* was then more than three decades in the past, her rendition of "On the Good Ship Lollipop" still came into my head when I thought of Shirley. Even *I* would have a hard time voting against Shirley Temple.

In his book *The Audacity of Hope*, President Barack Obama writes of three emotions—ambition, single-mindedness, and fear—that grip a politician in the throes of a campaign. As it turned out, I was only subject to the first two. I really wasn't afraid of losing. I thought I would make a good congressman, but if the public decided to pick someone else, there was probably a good reason for that, and I would happily return to venture capital.

There *was* another concern, though. It was not long before I realized that I actually knew very little about how our county worked and about the local problems faced by most of the constituents. True, I read the *New York Times* every day, had traveled extensively, ran a business, and was well educated. But issues like conservation, education, and infrastructure were all new to me, especially at the local level. I crammed a bit between public events, but for the most part I learned the hard way: in front of rooms full of skeptics, many of whom were well informed.

The overriding issue of the day was Vietnam. It seemed as though we might lose the war, and President Lyndon Johnson's popularity was waning each day because of it. Even so, it was not yet considered a lost cause. Nearly everyone in San Mateo County was grappling with the issue, and of course they all wanted to know how each of the congressional candidates felt about the war. Pete McCloskey, a tough-minded, Stanford-trained lawyer, carved out a distinctive and courageous position: if elected, he would sponsor legislation mandating an immediate withdrawal of all U.S. troops from Vietnam. As the weekly debates around San Mateo County began to attract standing-room-only crowds, McCloskey emerged as the star. He had served in the Korean War—as had I—so he certainly couldn't be dismissed as a "peacenik." General James Gavin, a bona fide World War II hero, had also endorsed him and his position.

Give a dozen individuals three minutes to explain their positions on Vietnam—expect most of them to run overtime—and you can quickly see why Vietnam consumed almost all of the allotted time at every event. On that front, McCloskey pretty much destroyed us. He had done his homework, and he spoke eloquently. The rest of us seemed to be making it up as we went along. My three minutes came and went in an uncomfortable blur.

Halfway through the campaign, I realized that I really needed more in-depth knowledge about Vietnam. I called a meeting of my campaign committee, during which somebody finally said, "Well, if you don't feel comfortable with your grasp of the facts, why don't you go to Vietnam and see the situation firsthand?"

I jumped on the idea. No one objected, and the following week I was on a CIA plane traveling from Saigon to Hue, flying over a beautiful country caught up in a tragedy of immense proportions. The Army effectively controlled my tour. I was briefed by colonels, generals, and even the U.S. ambassador. I was helicoptered into barren villages, now supposedly "pacified," but with few remaining residents. My original position—that we should "stay the course"—was being reinforced by every meeting, jeep ride, and face that was put in front of me.

The night before I was scheduled to leave Vietnam, a journalist and I were surveying the modest Saigon skyline from a third-floor hotel terrace. He spoke very little, but at the end of our evening together, he simply said, "Nothing is as it seems in Saigon."

When I landed at the San Francisco airport, I was met by Stu Leeb, who told me that during my absence, McCloskey had surged ahead of both Black and me. Polls were certainly not as sophisticated as they are today, but even so, Stu had it right. On my drive home, it seemed to me that every other car on Highway 101 sported a McCloskey bumper sticker. The race was over. A military victory in Vietnam was nowhere in sight, and the public was fed up with the steady diet of violence that they were being fed by the evening news, with no strategic goals being served by all that death and destruction. The country wanted to stop the war, and San Mateo County wanted Pete McCloskey to be its voice on the issue.

So I failed in my one and only attempt at electoral politics. I felt perfectly fine about that. After the race, I happily returned to my position as senior partner of Sutter Hill. And although fourteen years intervened between that race and my next effort at public service, I've always viewed that race against Pete McCloskey and Shirley Temple Black as a prelude to what was to follow.

Reagan to the Rescue

In some ways, 1980 looked a lot like 1967. The country was exhausted and confused, not certain of where it should go next. This time, though, it wasn't the senseless carnage of Vietnam. Instead, we were tired of long lines at the gas station, rampant inflation, a stagnant economy, and the humiliating spectacle of our citizens being held hostage in the U.S. embassy in Tehran after being captured during the Iranian revolution of 1979.

Most of all, we were tired of President Jimmy Carter. He had seemed like a breath of fresh air in the wake of the sordid ending of the Nixon administration, but after four years in the White House, he too seemed exhausted. He appeared incapable of leading the nation. "Stagflation," a new word in the economic dictionary, had him by the throat. He had no

economic answers to offer the nation, even though he had been a successful small businessman and the governor of Georgia before becoming
president.

The country wanted a change. We wanted a leader with new
ideas and the willpower and persuasiveness to deliver on those ideas
successfully.

As it turned out, Ronald Reagan was that man. Reagan had but three
simple ideas. First, cut taxes so that business and entrepreneurship could
prosper. Second, power up defense spending, both to ensure national
security and force the Soviet Union to engage in a ruinous spending spree.
Third, with the notable exception of defense, reduce the size of government in every way possible.

This simple but powerful vision did not just spring from Reagan's
head one day. It was shaped, tested, and refined during the years when the
former actor was governor of California (1967 through early 1975). Many
people helped build the intellectual scaffolding behind Reagan's vision,
but none was more important than the late William F. Buckley Jr., a dear
college friend of mine and longtime editor of the conservative *National
Review*.

During one of Buckley's visits to my house in Atherton, probably in
July 1979, we discussed a key reason for his California trip. He would
be dining that evening with the Reagans at their Bel Air mansion. The
following day, he would be meeting with the Reagan brain trust to continue putting the intellectual meat on the bones of the Reagan strategy.
I figured that I should take advantage of having the ear of someone
who had the ear of Reagan. While we were drying off after a swim, I
said to Buckley, "When you see Reagan, be sure to put in a plug for the
entrepreneur."

He flashed that broad, infectious grin of his. "Bill," he replied, "the
entrepreneur is what it's all about. Every part of the Reagan economic
strategy is designed to enhance the role of the entrepreneur." He pointed
out that lower taxes allowed the entrepreneur to spend more money on

research and other productive elements that were paying off so well in Silicon Valley. Yes, we might well face a bulging federal deficit if defense were beefed up and taxes were drastically reduced, but before long—Buckley asserted—the increased productivity brought about by lower taxes would start to whittle away at that deficit.

I didn't realize, at the time, that I was being given a sneak preview of the vision and strategy that would guide the nation for most of the 1980s. I certainly had no idea that I would play a role in *implementing* that strategy.

A New Life in Washington

Shortly after Reagan's inauguration in 1981, Vice President George H. W. Bush suggested that I serve in the administration as chairman and president of the Export–Import Bank of the United States (Ex–Im). I had known Vice President Bush for many years, and I admired him enormously. Even though I didn't know too much about the Ex–Im Bank, I enthusiastically accepted the offer. I was drawn to public service because my father's long career in government had influenced and intrigued me. I also really wanted to support the changes in government policy that the Reagan–Bush administration was proposing.

I soon learned that my unfamiliarity with the Bank wasn't an immediate problem, because Jim Baker—the recently installed chief of staff—had other plans for me in the short term. In a phone conversation, he asked if I would take the job of deputy director of presidential personnel for a few months before joining the Bank. Baker said that Pen James, then director of presidential personnel, wanted my help in organizing and modernizing his operation. Gradually, I realized what was going on: the Reaganites figured that because I was from Silicon Valley, I would be able to bring those personnel operations into the computer age. Any one of my business partners, starting with Pitch Johnson and moving forward, would have gotten a chuckle out of the notion of me as a technology guru.

"Great!" I said to the voice on the phone. "When do I start?"

"Yesterday," Baker said.

When I arrived in Washington a few days later, I realized why Baker had felt some urgency. In one underutilized corner of the White House basement were stacks and stacks of resumes—some 25,000 in all—from people who wanted to work for the new president. The resumes were neatly tied up with string and stacked in tidy bundles, where they were sure to languish if no one came up with a plan. With a couple of assistants, I undertook the task of setting up a computerized system to deal with this flood of job seekers.

After a few months, I finally got to the Ex–Im Bank. I sought out an old friend from college who worked there, Ray Albright, to give me a detailed brief about the Bank and its recent operations. It was an independent, reasonably nonpartisan government agency with the mission of promoting American exports. Basically, it borrowed money from the U.S. Treasury at government bond rates and then loaned that money on very favorable terms to foreign governments and companies that committed themselves to buying American-made goods. Some U.S. multinationals, like GE (jet engines and nuclear power technologies) and Boeing (aircraft), were skilled at using Ex–Im's expertise and resources. Thousands of other U.S. corporations used it to good advantage as well. During my tenure, I grew to realize that the Ex–Im Bank delivered an extraordinary service to all forms of international business. I would advise all entrepreneurs to investigate the Bank's offerings before engaging in any export activity.

In a way, my job at the Bank was similar to my job as a venture capitalist—evaluating projects, determining risk, developing relationships, and providing guidance to others. Meanwhile, there were skills that I learned in Washington, and later at the United Nations, which I was able to take advantage of when I returned to the private sector. These include sensitivity to other cultures, patience in negotiating through the labyrinth of bureaucracy, and a better understanding of the global implications of every action.

Now let me say a word about my office, which must be the *longest* office in Washington—some 65 feet from end to end. It was built by Jesse Jones: czar of the Reconstruction Finance Corporation, former secretary of commerce and the second chairman of the Ex–Im Bank (1936–1939). He was from Texas, and everything he touched had to be big. In this case, supposedly, he insisted that his office be the biggest in town. Jones had an enormous desk to match, which I was now inheriting. The office over-looked the White House across Lafayette Park, and it was said that Jones picked the location so that he could keep an eye on the young man in the White House, Franklin Delano Roosevelt.

I won't go into too much detail about my five years behind that big desk, but I like to think that I brought some good changes to the Bank. One was a reduction in unnecessary subsidies, without hurting the Bank's important task of adequately lubricating the financial machinery for American exporters to compete.

This wasn't always an easy balance to strike. Some members of Reagan's inner circle were putting pressure on the Bank by referring to it as a "cor-porate welfare" program. Reagan himself told a joint session of Congress in 1982 that he supported cutting Ex–Im's lending authority by a third, to $4.4 billion, thus adding fuel to the fire.[1] From my vantage point, I could see the need for government support for private industry when unfair practices were being used aggressively by other governments. I could also see the critics' point of view. At that time, average interest rates were 12.5 percent, but we were charging our corporate customers only 7.5 percent so that they could be competitive with other countries. In other words, our subsidy was 5 percent on every export loan. Meanwhile, other countries were offering even *higher* subsidies—a "subsidy arms race," if you will.

I decided to fly to Paris to participate directly in the ongoing multilat-eral negotiations aimed at addressing these problems. Both the Treasury Department and members of my own staff argued against my personal involvement, but I was determined to look for ways to break the deadlock. After failing in Paris to persuade France, England, Germany, and Japan to raise their interest rates closer to commercial rates, I decided on a new tactic: stop talking, and take action. Against the advice of almost everyone, I went back to Washington and raised Ex–Im's rates unilaterally to 12 percent, in order to reduce our subsidies and challenge other governments to do the same.

Our phones rang off the hook. Our customers, the exporters, were hopping mad. I made a few speeches. I went to see a very unhappy Jack Welch at General Electric. I debated Joe Wilson, then president of Boeing, on the *MacNeil/Lehrer NewsHour,* and then again on Ted Koppel's *Nightline.* It wasn't fun, but I felt I had a good case. If we kept subsidizing Singapore Airlines (for example) at the prevailing rates, the U.S. taxpayer would be a major investor in every jet that airline bought from Boeing. In other words, I argued, we had another stakeholder, and one who wasn't being treated very well: the American taxpayer.

The next two months were not easy for me. One highlight was the extraordinary loyalty of my staff, many of whom had advised against my unilateral move. They took the heat along with me for those two difficult months—thus belying the conventional wisdom about disloyal and disinterested Washington bureaucrats—and I will always be grateful to them.

Then came one of the best calls I received in all of my days in Washington. It was Warren Glick, my general counsel and brilliant adviser. "The Europeans and Japanese have just raised their rates to 10.75 percent," he said excitedly. I hung up and immediately gave orders to lower our rate to 10.75 percent. Shortly thereafter, we negotiated a rate system based on LIBOR, a London-based interest rate system that is adjusted every day. The United States and all of our economic competitors put pens to this agreement. Henceforth, yes, exporters would still be helped and taxpayers would still pay some subsidy, but commercial banks would be the lenders of first resort, and governments would be the lenders of last resort. A version of this agreement is still in effect today.

Advice from the Most Trusted Man in America

One thing I had to learn quickly at Ex–Im was how to go from being a fairly private person to being a fairly public person. The issue came to a head early in my tenure, when *60 Minutes* asked for an interview. The correspondent would be the intimidating Mike Wallace: feared by politicians and businesspeople alike. I knew that Wallace was notorious for reediting taped interviews and taking comments out of context. I decided to seek help from Walter Cronkite, who had just stepped down after a nineteen-year run as the anchor of the *CBS Evening News* and topped every poll as the "most trusted man in America." We were coming out of the shower stalls at our Hillbillies camp at the Bohemian Grove, that unique California "boys' camp" extraordinaire.

"Walter," I said, "Ex–Im made a questionable loan to Zaire before my time, and Mike Wallace will be interviewing me about it this coming week. I am really concerned. What can I do?"

It wasn't a fair request. Both he and Wallace worked for CBS, and I was putting him in a tough spot. But he responded immediately, in that warm and wonderful gravelly voice. "Bill, here is what I suggest. Get a tape recorder, put it in your office so that you can run it during the interview, and tell Mike what you plan to do. That way you are protected from his taking anything out of context, and he is forewarned."

When I arrived at the office early the following week, Linda Rheem, my exceptionally capable and dedicated administrative assistant, told me that they were already setting up for the interview. It was true: leaning up against Jesse Jones's enormous desk was Mike Wallace himself, watching his crew set up. We shook hands and chatted about our favorite sport—tennis—and about two of our favorite mutual friends, Bill Buckley and Walter Cronkite. I casually told him about Cronkite's idea of the tape recorder, and he said, "Fine. No problem." He was relaxed and genial—nothing like the fire-eater I had seen on TV. Because of the way he was perched against my desk, his suit jacket was hanging open, and I noted that the label indicated that the suit had been made in Toronto, Canada. That stuck in my mind for some reason.

The crew was ready. I turned on my tape recorder, and Wallace asked his first question: "What do you think of World Bank reports?"

Without giving it a second thought, I said, "Oh, I think very highly of them." Actually, I was just relying on the World Bank's solid reputation rather than personal knowledge of their reports.

Wallace pounced. "So would it surprise you to know that the last report said that the Ex–Im made a miserable mistake by lending $500 million to Zaire for building a power line across the country? President Mobutu, by the way, has three chateaus in Belgium and a huge Swiss bank account. I guess that since you like their reports so much, you must agree with the World Bank that *your* bank made a big mistake."

Things are not going well, I thought to myself. But as I was fumbling for an answer, the cameraman, somewhat flustered, announced that something had gone wrong with the camera and asked if we could do that take again. Naturally, I had no problem with that.

So after a moment, Wallace asked again, "What do you think of the World Bank reports?"

I smiled and said, "Well, some are good, Mike, and some are bad." He cracked up in spite of himself, and we both relaxed.

At one point, he brought up the widespread allegations that President Mobutu was skimming money from big government contracts and putting it in his own pocket. "He probably put that cash you gave him in his own account!" he said. Speaking slowly and precisely, I pointed out that Ex–Im never gave cash to anybody. "We pay the exporter, and the exporter ships the product. You can't put a Caterpillar tractor in a Swiss bank account." *This was starting to be fun.*

After some more sparring, Wallace took a new tack, acknowledging that the Ex–Im Bank *did* do some good things. "I guess you really do help the exporters reach markets in the developing world," he said. "But the big problem in this country is that imports keep growing. Our exports aren't increasing fast enough to keep up with imports, and so the trade gap keeps widening."

Now it was my turn to pounce. "You are *exactly* right, Mike. We need to urge more of our fellow citizens to buy American. For example, it's too bad that you didn't buy an American-made suit instead of that Canadian suit you're wearing."

Surprisingly, Wallace denied on camera that the suit was made in Canada. But I wasn't particularly surprised that *60 Minutes* never wound up airing our interview.

China: From Rice to Riches

I met scores of world leaders during my missing decade, but none impressed me more than Deng Xiaoping of China and Manmohan Singh of India—men of enormous vision, who were able to see into their countries' respective futures and remake their economies to reflect those visions.

My first visit to China came in October 1981. I was traveling with Don Regan, then secretary of the treasury, and we were attending the second annual China–U.S. Cooperation Meeting, where topics such as economics, finance, trade, and the $39 billion Three Gorges Dam project were discussed.

Just a few months prior to our meeting, the Ex–Im Bank had made the first ever U.S. loan to China to help finance the purchase of equipment needed to manufacture turbine generators, boilers, and air preheaters. Electric power generation was a high priority for China, and U.S. exporters were eager to begin selling their equipment into the new Chinese market. The loan was for $57 million—a figure that seemed high at the time. Today, however, thirty years later, the United States owes China something like *one trillion dollars.*

Our private meeting with Deng took place in Zhongnanhai, a sprawling government complex reserved for the nation's senior leaders, secure behind a giant wall in the center of Beijing and adjacent to the Forbidden

City. When Deng—then seventy-seven years old—entered the conference room, the energy level went up notably. He greeted us with an electrifying grin. When he sat down, his feet didn't quite reach the floor, and his tiny frame looked even more diminutive once he settled into his throne-like chair. But what Deng lacked in physical stature, he more than made up for with his commanding presence. His energy was palpable, his enthusiasm contagious, and his authority unquestionable. After a few minutes of informal chitchat, Deng casually said, "I am undertaking an experiment." Our ears perked up. "My home, Sichuan, was poverty-stricken when Mao died. For years, the citizens had been ordered to grow rice for the iron rice bowl, and only rice. They were all very poor, so when I took over in 1979, I told them that they could grow whatever they wanted. They switched their crops to tobacco and cotton, and now, just two years later, they are all becoming rich."

He flashed a bright, oversized smile. "That's not all," he continued. "I'm going to experiment with thirteen other provinces and tell them to grow anything they want, to trade with whomever they want in the world, and to open up and freely exploit their resources, both human and natural. I am encouraging everyone to be rich." Today, Deng is known as the father of China's "socialist market economy"—a far-reaching transformation that has astounded the world—and we were being given a sneak preview.

We didn't attempt to conceal our enthusiasm. Regan expressed our wholehearted support for Deng's experiment and observed that the entrepreneurial spirit of the Chinese people—visible in expatriate communities around the world—would surely help validate Deng's vision. Then, in something of a throwaway question, Regan asked, "What will be the per-capita income in China in the year 2000?"

Deng answered without a moment of hesitation: "$1,000."

The five other Chinese officials in the room instantaneously erupted with excited chatter in Chinese and the government interpreter said not a word. After several minutes of heated debate, Deng raised his hand, and the cacophony immediately stopped.

"The income per capita in China will be between $800 and $1,000 in the year 2000," he continued, slightly revising his previous statement. As we later learned, his "experiment" in opening up the Chinese economy had been so carefully planned that his associates did not want his public statements to stray from any aspect of that plan. But in retrospect, it's amazing just how on-target both Deng and his plan turned out to be. In the year 2000, nineteen years after Deng's prediction, the Chinese income per capita was $850. Today, it is nearly $3,500.

In *Modernization and Revolution in China,* the authors cite an issue of the *People's Daily News* in which a peasant from Hebei said, "In 1982, I became prosperous on the sly. In 1983, I had to be brave to remain prosperous. In 1984, I can be prosperous without any worry."[2] Only Deng's personal vision—and commitment to realizing it—made that kind of transformation possible. "To be rich is glorious," Deng told his people. It was a message that they were more than ready to hear. I am convinced that he had a greater positive influence on a larger number of people, especially entrepreneurs, than any other single individual in the twentieth century.

Life at the United Nations

By 1986, I had been running the Ex–Im Bank for five years. Phyllis and I had enjoyed our experience in Washington immensely, but we were coming to the conclusion that it was time for us to go home to California. Then came the call from Bob Tuttle, then White House director of personnel. He was offering me the opportunity to move to New York City and run the United Nations Development Programme (UNDP).

The UNDP is the world's largest source of multilateral development grants and is responsible for coordinating an amazing range of UN initiatives: UNICEF, environmental programs, economic programs, and population efforts.

"It's a big job," Tuttle continued. "You would have the title of under-secretary-general, and you would be the number two ranking person at the United Nations. Only the secretary-general would outrank you. You are just what we need at the United Nations, because you would bring a

businesslike approach to the job," and you could help promote free enterprise and entrepreneurship throughout the developing world.

Phyllis encouraged me to go for it. I called four or five friends for
advice, including Vice President Bush. He had been the U.S. ambassador
to the United Nations and said he thought that I could do some good
there. Secretary-General Javier Perez de Cuellar met with me and agreed
to nominate me for the job. Before long, I was in my new office, and
Phyllis and I were back in the city that my father had left nearly fifty years
earlier.

Arthur Brown, my deputy, was one of the best men with whom I
have ever worked. He was a brainy, kind, hardworking individual. Born
in Jamaica and well educated, he had been chairman of Air Jamaica and
later chairman of the Central Bank of Jamaica. Without Brown, I would
have been lost in a fathomless sea: an inscrutable organizational culture,
a tangle of complex rules and regulations, and so on. With Brown, everything seemed logical and somehow went smoothly.

UNDP was then composed of about 8,000 people, 80 percent of whom
were stationed abroad. (At the New York headquarters, we had at least one
person from every country in the world.) The organization oversaw about
10,000 separate projects, all serving the developing world. These varied
from bamboo housing in Central America to nurses' training in Sudan to
coaching new mothers in Mozambique to starting the first-ever newspaper
in Bhutan. The list went on endlessly. Each project up to a certain size was
approved in the field by the in-country resident representative (ResRep);
larger projects came to headquarters for consideration. By UNDP policy,
no ResRep could be a citizen of the country in which he or she served.

My job was to oversee the management of these ResReps and the
support staff behind them, to coordinate with other UN aid agencies, and
to raise the money needed each year for the UNDP projects. Needless to
say, my learning curve was straight up. I was busier than I had ever been
in my life.

Let me address some misconceptions about the United Nations and
its programs head-on. First of all, the UNDP projects were well vetted and well managed. Cash control was easy, because no one handled

cash. The funds were delivered directly to the project management and therefore never went through the sometimes-sticky hands of government officials. Both the ResRep and the country's government had to approve each project; neither could do so alone. By and large, the projects were highly successful, and as a result, UNDP was and continues to be well respected in both the developing countries and the donor countries.

None of our funds came from the UN budget. We at UNDP raised our money by direct appeal to the governments of the donor countries. I personally went to each of the donor countries at least once a year to make my pitch. In that job, I received expert help from Sarah Papineau, a Cambridge-trained British woman who was born and raised in South Africa. Our fundraising peaked in 1993—the year I left UNDP—at $1.5 billion.

Most of the wealthy countries were happy to help. The United States contributed about 10 percent of the total, closely followed by Japan and the always-generous Nordic countries. The French also did their part, although they always made me spend an agonizing five minutes speaking only French before we were allowed to switch to English for the rest of our meeting.[3] (I love the language; I'm just not very skilled at it!) Our combined efforts were not as significant as the Marshall Plan, but they were an inspired, effective, and multilateral attempt to make the world a better place. I soon came to believe—and still feel strongly today—that the United Nations deserves far more credit than it has received for its multifaceted aid programs in the developing world. If the United Nations had done nothing more than the tremendous feat of eradicating smallpox worldwide—which it did, thus ending a millennia-old plague—it would have earned its keep many times over.

The Human Development Report

One UNDP project of which I am particularly proud is the *Human Development Report*. Not surprisingly, the United Nations maintained detailed statistics regarding all of its diverse activities. Although this information had the potential to be very valuable to officials in nongovernmental organizations (NGOs) and governments around the world, it was never collected and synthesized in one place. The limited data analyses that were made were never distributed outside of the United Nations.

One day, an extraordinary man—Mahbub ul Haq—came to visit me in my office. I had met him on a visit to Pakistan when he was chief of staff to President Zia, and I had been impressed by his intelligence and political savvy. "Bill," he said, "I'm sure someone could pull together all of the information stored here in the United Nations and make it useful to the developing world in some way."

I grasped his point immediately and agreed. I love good data. "Mahbub, you have to do this," I said, "and I will give you my total support."

"But Bill, the fact is, I can't live on a UN salary."

A few days later, I bent the UN rules a bit and hired Mahbub ul Haq as a full-time consultant at a fee that was larger than my own salary. He was worth every penny. When people ask me about the best investment I ever made at the United Nations, I often point to the decision to hire Mahbub ul Haq.

Mahbub and I worked closely for the next months. We pulled together a superb team, and collectively, we came up with a novel idea—a "Human Development Index" (HDI)—which ranked countries from 1 to 164 along dimensions like income, literacy, and life expectancy. That index served as the intellectual backbone of the first *Human Development Report,* issued in 1990.

Nearly 50,000 copies of the *Human Development Report* are now published every year.[4] It is in almost every major library in the world, and— just as important—sits on the desks of thousands of government leaders around the globe, in part because it has engendered a competitive spirit among them. Every country rich or poor wants to move up on the HDI scale, and most are taking action to make that happen.

Promoting Entrepreneurship and the Free Market

While at the United Nations, I continued to advocate for free enterprise and the private sector. My timing turned out to be extraordinarily good:

I was at UNDP when the Berlin Wall came down. Next, the dissolution
of the tottering Soviet Union led to the creation of fifteen new nations.
In many of those countries, the resources of the United Nations were
sorely needed. We gave impartial guidance on the technical aspects of
setting up new governments, supported the efforts of many NGOs to
encourage social progress after years of neglect, and helped stimulate
a private-sector economy after the oppressive yoke of communism was
lifted.

I personally opened nine new UNDP offices, mostly in former Soviet
states, and I made a point of staffing them with some of our very best
people. I brought my former partner Pitch Johnson with me to several of
these countries. Because he had been a professor at the Stanford Graduate
School of Business teaching entrepreneurship and venture capital, I knew
that he would be the ideal person to convey the excitement and productivity of free enterprise and help to unleash the private energy of these
formerly communist countries.

In each country, the UNDP team served as leader and coordinator for
all UN activities there. It was a huge job, and our resources were stretched
thin. But donor countries proved very supportive, and we helped effect
major economic transitions without serious disruption.

Each country was different, of course. When I visited Belarus, I got
the distinct impression that freedom was not what the backward-looking
leaders of that unhappy country wanted. The statue of Lenin in the heart
of Minsk—the capital of Belarus—was still lovingly maintained.

Romania presented a sharp contrast. I was there in January 1990, a
few weeks after the brutal dictator Nicolae Ceausescu and his wife were
executed by a military firing squad. The country was in a state of elation.
Bucharest's University Square was awash in jubilant humanity—cheering,
dancing, and celebrating as they breathed the unaccustomed air of freedom. A humorous sidenote of that visit came when I gave a speech in
Bucharest, which was broadcast on Romanian television. I was attempting
to reassure the Romanian people that the United Nations was going to do

everything it could to help them establish a new government. Because I was sitting in Bucharest's UN office when I made the speech, a picture of UN Secretary-General Javier Perez de Cuellar was hanging on the wall behind me. Word filtered back to me that the speech had made a lot of Romanians nervous—not because of what I said, but because they didn't know whose picture was behind me, and they feared that this stern-looking character was the new dictator waiting in the wings.

The free-market system is now well established in almost every one of the countries that were released from Soviet domination. I am proud of the significant part that the United Nations Development Programme played in that transition and of the people who made it happen.

Empowering Women in Development

While I'm on the subject of advocacy—and on my way back to the subject of vision and leadership—I should mention something about our work at UNDP to advance the cause of women.

I would never claim to be the most progressive fellow on the planet, but my American upbringing gave me a liberal attitude when it came to the role of women in society. I didn't realize exactly how "liberal," in a relative sense, until my positions at the Ex–Im Bank and at UNDP took me abroad, and I saw firsthand the restrictions on women in many societies.

I decided to try to do something about those inequities by focusing on the issue of women in development. I was pleased by the wholehearted support I received from my team at UNDP on this front. We powered up a division called "Women in Development," which reported directly to me, and the mission of which was to promote gender equality and women's empowerment, particularly in the developing world. As part of that larger effort, we promoted many deserving women to key management jobs, particularly the all-important job of resident representative—a rank equivalent to ambassador in diplomatic circles.

By far my most satisfying accomplishment in this area came in 1992 when I decided to fire the sexist and arrogant man who was then serving as assistant administrator for Africa at the UNDP. My choice to succeed him was a woman named Ellen Johnson Sirleaf. She had been a vice president of the World Bank and had already established herself as a no-nonsense, dead honest, and ethical leader. The man she replaced lived up to my low expectations of him: he was planning to run for president of the small West African nation of Burkina Faso until he was charged with murdering his wife.

I met with Sirleaf in Paris, hoping to persuade her to take the job. I told her that if she agreed, she would be in a position to do more good for Africa than she would have in almost any other position in the world—which I really believe to be true. Luckily for me, she accepted the offer, and by force of personality, strong leadership, and determination, she emerged as one of the most outstanding talents in the United Nations over the following five years.

But there was still more distinction in her future. Here's an excerpt from her inaugural address, delivered on January 16, 2006, when she took over as president of Liberia:

> Fellow Liberians, we know that if we are to achieve our economic and income distribution goals, we must take on forcibly and effectively the debilitating cancer of corruption. Corruption erodes faith in government because of the mismanagement and misapplication of public resources. It weakens accountability, transparency, and justice. Corruption short-changes and undermines key decision- and policy-making processes. It stifles private investments, which create jobs, and assures support from our partners. Corruption is a national cancer that creates hostility, distrust, and anger.[5]

One episode that cemented President Sirleaf's credibility in Liberia came immediately after she took office. She personally went to the offices of the Liberian Treasury Department in Lagos, where she had once worked, and fired the entire department for corruption.

I saw Sirleaf in Redwood City, California, a few years later when she was engaged in a two-week speaking tour of seventeen U.S. cities in an effort to bring our countries together and gain financial backing for her anticorruption campaign in Liberia. In just a few short years, she had already led the country to a new level of respect. When people ask me about the best decisions I've ever made, my investment in this remarkable woman is one that comes to mind.

Cuba: Entrepreneurship Stifled

So far in this chapter, I've only talked about powerful visions that improve the common good. But there are corrupt visions, as well, and some of them can be quite powerful.

I met with Fidel Castro in February 1990, just as communism was collapsing all across the Soviet bloc. I was in Cuba representing the UNDP, and during my visit, I did my best to separate myself from the hostility between our two nations so that I could objectively evaluate the United Nations' agricultural, education, and health programs in Cuba.

There's no other way to summarize it: I was simply appalled at the striking level of poverty and the lack of development in Castro's Cuba. It was as if the country had been frozen in the Eisenhower era. The few cars on the streets were all American-made 1950s models, and the severe poverty, lack of food, and poor living conditions were shocking to my American eyes. Hundreds of billboards, all ominously proclaiming "SOCIALISM OR DEATH," littered the streets of Havana.

It was a cool evening when I finally met Castro himself. We were in the home of the UNDP ResRep, and we were seated around a long rectangular table in a beautiful garden of lush flowers. Castro was a commanding presence, dressed in his trademark khaki military uniform, which was starched and pressed to perfection. His beard was more salt than pepper, and he had probably loosened his belt a notch or two since coming to power, but overall he appeared to be in good health.

We spent five hours sitting directly across that table from each other, carrying on a deep and animated conversation about a wide variety of topics. We were both sixty-two years of age and of similar size and physical stature. Yet in terms of our backgrounds, politics, and outlook, we could not have been more different. Under the circumstances, we were about as friendly as foes could be.

During our conversation, I felt compelled to take full advantage of the fact that Fidel Castro was going to be with me all evening long. I momentarily stepped out of my role as the head of the UNDP, and in an attempt to liven up the conversation, I said, "To be honest, I've been to about sixty developing countries, but I've never seen an economy in worse shape than yours." He shot back, "Our economy wouldn't be so bad if your country lifted the embargo."

The Cuban government's human rights abuses, including torture, unfair trials, arbitrary imprisonment, and extrajudicial executions, came to mind. So I continued to prod: "The United States placed the embargo because of the human rights violations here in Cuba."

He called down the table to his yes-man: "Carlos, do we have any human rights problems here?"

Carlos, the official who had arranged the dinner, had earnestly tried to have us meet in a cooperative and cordial way, yet I was testing the waters to see how far I could swim. Carlos, visibly shaken, hastily replied, "No, no, Fidel. No, no."

Castro continued, "By the way, if you want to talk about human rights problems, what about New York City and all of those poor people there?" He had visited New York City in 1959, at a time when he was still received as an up-and-coming leader, lunching with bankers on Wall Street, speaking to an audience of 30,000 in Central Park, and even feeding a Bengal tiger at the Bronx Zoo.

I said, "Well, we do have some poverty in New York, but our free-enterprise system encourages entrepreneurship and economic development, and has led to enormous wealth and a higher standard of living for the vast majority of Americans." Castro's reaction was a heated denial that free enterprise was needed for a healthy economy.

Thinking that this had gone as far as I should test it, I said, "Fidel, maybe we should talk about something less controversial, like UNDP programs here."

"No, I'm having fun! Aren't you having fun?" he asked. I really was, so I continued. "Who do you think will win the Nicaraguan elections?" I asked him.

"Ortega, two to one," he confidently replied.

Daniel Ortega was the leader of the Sandinista National Liberation Front—the ideology of which was in line with that of the communist party—but he faced a strong challenger in Violeta Chamorro of the anti-Sandinista alliance. "Well, I think that Chamorro's going to win," I said. Castro paused for a moment to savor a bite of meat that had been approved by his official food taster. "Ortega, 53 percent," he said flatly.

I reached for my wallet, pulled out a bill, and said, "I'll bet you $20 even that Chamorro wins."

Castro snapped his fingers at his assistant. "Carlos, give me twenty pesos."

After the bills were passed to him, we eyed each other again. We both knew what the other was thinking: *twenty dollars is worth a whole lot more than twenty pesos.* I chose not to point that out. But Castro pulled out a pen, and—with a hint of a smile—signed and dated each of his bills. Instantaneously their value skyrocketed.

In diplomacy, positioning is everything. With a wink, I took out my pen and signed my bill as well, but of course, its value remained grounded at $20. We exchanged bills and sealed our bet with a handshake.

I'm pleased that Ortega's Sandinistas ended up suffering a stunning defeat, with Chamorro winning 55 percent of the vote. I never did get my $20 back, but the Cuban representative to the United Nations approached me a few times over the next few years to say, "By the way, Fidel knows that he still owes you $20."

Oddly enough, several years later, a friend showed me a copy of a handwritten letter that a twelve-year-old Castro had sent to then-President Franklin Roosevelt on November 27, 1940, congratulating him on his recent election and addressing him as none other than "My good friend Roosevelt." He then went on to write in slightly broken English, "If you like, give me a ten dollar bill green american...because never I have not seen a ten dollar bill green american, and I would like to have one of them."

His childhood aspiration to own a $10 bill may not have come true, but Castro did manage to make off with my $20!

India: Opening the Doors of Entrepreneurship

I first met Manmohan Singh, the current prime minister of India, in England in 1990. Singh had just finished his stint as the deputy chairman of the Indian Planning commission, which was responsible for the country's five-year economic plan. We both belonged to a group called the Tidewater Associates—a few dozen people who would meet each year in a donor country to discuss potential approaches to improving the lives of those in the developing world. That year's group included Barber Conable, president of the World Bank; Jim Grant, president of UNICEF; as well as several finance ministers and dignitaries from both the developed and the developing world. We met in Kent, England, at the elegant Leeds Castle—a stone fortress that dates to the year 1119 and is set on two islands.

The flap-flap of helicopter blades announced the arrival of Princess Anne, who joined our group for dinner in the baronial hall of the castle. An excellent host, the princess charmed us with the history of the castle, which had once been home to the ill-fated Anne Boleyn. The next morning Princess Anne returned to her own castle, and the rest of us got down to business.

The focus of our meeting was on stimulating employment in the developing world. I listened as, one by one, the members of our group shared ideas about how governments could start employment programs, or buy more from cooperatives—enabling farmers to sell their produce at a fair price—or some similarly well-intentioned notion. *All good ideas*, I found myself thinking, *but no one is hitting the nail on the head.*

By the time the group took its lunch break, neither Singh nor I had entered the discussion. But shortly after we had completed our meal, I stood up and declared that everyone seemed to be focused on increasing the role of government in the economy of these developing nations, despite the fact that it was government interference that was hindering economic progress.

"No one this morning even *mentioned* the role of the private sector," I continued, "and that is where the creation of most jobs should occur. In my opinion, governments do best when they get out of the way of private enterprise; when they open up their borders to free trade with foreign countries; when they allow businesses to form in small, out-of-the-way towns without forcing the entrepreneur to travel to the capital to get a permit; when taxes are kept low so that private risk is rewarded; and when governments stand on the sidelines and encourage and applaud the energetic and hardworking entrepreneurs in their countries. That's when governments can concentrate their effort instead on other important issues, such as infrastructure and law and order."

Some members of the group seemed to be nodding in apparent agreement. Then the fifty-eight-year-old Singh, wearing the pale blue turban of his Sikh faith, stood up and quietly took command.

"We in India also believe in the private sector, but only as a part of our mixed economy," he said. He spoke eloquently and made a cogent argument for his point of view, kicking off an animated discussion that lasted all afternoon. Before leaving, I intervened once again, advising Singh and the other distinguished guests to return to their countries and open up their economies to free enterprise as much as they possibly could.

I left Leeds Castle that day with great admiration for Singh, but I found that I couldn't shake the thought that India's "mixed economy," as

Singh put it, was nothing more than a euphemism for socialism. I hoped that we would meet again and continue our dialogue.

Happily, we did. I left my post as the head of the UNDP at the end of 1993 and returned to California, where I soon encountered my future business partner, Robin Richards. With our combined international experience and strong affinity for venture capital, she and I decided over French toast and eggs that we wanted to establish an international venture capital fund. I will go into detail about this fund in the next chapter.

In 1994, soon after our decision to focus on India was made, Robin and I found ourselves sitting in an elegant meeting room in the Ministry of Finance building in New Delhi. Singh, who had been finance minister for the previous two years, had driven a rapid and widespread transformation in the country's economy: away from a planned economy to a more freewheeling system. The impediments to trade had been swept aside, entrepreneurship was encouraged, and the government was actively pulling back from the "License Raj" system, which imposed a plethora of restrictions on private business. At one time, it took the blessing of *eighty* separate government agencies—I'm not exaggerating—to approve the creation of a single private business.

It was this creaky old system that was being swept aside by Singh's astonishing reforms, which had led to an annual increase in GDP from around 3 percent in the 1980s to 7.5 percent by the late 2000s. In fact, it was those breathtaking changes that had helped to encourage Robin and me to invest in India.

Singh walked into the room and greeted us with a big smile. As we shook hands, I said, "Thank you for agreeing to meet with us. And by the way, congratulations on taking all of the advice that I gave you at Leeds. It looks like it's working out for you!"

I couldn't help but chuckle at my having jokingly taken credit for unlocking the Indian economy. Fortunately, the finance minister of India laughed along with me.

Looking Back

Once I had returned to Silicon Valley, I looked back at what I had learned during my twelve years at the Ex–Im Bank and the United Nations. One observation really stood out in my mind: it became very obvious to me that the world was shrinking rapidly. Both jobs had taken me outside of America, so I knew firsthand that the developing world was exploding at an exponential rate and that it wouldn't be long before the trickle of talented immigrant entrepreneurs became a flood. In addition, I realized that the most alert venture capitalists would soon be finding their way to these developing countries, where the gates of entrepreneurship were just starting to open.

CHAPTER 5

To India and Back

Why not go out on a limb? That's where the fruit is.

—*Mark Twain*

FTER MY "MISSING" DECADE, my challenge was to figure out what to do with myself—and specifically, how to integrate my twelve years of international experience with my previous two decades of exciting work in the venture capital industry.

In 1993, I decided to leave the United Nations Development Programme (UNDP), and Phyllis and I moved back to our home in Atherton, California. I watched the grass grow for a bit, but before the lawn even had to be mowed, I was already itching to get out and do something again. Based on my time in Washington DC and New York, during which I had visited 101 developing countries, it was obvious to me that venture capital—and lots of it—was needed in the developing world. Asia was changing quickly. Almost every day, I would read about the loosening of another bureaucratic restriction, which would further unleash the abundant entrepreneurial energy that was emerging in both India and China. Other parts of the developing world weren't changing as quickly as those two Asian powerhouses, but they were certainly going through their own version of entrepreneurial ferment.

It has always been clear to me that the private sector does far more for economic development than any government programs. Granted, government is needed to regulate excess in private sector activity—such as monopolies and oppressive labor practices—but government is also prone to excesses of its own. In the early 1990s, after years of socialism and communism, it was important for governments around the globe to just *get out of the way* of the private sector.

Meeting My New Partner

Because I needed to replenish my wallet and the developing world needed venture capital to support its entrepreneurs, it seemed that the stars were all aligning. I could help promote the private sector in the developing world, as I had been trying to do for the past seven years at the UNDP. Moreover, I could get back into private life and private business by somehow connecting these two wonderful phases of my life. Connecting all these dots, I decided that I wanted to start a venture fund that was international in scope—probably with an Asian or East Asian focus—because I had learned that unfettered entrepreneurship was beginning to bring rapid growth to that part of the world, and I wanted to participate.

"If you want to do *that*," said my friend Bill McGlashan, "come with me tonight to the GSB." He explained that while on vacation in the Czech Republic during that previous summer, he had run into a young woman—then between her first and second years at the Stanford Graduate School of Business—who was talking in very similar terms. Since then, they had stayed in touch, and the young woman—Robin Richards—had pulled together a team of Stanford students to study an idea that Bill had put on the table: investing in private companies in Chile, through a friend of his who lived in that country. "So they've been looking at South America, rather than Asia," he continued. "But you should definitely come take a look."

Bill had been an entrepreneur in residence at Sutter Hill Ventures and had successfully launched and managed a medical instrument company.

He was a good friend and had excellent judgment. If anyone knew how to help move my vague inclinations toward reality, it was Bill.

I arrived at Stanford at 8 P.M. Bill was already there, as were the five students. The student team included a Nicaraguan student, Robin Richards, and three other classmates. That evening, they would be making their final report to Bill on investment opportunities in Chile. What were the likely risks? What were the potential rewards?

Each member of the team took the floor in turn, and presented an in-depth perspective on a particular slice of reality in Chile: the economy, the political situation, legal and regulatory issues that might be brought to bear, industries that seemed like good bets to investigate for a potentially profitable investment, and so on.

I thought that all the students did reasonably well—asking and answering good questions. But I took particular notice of Robin, who (as I knew from Bill) had put this particular team together and had managed its work. She was a tall, dark-haired Southerner, who tended to talk softly, slowly, and economically. She didn't dominate the group, certainly; but she filled in the blanks, kept things moving, and—quietly, effectively—made her team shine.

As I recall, their collective conclusion was that Bill McGlashan should proceed with his plans to invest with his Chilean friend. He never did, so you couldn't say that that meeting changed his life. But it certainly changed mine.

I thought no more about Robin Richards until a week or two later, when on a Tuesday morning, my brand-new fax machine extruded a single sheet of paper with some writing on it.

Remember that I had just spent a decade being a relative big shot in two huge bureaucracies. I had been surrounded by smart people—many of them young and technically savvy—who jumped at every chance to make my life easier. As a result, I was thoroughly unprepared to set up a 1994-era home office. Luckily, some friends had helped me out, including setting up my fax machine.

"Hi," the fax read. "I would like to talk to you about venture capital. Robin." I was pleasantly surprised. First, my fax machine was actually working. (This was my very first incoming fax.) Second, I had forgotten that I had given Robin a business card, on which I had scribbled my new fax number.

The following Saturday morning, Robin and I were sitting together at Il Fornaio in Palo Alto, discussing my plans to start a venture capital company focused on Asia. She remembers that I had French toast slathered in butter and syrup; I remember that she was full of interesting ideas about how to advance my plan.

I've often been told that I have good instincts about people. In my entire professional career, I've never been more certain of my instinct than I was over breakfast that morning, sizing up this Robin Richards character. At the end of a three-hour brunch, we were partners.

If my colleagues in the venture capital community thought about this outcome at all, they must have thought I was nuts. I had broken the cardinal rule of venture capital: *Do your homework, and check all references.* So maybe this quick decision deserves a little more explanation.

I generally make decisions quickly when it comes to appraising people. I asked my wife, Phyllis, to marry me three days after we met. We were on a boat headed for Europe: Phyllis with another man's engagement ring on her finger and her sister by her side, and me with nothing but Phyllis on my mind. Fifty-seven years later, it seems to be working. She is still the love of my life.

As I was sizing up Robin over brunch, I ticked off the attributes that I thought would complement my own skill set and experience. First, she was young. In many professions this is a disadvantage, but in venture capital, this can be a major advantage. The "new, new thing" almost always springs from the mind of a brilliant youth. I was sixty-five. I surely needed someone who would know about the breaking waves.

Clearly, Robin was a networker, as evidenced by her reaching out to Bill McGlashan and to a variety of students for the Chile project, and to me after the project was completed. A venture capitalist needs this quality, especially if the firm is small and can't afford specialists.

Next, she was *sharp*. Her Phi Beta Kappa credentials spoke volumes. In our three-hour mutual interview, the power of her big brain became more and more evident to me. This kind of brainpower is a blessing and goes a long way toward qualifying a person to be an extraordinary partner in a venture capital company.

In addition, Robin had the gift of warmth and sensitivity as a part of her exceptionally appealing personality. At our breakfast—and over the subsequent sixteen years—I rarely heard her make a suggestion to me or anyone else without saying, "If you don't mind" or adding, "Assuming it's okay with you." She always gives others the chance to talk, give opinions, or disagree. To me, these traits all point to an underlying quality of *empathy*, which I think is an essential characteristic of a good leader. Sensitivity and the ability to listen are terribly important to the venture capitalist—both in deciding which entrepreneur to back and then helping him to succeed. Again, these are among the many faces of empathy.

As a rule, experience is sine qua non when it comes to picking a partner for a venture capital firm and particularly for a small, new firm. I had twenty years of experience in venture capital by the time I met Robin, so this was not the highest priority on my list. That said, Robin did have some experience in the field. She had worked with the former vice president and CFO of Coca-Cola in his personal venture company. So even at twenty-eight, she did have some relevant experience.

Balance within the firm is the second-to-last thing I'd point to, if you're considering a new partner. Robin was young; I was "experienced" (a gentle euphemism for "old"). Robin was female; I was male. Robin was from the South; I was from the Northeast. Looking back, I'd admit that we did lack some kinds of balance. Neither of us had an engineering degree, and we would be investing almost exclusively in technical startups. Neither of us was of Indian heritage, and we ended up exclusively doing deals in India. It's good to have a "serial entrepreneur" on your team, as well, so ideally, Robin or I would have been an Indian entrepreneur with an MIT degree.

But with only two people, it is impossible to get it all. We later rounded out our team by hiring two Indian partners: one with a strong financial background and the other with an engineering degree.

Finally, it is important to have *compatibility* on your team. Not just compatibility in a social sense, but also passion for accomplishing the mission of building successful companies. Robin and I were totally compatible in this sense. We were dead serious in our objective. We talked about this more than anything else at our first breakfast, and in our subsequent years together. We never took our eye off that ball.

I believe that there were a couple of factors that persuaded Robin to sign up with an old retread venture capitalist. She liked what she knew about the industry, which even then had a bit of glamour to it. Based on her research at Stanford, she liked the idea of trying to take venture capital abroad. And finally, she probably thought that I could help show her the ropes, both in terms of venture investments and the international community.[1]

But I'm getting a little ahead of myself here. With all of my experience at the Export–Import Bank (Ex–Im) and the United Nations, I was convinced that Asia was the right place to be. Before we could figure out which country to focus on, we would have to do some research, and—as I've tried to stress in previous chapters—the best research is generally done on the ground. And before doing *that*, Robin had to finish her second year at Stanford GSB and get her MBA.

The day after her graduation in 1994, Robin and I were on a plane headed to China.

Scoping Out China

I was excited to see the progress China was making by 1994. Remember that I had made my first trip to China in 1981, when then Secretary of the Treasury Don Regan and I had the privilege of meeting the legendary Deng Xiaoping. In the intervening thirteen years, thanks in large part to

Deng's vision, China had moved into the twentieth century and now had its sights firmly set on the twenty-first.

The highway from the Beijing Airport into the city was now up to modern standards. Our hotel in Beijing was well managed and well maintained. Cars were gradually replacing bicycles, although the latter were still the preferred mode of transportation, lined up ten abreast at red lights. Robin and I visited the Forbidden City, Tiananmen Square, and a few other impressive locales in Beijing, mostly just taking in the sights and sounds.

Then we moved on to Shanghai, where much of the business of China was (and is) done. Our objective there was to pick the brains of enough businessmen and government officials to figure out if we wanted to locate Draper International there. Many people made an extra effort to be helpful, the evening banquets were sumptuous and plentiful, and the entertainment was largely karaoke.

Shanghai was a city under siege, reeling from an invasion of cranes and cement trucks. Pudong, the "New Open Economic Development Zone" launched in 1990, was visible on the other side of the Huangpu River. Even though it was only half built by the time of our visit, it was well on its way to becoming China's commercial and financial hub. We were told that Raychem was the biggest industrial company in Pudong, with both offices and a plant in that booming quarter of the city. This was an interesting coincidence because, as I mentioned earlier, Raychem was the big success in which General Fred Anderson had invested at the time Draper Gaither & Anderson was founded.

Despite the best efforts of a helpful young man who took us under his wing, and even with the obvious progress all around us, my new partner and I felt slightly overwhelmed. At the end of the day, we decided that the prospect of negotiating private deals through an interpreter was simply too much. Also, how could we do our due diligence if we could only communicate through an interpreter? Another overarching problem for us was the lack of true freedom of ideas, democracy, and the rule of law.

So we were skeptical about China. Yes, it might have been a great setting for large companies like GE that needed a huge supply of inexpensive, smart, and hardworking employees, but for a miniscule venture capital firm that wanted to check out possible investments on its own, China was probably a bad fit.

Nevertheless, we hopped on a plane to Hong Kong, the British enclave that was soon to become part of China again. I had become acquainted with Chris Patten, the governor of Hong Kong, when he had managed the Overseas Development Administration (ODA) for Great Britain. ODA doled out the British contributions for international organizations, including UNDP; and like USAID, ODA had its own programs aimed at helping the developing world. Patten was a talented and promising young diplomat when I first met him, and I could always count on his support when I carried my little tin cup to London on behalf of UNDP and its 10,000 projects all over the world.

Patten graciously welcomed us at the governor's mansion. He introduced us to several people who he thought could be helpful to us, and he unabashedly laid out the many, many advantages of locating our new business right there in Hong Kong.

That night we met a colorful character, Jack Perkowski, and his drop-dead-beautiful Chinese significant other. Perkowski had spent twenty years on Wall Street, and in the early 1990s, had taken off for points in the Far East to enhance his fortune. We all had dinner in an elegant high-rise setting, which I believe was a part of Perkowski's office. He eloquently argued the case for us to overcome our reservations, go back to China, and set up shop there. It was safe, he told us, and a great long-term investment. "After all," he said with emphasis, "I have put my money where my mouth is."

I smiled. He had also put some of *my* money where his mouth was. A few months earlier, Perkowski had passed through Silicon Valley and rounded up a series of significant personal investments from me and several of my friends, including Bill Edwards and John Bryan. The funds were to be used for two ventures: a roll-up of a bunch of Chinese auto-parts plants, and a buyout of the second-largest beer company in China. I had invested $500,000 in the latter venture, along with Miller Brewing Company, which was in for a 10 percent piece of the action. I had been out of the venture capital business for twelve years, but I thought this brewery deal was a lead-pipe cinch.

Over dinner that night, with the wine flowing and the lights of Hong Kong twinkling far down below us, Perkowski and I professed our continued enthusiasm for his brilliant idea—1.2 billion people soon to be drinking our beer! It wasn't until later that I learned that the expansion plan for the beer company was a disaster and that the distributors were robbing the company blind. Perkowski's colleague Tim Clissold wrote a funny and insightful book, *Mr. China*, about ASIMCO Technologies, Perkowski's auto-parts business. My understanding is that the book has sold better than either our beer or his auto parts.

Robin and I said good night to Perkowski and his girlfriend. Walking back to our hotel, we sat on a park bench and watched the boats plying the waters of the Yangtze River. Once more, we discussed our China options. Yes, the country was rapidly modernizing. Yes, the former mayor of Shanghai, the extraordinarily competent Zhu Rongji had been installed as the Premier of the People's Republic of China and was pushing hard to make Deng Xiaoping's "experiment" a success. Yes, Hong Kong—with its can-do, capitalist energy—was soon to be a part of China, and that seemed to bode well for mainland China (rather than spell doom for Hong Kong). But it still didn't feel right for us. We decided to ignore the advice that Patten, Perkowski, and so many others whom we had encountered in the past few days had given us. China may have already been ripe for venture capital, but these two particular venture capitalists weren't yet ready to take on this country. We would leave China to other risk takers.

Zeroing in on India

I won't bore you with the details of our two other trips in the same vein. Suffice it to say that we did our research on the ground in both

Indonesia and Vietnam, and although we found positive elements in both countries, we soon crossed them off our list. Maybe if one of us spoke Vietnamese, or had ties to one of the large families that dominated the Indonesian economy, things would have been very different. But we didn't.

On the long flight from Vietnam back to San Francisco, we already knew that our next business trip would be to India. I had been there a number of times, and Robin had already made plans to go with some Stanford friends on an Indian vacation that summer. I honestly thought India would be perfect for us. India had what China lacked—democracy, rule of law, and an English-speaking business community. In addition, India had a dynamic entrepreneurial population; some of these entrepreneurs had made their way to Silicon Valley and had already demonstrated their natural energy, creativity, and business acumen. Also, as I mentioned before, Finance Minister Manmohan Singh had been in place for two years and had aggressively relaxed government regulations restricting free enterprise and entrepreneurship. Another factor that we took into consideration was India's significant edge over China at the time; namely that English was then a prerequisite for computer software design, and we expected that many of our new companies would be focused on computer software. Last but not least, we both loved Indian food.

How to introduce India? The most mysterious, magnetic, and exotic country in the world? The largest democracy ever, anywhere? A land of 13 languages and 113 dialects, spoken by more than a billion people? A land of maharajas and occasional mayhem? India, India, India!

Our plane landed at the Bombay (this was before the city was renamed Mumbai in 1995) airport at 12:30 A.M. Owing to severe domestic congestion in the daytime at this then-antiquated facility, all foreign planes were required to land at night. We felt the stifling hand of bureaucracy as we crept through the molasses-like mire of customs. More endless, slow-moving lines; more forms; more stamps; still more lines. We were tired and on the verge of being demoralized.

Inside the airport, it was quiet and calm. There were bodies lying everywhere—bodies of people whom we assumed to be asleep—but it was relatively peaceful. Not so outside, where we were instantly overwhelmed by a throng of pushers and shovers, looking for either a handout or offering some service that they could perform to earn a small tip. The air was stale, but the colorful saris and dhotis were a pleasure to see. Even in the early hours of the morning, the sheer masses of human beings were staggering.

Our adventure was beginning.

Doing Business in India

Once Robin and I had finalized our decision to invest in India, I flew back to Washington DC to speak with the people at the Overseas Private Investment Corporation (OPIC). This may sound like just another of the many private hedge funds that have sprung up in recent years, but in fact, OPIC is a U.S. government agency, somewhat similar to the Ex–Im Bank. OPIC's mission is to "mobilize and facilitate the participation of United States private capital and skills in the economic and social development of less developed countries and areas, and countries in transition from nonmarket to market economies."[2] In other words, it leverages new investments made by licensed American companies in any of the developing countries on OPIC's approved list. So, much like the SBIC program, OPIC lends American investors three dollars for every dollar of equity from the investor, who commits to invest in the developing world (e.g. India). As with the Ex–Im Bank, the theory is that when the government gives the private sector a judicious boost, everyone benefits.

Because of my track record in venture capital and my extensive international experience, Robin and I had no trouble obtaining verbal approval to proceed with our plans. Other roadblocks soon arose, however. For example, we had enormous difficulty completing the legal work needed to set up the very first United States–India venture capital partnership, mainly because the Indian government's regulations and OPIC's procedures didn't match up very well. In retrospect, it's a miracle that they matched up at all, because we were attempting to pioneer a new category in U.S. venture capital. Cutting through the dense thicket of regulations along our way was a daunting and sometimes horrendous challenge. Luckily, we had superb legal advice from Dan Frank—a partner in Cooley Godward's venture capital group—and we ended up clearing all of our hurdles safely.

One interesting angle was that in order to avoid paying capital gains taxes to both the U.S. and Indian governments—assuming, of course, that we were lucky enough to make capital gains on our investments!—we had to establish a "paper entity" in Mauritius. In other words, Draper International (the name of our newly established firm) was obligated to have legal and accounting representation in Mauritius, and Robin and I were required to hold a "meeting" or two there. Let me say quickly that this wasn't all bad. Mauritius—once the sole home of the now-extinct dodo bird—is a beautiful island nation in the middle of the Indian Ocean off the coast of Africa. I knew Penne Korth, then the U.S. ambassador to Mauritius, and the local paper published our picture on its front page during one of my visits. Korth introduced me to the prime minister, who gave me a wooden replica of an old sailing ship—an iconic product of the island.

This may sound like a quaint detour, but it wasn't and isn't. Today, every U.S. investor still uses this circuitous route to make investments in India. The Indian population in Mauritius is substantial, and—thanks to a long-standing positive relationship between the governments of those two countries—large amounts of money flow to Mauritius this way, benefiting the local population. Yes, it's perfectly aboveboard and legal for a U.S. citizen to invest in this manner; and yes, I always felt a little uneasy about paying Mauritian accounting and legal fees for "meetings" that were more or less a sham. That said, I tend to agree with what Will Rogers, the cowboy philosopher, once said: "Be thankful we're not getting all the government we're paying for."

On one of our first trips to India, we met Kiran Nadkarni, a gentle, cheerful Brahmin who was doing some astute investing in the Indian private sector as an employee of ICICI—then India's second-largest bank, with assets totaling $77 billion.[3] We had been introduced to Nadkarni through a friend of Robin's, and we wanted him to be one of our partners and open an office for Draper International in Bangalore, where he lived and where some interesting electronic and computer software companies were already starting to emerge. At one point during our negotiations to set up that partnership, he agreed to meet me in New York. Things did not get off to a good start: as he was stepping out of his cab to meet me at the Yale Club, he lost his footing and broke his ankle.

Of course, I accompanied him in the ambulance to the emergency room at Bellevue Hospital in New York City. As he lay on his stretcher, I took the opportunity to resume our negotiations and twisted his arm—not literally!—to join Robin and me in our Indian venture. Today, I think that he's happy that he signed up with us, but on that day, he must have wondered whether I had taken unfair advantage of the situation.

In Nadkarni, we had our "on-the-ground" Indian partner—based in Bangalore, as it turned out—and Draper International was really underway. We later recruited Abhay Havaldar, an energetic, lean, and handsome man who had been on the Indian marketing team of Hewlett-Packard's affiliate HCL-HP. Havaldar was a perfect complement to Nadkarni, who was a financial wizard but was inexperienced in sales and marketing. I'll take this opportunity to make this key point: it's essential to have both financial talent and marketing expertise in a venture capital company—or in any entrepreneurial enterprise, for that matter. The two new partners were asked to identify opportunities, investigate the potential of each one, check references on the entrepreneurs and teams involved, and give us their recommendations in preparation for our quarterly visits.

Nadkarni and Havaldar are both likeable, have good people instincts, and are blessed with high energy levels. Between the two of them, they teed up literally hundreds of potential deals—mostly technology-driven companies—during the next six years, from which Robin and I selected and successfully pursued nearly three dozen, negotiating satisfactory terms and investing Draper International's money.

Havaldar lived in Mumbai, so we set up our second office in his home there, which worked pretty well. In hindsight, I think it might have been better for reasons of synergy to have had both men in the same office. Mumbai is about the same distance from Delhi as Los Angeles is from Seattle—that is to say, not right around the corner—and so there were some inevitable disconnects. On the other hand, we had the advantage of far broader coverage as a result of having two offices, and Mumbai ended up being the source of many lucrative deals.

One proposal that we particularly liked described a new online portal, similar to Yahoo. It was to be based in Mumbai and called "Rediff.com." The company's founder, Ajit Balakrishnan, was also the founder and partner in one of India's premier advertising agencies, Rediffusion Advertising. The idea was that his partner would continue to run the ad agency, and Balakrishnan would run Rediff.com. In 1996, we did our due diligence, and—together with the New York–based private equity firm Warburg Pincus—we bought 30 percent of the new company. Rediff launched on February 8, 1997, and today, it is the largest Indian portal for news, entertainment, and shopping.

There was an unusual aspect of this investment. The company issued Indian rupee stock to us, and a few years later, when it needed more money, it went public on the NASDAQ exchange. In doing so, it issued American depositary receipts (ADRs), a different type of stock from ours but essentially of equal value. Of course, we wanted to sell our stock when the internet bubble was ballooning. But because the company had not gone public on the Mumbai exchange, we were not allowed to sell: the company needed three years of profitability before it could go out on the Mumbai exchange, and Rediff had no such record.

As of this writing, Draper International has distributed or sold all but one of its stocks. In just six years, we returned sixteen times our limited partners' money—not a bad track record, considering that we were exploring more or less uncharted territory. The stock we haven't sold? It's Rediff, which still hasn't hit the three-year profitability threshold, and therefore still can't go public on the Mumbai exchange. On the other hand, we're not all that eager to sell, because the NASDAQ stock is down and the company has some unique characteristics.

And so we wait. Sometimes it feels like we are waiting for Godot. Again, this is venture capital. Earning sixteen times your investment may sound great—and it *is* great—but you have to be patient and willing to live with uncertainty most of the time.

Several of our Draper International companies decided to locate their headquarters in the United States, instead of in India, with corporation-friendly Delaware and tech-rich California being the home states of choice. The U.S. regulatory environment sometimes can be faulted for being intrusive or misguided, but at least the rules are clear—a great boon to doing business. Our companies' top management tended to be based in the United States, so it just made sense for them to incorporate here. (When they did so, problems such as those we experienced with Rediff didn't arise.) But in every one of our investments, most of the employees were based in India. In order to qualify for OPIC's three-to-one leverage, the bulk of our money (essentially payroll) had to be spent in India. Remember, OPIC policy is geared to promoting U.S. investments in developing countries.

Ramp Networks Inc., was headquartered in Mountain View, California, although the majority of its employees lived in India (and so it qualified for our India fund). Ramp Networks was a pioneer in internet access and security appliances, specifically designed for small-office applications. The Ramp product was reliable, simple, and cheap: three good characteristics in the rough-and-tumble high-tech marketplace.

Ramp's founder, Mahesh Veerina, was a young and relatively untested entrepreneur with deep engineering skills and an engaging smile. Short in stature but long in leadership potential, Veerina was skillfully mentored by one of my favorite venture capitalists, Tony Sun of Venrock, who served as chairman of Ramp's board, on which I also served. I've written in earlier chapters about the wisdom of betting on great people. Veerina and

Sun are both wonderful people who work hard, keep their antennas up, and have sound judgment without being encumbered by big egos. One was a budding entrepreneur; the other, a wise and experienced venture capitalist. Ramp was therefore a good bet. The company quickly achieved amazing success, went public, and reached a market capitalization of over $450 million.[4]

When Ramp went public, I stepped off the board and sold my shares. As it turned out, I sold them at their peak value—the only time that I have ever succeeded in doing that. It was pure luck rather than good planning. As with most kinds of investments, there's no such thing as a crystal ball, and venture capitalists would surely drive themselves crazy if they spent a lot of time worrying about whether they are selling a little too soon or too late. We'll return to the subject of exit strategies in Chapter 7.

Ramp Networks was acquired by Nokia in 2001; Veerina served as the vice president of Nokia's Small Office Products group for one year and then went on to found Azingo Inc., which develops next-generation mobile phone software.

Winning with Raj Jaswa and Selectica

Perhaps one more Indian case study, this time in a little greater depth, will help demonstrate how Draper International made its investments in India—and more generally, how opportunity can be spotted and pursued in new corners of the world.

One of the first things I did after Robin Richards and I set up shop in India was to join The Indus Entrepreneurs (TiE). This group was set up in 1992 by a team of Silicon Valley entrepreneurs who wanted to help foster entrepreneurship and promote a network among immigrants from their home countries of India, Pakistan, and Bangladesh (the "Indus" countries). At that time, TiE met more or less on a monthly basis and was composed of between three and four dozen people. As I recall, I was one of the few members—actually probably the *only* member—with no family or cultural ties to South Asia. But I liked the group's stated goals (in particular, their intention to bring together the entrepreneurial spirit of Silicon Valley with the South Asian tradition of guru–shishya, ("teacher–disciple," or in my terminology, student–mentor).

I won't go deeper into TiE in this context, other than to point out that since 1992, the group has helped launch businesses with a collective market value of more than $200 billion. It has grown to include some 13,000 members in 13 countries, and a ticket to its annual conference in May is always a prized commodity among the entrepreneurs of Silicon Valley.[5]

At some point shortly after I joined TiE, I made the acquaintance of a young man named Raj Jaswa, an Indian-born, Canadian-trained engineer who was already making an impact in the memory-chip field. After working for a few years at Intel, Jaswa cofounded a small chip-maker company called OPTi, whose sales grew from nothing in 1988 to $163 million in 1995, largely on the strength of its sales of performance-enhancing semiconductor chipsets for use in Intel's 486 microprocessor (in turn used in PCs made by IBM, HP, and others). It was a great ride, but when Intel switched to its new Pentium chip, OPTi was out of luck.[6]

Jaswa walked away from OPTi with several million dollars and thought briefly about retiring from business. But he was too young—still in his early 40s—too energetic, and (through TiE) too surrounded by good ideas and interesting people to leave entrepreneurship behind. In June 1996, he teamed up with another TiE member—a computer scientist and artificial intelligence expert named Sanjay Mittal—to found a company called Selectica, aimed at providing high-performance enterprise software for contract-management and sales-configuration systems.

Despite their respective stellar records and credentials, Jaswa and Mittal had trouble raising money for their new venture. We became aware of Selectica by a pretty roundabout route: one of Jaswa's partners in India had a breakfast meeting with one of my Draper International partners, Abhay Havaldar, at the train station in Pune, India, and Havaldar subsequently emailed Robin and me to say that the struggling company—and its leaders—looked interesting. Because this seemed less an Indian opportunity and more of a U.S. one, we arranged for Jaswa to make a pitch to

Draper Fisher Associates (Steve Jurvetson's name was not yet on the door). John Fisher, in particular, liked what he was seeing, but unfortunately, the venture capital syndicate that Draper Fisher Associates was trying to help put together came unglued. The reason this happened was pretty common in the venture field: other lead members of the proposed syndicate learned that some heavy hitters in the venture capital community—names like Mayfield and Kleiner Perkins—had already invested in a company with similar-looking software products and decided that this particular field looked too competitive. Jaswa had been looking for $4 million; now—in the closing months of 1996—he had nothing.

Early in 1997, Jaswa sent me an email in which he asserted that he still believed in Selectica and that he and his partner Sanjay Mittal would appreciate the chance to come over to my office in San Francisco to talk with me about it. When they came, they told me that they still felt that the company had great potential, were willing to put their own money into it, and would welcome my participation.

Thanks to Jaswa and Mittal's convincing plea, we at Draper International jumped in, providing enough seed capital to get the company off the ground. But Draper International was billing itself as an "India fund," and obviously, we needed to invest in companies that had a strong presence in that country. Luckily, Jaswa and his team already had plans to build up Selectica's Indian operations. And so, about six months after the company's launch, Jaswa started steering resources toward India—to the extent that within three or four years, fully half of the company's roughly 800 engineers were based there.

This was good for Draper International, but it was *really* good for Selectica. The company went into its battles for customers with a significant built-in cost advantage. (Especially back then, Indian engineers cost much less than their American counterparts.) One competitor, Calico, lost the business of Cisco Systems and Siemens to Selectica, and it eventually went bankrupt. Another one, Trilogy, lost GE Medical, IBM, and HP to Selectica. Yes, Selectica had strong products, but its low-cost base and fast cycle times were also vital co-contributors to its success.

Over the next six months, Selectica made substantial progress in the "configuration market," using its "ACE" software to help large companies like Dell, 3Com, and Cisco Systems sell products and services on the web.[7] When they came up for their next round of financing, Draper Fisher was ready and willing to step in and lead that round, with Draper International again participating. (These are the "son" and "father" generations, respectively, if you're having trouble keeping these similar-sounding names straight.)

One interesting fork in the road came when Jaswa approached me about a representative from Draper International taking a seat on the Selectica board. Robin was very excited about Selectica and its prospects, so I suggested to Jaswa that she take the seat. He approached her, and she readily agreed.

Nothing about Selectica's first several years of operation was easy. They were trying to break into an extremely competitive market, against competitors who either had a multiyear lead in that space, deeper funding, or both. Companies like Calico and Trilogy were well established with strong reputations, and the trade press tended to write stories about how one of those competitors was likely to emerge as the top dog in the industry. At one point, one of the younger and less experienced venture capitalists on Selectica's board voiced an opinion that may have been shared by others around the table: *Our bankers are making no inroads selling our stock to institutional investors. We need more money, and we need it fast. I think it's time to consider swapping out our CEO.*

I was appalled. I attended a board meeting with Robin and said that I had full confidence in Raj Jaswa, who had already overcome significant challenges that Selectica had faced in terms of competition. I also told them that I was astonished at the suggestion that turmoil at the top of our company would be well received in the marketplace. The proposal to replace Jaswa was quietly shelved.

With our help, Jaswa was able to raise the money that he needed. In all, Selectica went through four rounds of funding, for a total of around $36 million. Draper International participated in all four rounds, putting in a total of around $3 million. This made us the largest single equity holder in the company, at around 11 percent of the total. Robin and I felt pretty good about that stake. We knew we had 11 percent of something pretty significant. The company continued to grab market share and gain new ground in its extremely competitive niche.

Selectica went public on March 10, 2000, offering four million shares at $30 a share. On March 11, a share of Selectica was trading for $150. In other words, the company's market capitalization was a dizzying $5 *billion*. It was one of the biggest IPOs of 2000, and there were 446 IPOs that year. On paper, at least, the $3 million and change that Robin and I had put into Selectica had turned into $600 million.

Yes, that kind of return was cause for celebration. Robin and I had every intention of making money through our efforts under Draper International's flag, and this success (among others) validated our business model at the same time that it made us wealthier. But we took as much satisfaction, if not more, from the fact that we were playing a small but measurable role in helping India make its transition from an economy that was oppressively regulated to free-market oriented, one that was sluggish to one that is dynamic. And although the venture industry in India still has a long way to go before it achieves an impact that corresponds to the U.S. venture sector, the process is well underway. I'm happy to be able to say that Draper International made a contribution to the development of India's economy.

CHAPTER 6

From International to Global

In the broad earth of ours,
Amid the measureless grossness and the slag,
Enclosed and safe within its central heart,
Nestles the seed perfection.

—Walt Whitman

VENTURE CAPITAL IS A fast-moving industry. It thrives on the cutting edge of innovation, and for the past century or so, nothing has moved faster than technical innovation. So when it comes to venture capital, yesterday's news is old news indeed.

In the last chapter, I described how in 1994, Robin Richards and I did our Asian due diligence and ultimately decided that India was where we would hang our hats as "Draper International": the first U.S.-based venture capital firm focused on India. I think it's fair to say that for its time, Draper International was a pretty adventurous and innovative business. I also think it's fair to say that to some extent, Robin and I were re-creating the classic venture capital partnership. True, she and I were of different age, cohorts and genders, and our field of operation—India—was untested and exotic. But Draper International was similar in fundamental ways to the business in which Pitch Johnson and I had participated fifty years ago in the orchards of what would become Silicon Valley.

In the interest of bringing our story up to date—that is, presenting today's and tomorrow's news—I want to devote a piece of this chapter to my son Tim's international activities, which clearly represent a new and highly successful approach to global venture capital. I also want to carry forward a theme that I introduced in my telling of the Selectica story in the previous chapter: entrepreneurial immigrants to this country are making a hugely important contribution to the American economy.

The DFJ Global Network: A Powerful New Model

Where do great new ideas come from? My son, Tim, credits Silicon Valley entrepreneur and childhood friend Tony Perkins with helping to set the stage for a global entrepreneurial culture. Perkins's own businesses haven't become huge, but they have helped create what Perkins now refers to as the "global Silicon Valley." For example, he founded the Churchill Club, where great entrepreneurs are invited to make speeches to audiences of their peers (or would-be peers). Also in the audience, and circulating before and after the speech, are the lawyers, accountants, and bankers who specialize in helping entrepreneurs with their startups. "The Churchill Club," says Tim, "is similar to The Indus Entrepreneurs [TiE] in that it creates this great atmosphere for networking and providing guidance to young entrepreneurs." Perkins continued to promote the notion of "Silicon Valley" as a distinctive context for entrepreneurship and also helped build an entrepreneurial community through the magazines he founded: *Upside* and *Red Herring*.

His next venture, an online magazine called *AlwaysOn*, carried this global networking concept yet another step forward, creating a worldwide virtual community of entrepreneurs and would-be entrepreneurs. Again,

Perkins's story is less about magazines and money, and more about how a vision of a certain kind of world can actually bring that world into being.

So Tim had Perkins's innovative approach to business culture to draw from. He also had some interesting experiences of his own in the early 1990s, which involved pushing venture capital out toward new horizons and figuring out what ingredients were necessary to sustain a vibrant venture capital and entrepreneurial community. As he recalls:

> It started in Alaska. It was necessity—always the mother of invention. I was out of money at the time, and I got this letter from the government of Alaska, saying, "Bring venture capital up to us. Tell us about venture capital."
>
> It was the same letter that a whole lot of venture capitalists got, but I was the only one who followed up on it. I had never been to Alaska, so I just went up. After about three years, we finally put together a $6 million Alaska fund that was half to be invested in Alaska, and half outside of Alaska. This was 1991. Truth be told, the Alaskan government was very suspicious. As soon as they gave us their commitment, I remember one guy up there said, "Well, *that* money's gone." Fortunately, it wasn't gone. True, we lost a lot of the money in Alaska, investing in things like *Alaska Men* magazine, salmon-skin wallets, and a fish head splitter. But we more than made up for it with the investments that we made down here in Silicon Valley. The Alaskan government was very satisfied in the end.
>
> So that was fun. It was a great experience, and I realized that the investments we made in Alaska didn't work out so well because the economy there is all natural resource based—basically, oil and real estate. On the other hand, it was clear that you could do venture capital in other parts of the country, so we started to think about that.
>
> Then I got a call from a Harvard Business School grad in Utah, Todd Stevens, who said, "Hey, we're starting an SBIC here with Zions Bank. Tim, can we get your firm to run it?" And I thought, *Well, gee; let's try that.* So now we had a fund in Utah. That one was $5 million, and we were able to borrow $15 million against it through the SBIC

program, and so we started investing there. And that seemed to be working. More food for thought.[1]

With all of these experiences in mind, Tim and his Draper Fisher
Jurvetson (DFJ) colleagues created a network of venture capitalists from
all around the world—a unique model for venture capital that combines
global reach and local presence.[2] The DFJ Network is a federation of independent local funds, with each partner fund governing itself and having
its own limited partners. A system of economic incentives ensures that
the interests of the various funds stay aligned: the management company
maintains a minority interest in the general partnership of each partner
fund, and the network has a shared pool of financial carry, in which each
network partner participates and is thereby rewarded by the success of any
partner fund.

Other less tangible bonds tie the DFJ Network together. Partner
funds, their limited partners, and their portfolio companies are brought
together several times each year to build direct personal relationships.
The result? Intelligence sharing, help with fundraising, deal syndication, and what DFJ refers to as "Rolodex power": vital connections
wherever they are needed. If a lead network partner is looking to bring
in a syndication partner with a specific geographic or sector focus, for
example, it can often find that partner within the DFJ Network. Simply
put, it works: to date, the DFJ Network has coinvested more than one
hundred times.

As of August 2010, there were sixteen active partner funds around
the globe. Their "deal flow" consists of literally tens of thousands of business plans submitted each year, which—according to Tim—continue to
expand in size, scope, and quality.

Again harkening back to the lessons learned and taught by Tony
Perkins, Tim identified five factors that have to be in place for these networks to think seriously about setting up an alliance with a new venture
fund in a new region. First, there needs to be the potential for a club-
like community resource—some kind of common-ground, watering-hole

context—in which entrepreneurs are able to meet other entrepreneurs in a relaxed but purposeful sort of way. Second, there must be a good technology-oriented university somewhere in the region. (True, "somewhere in the region" gets more and more broadly defined in this age of the internet and instantaneous global communication, but it still helps to have a reasonably local technical resource.) Third, it is necessary to have at least the beginnings of a local venture capital community and some angel investors to play their particular niche role. Fourth, the local press needs to be informed about and reasonably sympathetic to entrepreneurship and venture capital. Finally and most importantly, a government receptive to entrepreneurship is essential.

The DFJ Network has seeded companies that have become multibillion dollar successes on three different continents. It is composed of more than 140 venture capital professionals with over 600 portfolio companies funded and around $7 billion of capital under management. It's a great model. I wish I had thought of it. But the fact is, great models and powerful ideas have their own time and place. You can't rush them. The world was becoming "international" in my heyday; it's "global" today. Accordingly, Tim and his colleagues have drawn on their own experiences—and the lessons of history—to create something new. As Tim puts it:

> When Grandpa started venture capital out here, "Silicon Valley" was nothing more than apricot orchards. When we were growing up, there were very few stores in Menlo Park and Palo Alto. These were tiny little communities that didn't have a lot of commerce. Then the whole economy *took off* around technology, entrepreneurship and venture capital. And I got to see that whole thing happen. So it was something I understood in my soul—in my very roots—so when I went to other locations, I knew what was needed to make that culture happen in those places.[3]

Tim and his colleagues are still making it happen in other locations, all around the world.

P.S. I Love You

The DFJ Network is just one example of how venture capitalists can branch out into other areas. But there are several entrepreneurs who provide an interesting counterpoint to the DFJ Network. While Tim and his partners sought to replicate the "mother ship" of entrepreneur-ship and venture capital elsewhere in the world, a steady stream of cre-ative people were simultaneously making an effort—sometimes a heroic one—to come to the United States and do business here in the land of opportunity.

In a lot of cases, it's the combination of an immigrant entrepreneur and an American counterpart who come up with the next big thing. I'm not sure why this is so, except to say that combining the perspective of an outsider and an insider can be a very potent formula.

The best example I can think of comes from DFJ's own experi-ence with Hotmail: the hugely successful free email service that literally changed the way the world communicates.[4] One day in 1995, two young, would-be entrepreneurs—Sabeer Bhatia and Jack Smith—approached John Fisher and Steve Jurvetson of DFJ looking for funding for one of their ideas. Bhatia, an Indian immigrant, is a confident, strong, determined marketing type, and Smith is a skilled American engineer. They floated one idea, an internet personal database called Javasoft, which Fisher and Jurvetson politely shot down. Then they floated a second idea: free web-based email.

The idea had popped into Smith's head one night when he was driv-ing home from work, and he had called his friend Bhatia—with whom he had worked both at Firepower Systems and Apple Computer—on his cell phone to run it by him. Bhatia listened briefly and interrupted his friend: *Don't say another word. Call me back on a secure line.*[5]

Tim and his colleagues, particularly Steve Jurvetson, the technical brains behind the firm, agreed that this free email idea looked interesting, especially given that the dominant players at the time—including America Online (AOL), Lotus Notes, and cc:Mail—involved monthly subscription fees. Steve recalls that while he was negotiating the terms of the potential investment in Hotmail, Bhatia mentioned that he had a meeting with Mike Moritz of Sequoia Capital the following day. Steve, still with the sour taste of losing Yahoo to Sequoia in his mouth, didn't need to hear anything else. They struck a deal.

So, how was the world going to hear about Hotmail? For the foreseeable future, the product was going to be given away, which pretty much ruled out expensive billboard, radio, and TV campaigns.

Tim asked if there was some way Bhatia and Smith could add a persistent message at the bottom of every email that would serve as the much-needed free advertising. There was a long pause. Tim plunged ahead: "How about something eye-grabbing and memorable? Like, 'P.S. I love you. Get your free email at Hotmail.'"

Bhatia looked horrified and attempted to move on to the next item on the agenda. Tim pushed on, asking Smith if such a message was technically possible to include at the bottom of each email. Smith acknowledged that yes, it was *possible*—his tone effectively conveying his sense that it was a terrible idea. The meeting moved on, with the challenge of marketing Hotmail left hanging.

A few days later, Bhatia and Smith called Tim. *Yes*, they said; they were willing to go with the viral marketing concept that Tim had proposed. *No*, they were not going to include the memorable "P.S. I love you" tagline—just the part about getting your free email at Hotmail. Tim readily agreed, although he continues to maintain that our planet would be a much more peaceful place today if Bhatia and Smith had taken his entire suggestion, rather than only half.

But even the partial tagline worked magic. Once hotmail was launched, Bhatia sent an early email—complete with the persistent end message—to a friend back home in India; within three weeks Hotmail had 100,000 registered users in India. "And at that time," Tim recalls with only slight exaggeration, "there probably weren't 100,000 *computers* in India." In less than two years, Hotmail grew from zero subscribers to more than nine million, quickly becoming the fastest proliferating product to date.

And so, "viral marketing"—a system of marketing that could spread digital products and services "virally" at zero cost to the company—was born. If a product becomes more valuable to the user when more of her friends and associates also have that product, then that product can go viral. Viral marketing has become a standard marketing technique for hundreds of successful companies in the digital world, including Microsoft when they acquired Hotmail, Yahoo when they acquired Four 11's Rocketmail (who used the same model), Google's Gmail, Facebook, Skype, Twitter, and Glam. Tim is often given credit for innovating this powerful marketing technique—truly, a game-changing accomplishment.

The problem of Hotmail's nonexistent revenue stream continued, however. Every time the company needed a new and bigger server, DFJ found itself on the hook for more money. As I noted in the last chapter, Tim hates to sell anything good, and he was convinced that Hotmail was *very* good. But both DFJ and Menlo Ventures, which had signed on after DFJ as a relatively early-stage partner, were feeling tapped out by their rapidly growing baby. The nail-biting Hotmail situation even prompted Doug Carlyle from Menlo Ventures to say to Tim, "What are you smoking over there at DFJ? Hotmail is just giving dollar bills away."

Enter the giant from Redmond, Washington: Microsoft. As part of its belated assault on the internet, Bill Gates's company dearly wanted Hotmail. (MSN, Microsoft's email entry, then had only around 2.3 million subscribers; acquiring Hotmail would instantly push Microsoft past AOL's subscriber base of 10 million.[6]) Months of negotiations began, and—after some spiraling upward, which from DFJ and Hotmail's point of view was very welcome—a price was agreed upon.

Then the question came down to the method of payment: stock or cash? The potential sellers wanted Microsoft stock, which they felt was undervalued; Microsoft—evidently agreeing with that assessment—wanted to pay cash. At one point, the Microsoft negotiators said, in effect, "If it has to be all stock, then we have nothing more to talk about." Tim and Bhatia shrugged, gathered up their papers, and walked out, leaving Tim's partner John Fisher and a few lawyers behind. There was a long and awkward silence. John finally said, "Look, guys: just do what we want, and you get the *prize*."

Microsoft capitulated and got the prize, with the approximately $400 million acquisition being announced on the last day of 1997.[7] At this point, Doug Carlyle of Menlo Ventures again approached Tim, but this time he magnanimously quipped, "What are you smoking over there at DFJ? We want some!"

Tim later marveled at Bhatia's steely resolve, calling him one of the toughest negotiators he had ever come across: "I was amazed then, and still am today, at Bhatia's willingness to put it all on the line." One significant difference between venture capitalists and entrepreneurs is that venture capitalists are almost always well diversified in their investments, while entrepreneurs have probably put all of their resources, time, and energy into one ambitious venture. Consequently, the success or failure of any one company has a much more dramatic impact on the entrepreneur than on the venture capitalist.

Betting on Baidu

Robin Li, an immigrant from China and founder of the Chinese search engine giant Baidu, was introduced to Tim and John Fisher in July 2000 by one of DFJ's former portfolio company's CEO, Scott Walchek.

To digress momentarily: Walchek had founded a company initially called Beyond News, a private-label push network in which Draper Associates invested $1.5 million in 1997. Just two months after the funding was finalized, the company lost its main customer to Microsoft and as a result decided to change its product, strategy, and name. Tim promised that he would "eat his hat" if Walchek could turn the company around. C2B Technologies (the company's new name) was a big success and within a year sold to the high-flying public company Inktomi for $130 million worth of stock. Inktomi stock soared, and in twenty months, the $130 million became worth $1.9 billion. And true to his word, Tim literally ate the bill of his baseball hat at the celebration party of C2B's acquisition.

With his newfound wealth, Walchek and his C2B partner Greg Newman started a boutique venture capital firm called Integrity Partners in 1999. A mutual friend introduced them to Robin Li, who at the time was working as a search engine engineer at Infoseek. Infoseek's CTO William I. Chang was very impressed with Li, saying, "Robin is possibly the single most brilliant and focused person I know. And his inventions, now widely adopted, are still the gold standards in Web search relevance."[8]

From his work here in Silicon Valley, Li understood the power of search technology, and he was determined to bring this technology to China for the first time. Li didn't lack ambition: he aimed to create the first double-byte search engine that would work with Chinese characters. In July 2000, Walchek—who had put in the seed funding for Li's company, Baidu—called his former board member, DFJ's John Fisher, and asked for a meeting.

Li impressed the partners at DFJ as a highly intelligent, creative, and determined individual, and they were also impressed with his technical experience and U.S. search engine background. Everyone was well aware of how large the Chinese market for internet search could become, and they were very excited about the prospect of establishing a company that could someday be the leader in what would likely be the world's largest market. DFJ's ePlanet Ventures—the first international partner of the DFJ global network—approved an $8 million investment for about 25 percent of the company.

Under Li's remarkable leadership, Baidu grew steadily from a raw startup to market leader in China and had its initial public offering on NASDAQ on August 5, 2005. In fact, Baidu's IPO was the biggest opening on NASDAQ since the dot-com peak of 2000, and it remains the most successful first-day foreign company IPO in U.S. market history.[9] "Baidu," which means "hundreds of times," represents the persistent search for the ideal.[10] With DFJ ePlanet's original $8 million investment currently being worth approximately $8 billion, I'd say that they've come pretty close to finding that ideal.

Software, Rockets, Hot Cars, and Elon Musk

Like Sabeer Bhatia, Martin Eberhard approached DFJ with both an immigrant partner and an idea. The partner was South African–born Elon Musk, and the idea was to create a new generation of electric car.

In general, venture capitalists don't usually take up with car companies. Car production is hugely capital intensive, and the auto industry is generally seen as mature, with substantial excess manufacturing capacity. (These two latter facts explain much of the misery that Detroit has gone through in recent years.) But Eberhard and Musk were proposing something radically different from the standard car: they wanted to produce the first electric car that wouldn't require the driver to sacrifice either performance (i.e., "How fast from zero to sixty?") or range (i.e., "How far can you go before having to plug it back into the wall?"). In addition, they wanted to produce a *beautiful* car—one that your typical California car nut would be proud to drive.

As multiple lines began to cross—an electric car that dollar for dollar could compete with a gasoline-powered car and appealed to environmentalists and driving enthusiasts alike—the DFJ partners began to get more and more interested in the idea. Briefly, they considered taking the entire venture with only one other venture firm as a partner; but eventually, the capital intensity of the company compelled DFJ to limit its own involvement to a series of smaller investments in this exciting startup.

Tesla Motors was incorporated in 2003. Prototypes were introduced to the public in mid-2006, and the first production-model Tesla was delivered to Chairman Musk in February 2008, with general production beginning the following month.

Today, the Tesla Roadster sells for about $100,000. Not a car for the everyman, to be sure, but competitive with Porsches and the higher-end Japanese performance cars. The company produced its one thousandth car in January 2010. The Tesla sedan—with a projected range of 300 miles—is currently scheduled for introduction in either 2011 or 2012 and should cost in the range of $60,000. In making the transition from roadster to sedan, Tesla is following a time-honored Silicon Valley tradition of playing to the egos and fancies of "early adopters." These are the customers who are willing to pay a premium for a hot, new product, making it possible for the company to use the experience gained through those early transactions to achieve design optimization, bring production numbers up, and ultimately bring prices down through economies of scale. Tesla also invented the neat trick of getting people to pay *in advance* for their cars, which meant that as a buyer, you plunk your money down and get on a waiting list—and in the process, help fund the company. Tesla went public on June 29, 2010, and reached a valuation of $2.2 billion that day.

I could go on for quite a few pages about the Tesla Roadster—which is a truly spectacular-looking little two-seater and one with a level of performance that the car magazines unexpectedly found themselves raving about—but our focus here is on the immigrant entrepreneur, who in this case is Elon Musk.

Born in South Africa in 1971, he became interested in technology at an early age, selling his first commercial software (a game he developed called *Blastar*) when he was all of twelve years old.[11] At age seventeen, he left his family and immigrated to Canada, where his mother's family was from. He then studied economics and physics at the University of Pennsylvania, where he decided that there were three "important problems" with which he wanted to get involved: the internet, space, and clean energy. He has been pursuing that ambitious agenda ever since—and with astounding success. While still in his twenties, he launched the internet startup Zip2, which he sold to Compaq in 1999 for $307 million in cash and $34 million in stock. He then cofounded PayPal, which was sold to eBay in 2002 for $1.5 billion in stock, making his 12 percent share of PayPal worth something like $180 million on paper.

In 2002, Musk used $100 million from the proceeds from these two sales to found Space Exploration Technologies (SpaceX) aimed at designing and building low-cost launch vehicles and craft for space flight. "Somehow," he told *Esquire*, "we have to reduce the cost of human spaceflight by a factor of 100. That's why I started SpaceX."[12] He has found believers, particularly Steve Jurvetson, who is a well-known space and rocket aficionado. DFJ soon became one of the funders of SpaceX, and in 2008, the company won a $1.6 billion contract from NASA to service the International Space Station after the planned retirement of the U.S. space shuttle fleet. On June 4, 2010, SpaceX's Falcon 9 rocket achieved Earth orbit nine minutes after lifting off from its Cape Canaveral launch pad. "This has really been a fantastic day," exulted Musk.[13]

Also in 2008, the National Wildlife Federation gave Musk its National Conservation Achievement Award for his work with both Tesla and SolarCity, a photovoltaics products and services company in which Musk is the primary investor (along with DFJ), and he also serves as chairman of the board.

Immigrant Elon Musk, a serial winner in the startup game, is the epitome of the American dream.

David Lee and Qume

As is the case with so many immigrant entrepreneurs, David Lee took a winding road on his way to Silicon Valley.[14] Lee was born in 1937 near Tiananmen Square in Beijing; he spent his early years in China, and after that he and his family lived for a short period in Taiwan. When the Korean War started in 1950, they again relocated, this time settling down in Buenos Aires, Argentina.

Lee's father had never been to the United States, but he knew that he wanted his son to attend college there and study engineering—a field about which he knew almost nothing but which sounded promising. He saved up $600 and, in 1956, sent his son to the United States. Lee soon focused his attention on Stanford, but the tuition ($400 for an out-of-state student) was beyond his reach. He decided instead to go to Montana State University, where the tuition was only $60. Many years later, Lee told me that he was fairly certain that at that time—in the late 1950s—there was only one Chinese family in Montana, in addition to himself. He recalled that children would follow him down the street because of the novelty: they had never seen an Asian before.

After graduating from Montana State, Lee went on to North Dakota State for his master's and then to Ohio State in hopes of earning his PhD. As it turned out, he never completed his doctoral degree. (Universities around the world may be annoyed to hear me say it, but I'm often interested in backing a really smart person who loses patience while pursuing a PhD and opts instead to pursue an intriguing opportunity in the "real world.") In 1963, Lee accepted a job offer from National Cash Register (NCR): the Dayton, Ohio–based company that had been founded in 1884 by the legendary John H. Patterson, who was one of the true pioneers of both large-scale manufacturing and distribution in the United States. In the 1950s, NCR had begun dabbling in business computers that used transistors, rather than vacuum tubes—for example, introducing in 1957 the "NCR 304," which was the first fully transistorized business computer—and was keeping its eye out for talented young engineers.[15]

In addition to a secure engineering job, NCR also offered to sponsor Lee to become a permanent resident. This was a rare opportunity back in the early 1960s, because only about fifty Chinese immigrants were allowed to become U.S. permanent residents each year. By that point, Lee knew that he wanted to stay in the United States, so NCR's offer was one that he couldn't refuse.

After a few years, however, Lee left NCR to join Friden, the Oakland, California–based company. In those days, Friden was one of the largest and most innovative calculator companies in the world and was rapidly making the transition from mechanical to electronic calculators. There he helped design the Friden EC-130, the first electronic calculator with four basic functionalities: addition, subtraction, multiplication, and division. This calculator—which to the modern eye appears truly prehistoric—was the size of an early 1990s-vintage desktop computer and sold for a staggering $1,995, roughly $13,800 in today's money. While at Friden, Lee also worked on the EC-132 (the first calculator with a square-root function) and also on the first calculator with printer tape.

In 1969, Lee and a group of experienced engineers left Friden to form Diablo Systems, a company that was partially funded by Sutter Hill Ventures; my Sutter Hill partner, Paul Wythes, joined the board. At Diablo Systems, Lee and his team developed the fastest printer in the world, which used interchangeable "daisy wheel" print heads to generate an astounding thirty characters per second. (To put this in perspective, the state-of-the-art AT&T printers of that era were printing approximately ten characters per second, and even the popular IBM "Selectric" technology—which also featured interchangeable print heads—could only crank out about fifteen characters per second.) Word about Diablo and its amazing printers spread rapidly. In 1972, Xerox acquired the company for $18 million, distinguishing it as the largest acquisition made in Silicon Valley up to that point.

After the acquisition by Xerox, Lee grew unhappy with the management above him—Xerox was in the habit of bringing in engineers from other divisions to serve as the general managers of their new acquisitions[16]—so he decided to leave Xerox and again sought guidance and funding from Sutter Hill Ventures. Lee wanted to create a next-generation "daisy wheel" printer—faster, quieter, and generally higher quality—and after hearing his convincing pitch, we decided to fund his new endeavor, which he called "Qume."

As was typical of the venture industry in the Valley in the early 1970s, we invested as a syndicate: Sutter Hill Ventures (as the lead investor) along with Mayfield and Kleiner Perkins. In his book *Valley Boy: The Education of Tom Perkins*, Tom Perkins threw us a nice bouquet for giving them this opportunity, which he said was Kleiner Perkins's first good investment after some two or three lemons. I like to think that this helped launch them on their amazingly successful venture capital run.[17] Tom returned the favor many times over by offering some of his best opportunities to Sutter Hill Ventures. I believe that this cooperative attitude in the early days of venture capital was healthy and productive for the entire industry. As the industry has scaled up and some large venture firms have become desperate to find bigger investments to "move the needle," this practice of sharing projects has substantially declined. For this and other reasons, the venture capital industry is far less profitable than it once was. That being said, I still have most of my money invested in venture capital, and I am very optimistic about its future.

Qume was formally launched in 1973, with its headquarters in Hayward. By the late 1970s, Qume had become the largest printer company in the world, with blue-chip customers like IBM, Exxon, Philips, and Erickson on its client roster. In December 1978, ITT—still a high-flying conglomerate at that point—bought Qume for what was then an unprecedented $164 million. For the second time in six years, David Lee found himself in the middle of the largest acquisition ever put together in Silicon Valley. If anyone had managed to not notice Lee up to that point, they surely didn't overlook him from that point on.

There's at least one person, however, that I'm sure Lee wished *had* overlooked him. Here, we need to go back to the spring of 1979. I was involved with the Harvard Business School Association of Northern California—then in its fifth year. We had a continuing tradition of what we called "Business Leader" dinners, at which we honored prominent West Coast titans of industry: people like David Packard (Hewlett-Packard), Ernie Arbuckle (Wells Fargo), and A. W. Clausen (Bank of America). But with entrepreneurs and venture capitalists becoming increasingly visible in the Valley, and with much of the economy's growing vitality coming out of that sector, we decided that we should launch another dinner series, this time honoring the "Entrepreneurial Company of the Year"—and, by extension, the entrepreneur behind that company.

I had just such a company in mind: Sutter Hill's own rising star, Qume, the incredibly accomplished David Lee, and Bob Schroeder—the new CEO whom Sutter Hill had identified and Lee had embraced.[18]

Although our membership at the time was loyal and energetic, it was still relatively small, and we struggled to fill the five tables at that first entrepreneurship dinner. (Today, something like a thousand people attend these annual events, and it's a place to see and be seen.)

I don't remember much about the speeches that were made that night, but what I *do* remember is how proud Lee and his wife were as we left the Bohemian Club, with him clutching his award as if it were the World Series trophy, and my wife, Phyllis, and I sharing in their pride. To me, even way back then, this felt like great progress: a Chinese-born American citizen making good and getting recognized for that achievement.

I also remember what happened after the awards dinner when the Lees and the Drapers returned to the Bohemian Garage on Taylor Street, a block away from the club. Lee had driven his brand-new BMW into San Francisco for the very first time, and I had recommended that he park it at the Bohemian Garage.

"I'm sorry, sir," the embarrassed garage attendant told Lee. "I have bad news. Your car has been stolen."

David Lee's jaw dropped. Phyllis and I gave the Lees a ride home, and although I'm afraid the whole experience was not quite the unmitigated pleasure we had expected, I am happy to report that the enduring memory from that evening was the honor that David had received. The car was eventually recovered, and Qume is always listed as the first recipient of the prestigious "Entrepreneurial Company of the Year" award—on a list that now includes prominent Silicon Valley startups such as Yahoo, Apple, Salesforce.com, Netflix, and Facebook.

How Lucky We Are

My main point in recounting my son Tim's innovations on the global venture capital front—and also in telling the stories of these immigrant entrepreneurs—is to underscore the fact that entrepreneurial talent can be found almost everywhere. True, as Tim points out, there are a number of preconditions that have to be in place before venture capitalists and entrepreneurs can find each other easily and profitably. But put those preconditions in place, and it's off to the entrepreneurial races—whether in this country or on the other side of the Earth.

Another point that emerges from these stories is that we in this country are extremely *lucky*. We're lucky to have inherited a relatively wide-open economic system and to have defended it successfully against the kinds of government intrusions that kill ambition and achievement. Equally, in spite of our intermittent lapses, we're very fortunate that we're a generally open, inquisitive, and generous people—for the most part receptive to good ideas from new and unexpected directions.

We're lucky that the incredibly bright Sabeer Bhatia decided to move to California to study electrical engineering at Caltech at age 19. (He was the only person *in the world* in 1988 to get a passing score on the notoriously difficult Caltech Transfer Exam.[19]) He arrived with just $250 in his pocket—the maximum amount that the Indian government allowed its citizens to take out of the country back in 1988. He didn't know a single person in this country, and at first, as he later confessed to *AsiaWeek* magazine, life in the United States wasn't easy:

> I felt I had made a big mistake. I knew nobody, people looked different, it was hard for them to understand my accent and me to understand theirs. I felt pretty lonely.[20]

We're lucky that Bhatia and so many of his countrymen have overcome culture shock and homesickness and stayed to contribute to the U.S. economy. Today, something like 30 percent of the software engineers in U.S. corporations come from India.[21] And on the entrepreneurial front, fully *half* of the companies that were launched in Silicon Valley between 1995 and 2005 had at least one immigrant as a key founder.[22] More generally, one estimate has it that over the past fifteen years, immigrants have started a quarter of the public companies in the United States that were venture backed.[23]

We are fortunate, indeed, that South African–born Elon Musk left his adopted country of Canada for the United States. Why did he do it? Because, he explained to a *Florida Today* reporter, "It is where great things are possible. I am nauseatingly pro-American."[24]

We're lucky that David Lee was—among his many other attributes—a farsighted and patient man, who made the extra effort to demonstrate that having a different skin color was at first a novelty, and after that, irrelevant:

> I was one of the early Chinese who came to this country [who was] also a technical person, and therefore I was able to take the step of starting something up. And that generated a lot of interest [in] other Chinese people in this country. And also it created an opportunity for everyone. And in the early days, there were many meetings, many occasions, [in which] I was the only Asian there; I was the only Chinese, you know, in the meeting, and I look at that as a very positive thing. The reason is very simple: They notice me. You go to a meeting; they are all European Americans, and I'm the only one with a different colored face, and so they know who I am. So they pay a little bit of attention . . .
>
> I remember that in the early days, I [was] the only Chinese American able to get venture support. And I remember after I sold Qume to ITT, I asked Sutter Hill and the other venture people to make a conference for the Asians to come in, to listen to them . . . And that started a lot of companies from that meeting. And therefore I believe that [it was] very important for the venture people to understand that Asians can manage companies. The Asians can do things just as well as any other people.[25]

We are also lucky that in this country, each generation of immigrants continues to open the door for the next. In a very real sense, as an early Chinese immigrant entrepreneur, David Lee paved the way for Baidu's Robin Li. Li and his generation, in turn, make it possible for other immigrants to make their contributions to the U.S. economy—and, by extension, to the global economy.

CHAPTER 7

Finding the Exit

Exit stage left, pursued by a bear.

—*William Shakespeare*

ENERALIZATIONS ARE USUALLY RISKY, but I'll open this chapter with a few of them. To the extent that laypeople think about venture capitalists, they tend to assume that we are focused from day one on what might be called our "exit strategy": how we're going to get our investment back—preferably increased many times over—and move on.

That's simply not the case. As I emphasized in previous chapters, most venture capitalists are focused on *value creation:* a process that extends far beyond establishing a high share price, or increasing that price. Like most entrepreneurs, venture capitalists are fascinated by the sheer challenge of building a business—the fun, the disappointments, the rough-and-tumble that goes along with turning a good idea into a profitable reality—and they enjoy helping to solve that challenge. We're in a very different position from, say, private equity investors, who generally invest in large companies started many years prior and increase their profitability through financial engineering and operational improvements. Think of the private equity community as the classical musicians, with the score (in the sense of the musical script) laid out in front of them. We in the venture community are the jazz musicians. There's no score. We get to improvise.

It's *not* all about the money. All investors, however—from the least sophisticated to the most—have to worry about how and when they will recoup the investments that they've made. They have to understand the larger market cycles and economic trends that will affect the value of that investment, and they have to make decisions about when to head for the exit.

What's different about venture capitalists and the entrepreneurs is that within the limits of those same cycles and trends, we have a great deal of latitude about how and when we will shape our "liquidity event." We can merge with a competitor. Or, we can pursue an initial public offering (IPO). In a bad IPO market, we can also go for an exchange of private stocks. Finding the exit is the subject of this chapter, and of course it's an important element in the venture capital ecosystem.

Going Public

Okay, the time has come to deal with IPOs. An initial public offering is exactly what the label declares: the first time a company's stock is offered to the public. It's also much more than that. As previously noted, it's a form of validation—a coming-of-age ritual. It's a translation of hopes and expectations into concrete reality. When you read one of those hackneyed stories about "overnight billionaires," they may be talking about the night before, and the day of, that IPO.

The timing of an IPO is driven only in part by the intrinsic value of the company involved. Just as important, and often far *more* so, is the state of the economy in general and the stock market in particular. Public offerings in general have slowed down dramatically in recent years, particularly after the 2008 collapse of Wall Street. In 1999, there were 486 IPOs nationwide; just ten years later, in 2009, there were only 63.[1]

Only two of the more than two dozen current Draper Richards L.P. portfolio companies—OpenTable and athenahealth—have had IPOs in the last few years. Both are well-established companies. (We stayed with athenahealth for seven years and with OpenTable for ten before they went public.) Both are healthy with strong prospects, and that was the reason to go public, despite the anemic state of the market.

This brings us directly to Rule Number One for entrepreneurs and their venture capitalists: *never consider a public offering unless you are confident that the company will deliver increasing profits and revenue after the offering, so that the public buyer will (almost certainly) make a gain.*

I believe that the public should never be offered speculative opportunities. I think underwriters should insist on steady earnings growth *before* selling the stock of any company to the public. And I'll go a step further, as indicated in Rule Number One above: the people in charge of a business that's being offered to the public need to be very sure that earnings will grow *after* the IPO. The best way to head off "buyer's remorse," and prevent a sagging stock price, is to outperform expectations in those first critical quarters as a public company.

I've always believed that founders of one of our portfolio companies— DivX, the digital media company introduced in Chapter 2 as an example of a niche-market company—made a mistake in offering its stock to the public when they did. Why? Because there were some significant strategy alterations and a few key personnel changes that arose soon after the offering, both of which led to disruption within the company. As noted, the basic codec (digital compression) product—which is still used extensively in most DVDs—was a fine product and was delivering profits, but the president became very excited about his new DivX project: "Stage 6." This was a video-sharing website which would allow users to upload and share high-quality video clips—a promising concept. It was clear, however, that it would not show earnings for years.

As it turned out, the situation involving Stage 6 was far worse than any of us expected. In fact, this new project was a complete money sink. Earnings plummeted, thus violating Rule Number One. We sold our stock, as did many others investors. The stock price plunged: the "rats off a sinking ship" mentality. Stage 6—which was simply too expensive to maintain—ended up having to be shut down.

The lesson? Well, make sure you can obey Rule Number One. Stage 6 should have been spun off as a private entity. Yes, it was exciting and sexy, and with a little bit of luck Stage 6 might have been received like YouTube or Hulu—in which case, of course, the stock would have soared. But that was simply too speculative a leap to take in the same time period that the company was trying to prove that its IPO had been a good idea. Two years earlier or later, fine; but not in the glare of the public spotlight, with the company's stock price so closely tied to its profitability.

There are many other questions that need to be answered before a CEO should recommend to the board—or the venture capitalists should recommend to their CEO—that it is time for an IPO. For example:

- **Do we really need the money?** Usually the answer is "yes," but sometimes it's "no." If the company is growing like crazy and has only a modest income stream, the answer is probably yes. If the company is just bumping along in a quiet niche, with no bright prospects in sight, the answer is probably no. Being thinly capitalized doesn't necessarily mean you need a big cash infusion.

- **Is the money going to be enough?** Usually a small company can sell about 20 percent of its stock in an IPO. How does our price-earnings ratio compare with those of our competitors? Run some scenarios, including some very conservative ones, and see what going public is likely to yield. If it's not enough, don't do it.

- **How's our timing?** I've already mentioned the critical impact of the state of the markets.

- **Do we need this for our acquisitions strategy?** Sometimes the best way to grow is to acquire other companies or other products, and sometimes you need a public stock in order to go that route. Of course, you're going to have to *perform* well to make that stock useful in the acquisitions process. In other words, a high stock multiple on earnings makes life much easier for the acquiring company.

- **Do we need this for recruitment and retention?** Liquidity can help attract new employees and keep current ones happy. Often privately held companies, in an effort to stay competitive on the human resource front, establish incentive programs that offer stock options. At some point, the employees will want to exercise their rights to buy the stock and sell it at a profit.

- **Do we need this for our image?** Rightly or wrongly, public ownership often lends prestige and credibility to the company in its sales efforts, general public relations, and the execution of its future strategies.

- **Do we have the horses?** Do we have a CEO who is ready to answer to the new public stockholders and accept responsibility for both the good and the bad as it unfolds in an uncertain future? Do we have a strong CFO who is experienced in IPOs? Do we have a seasoned board with a clear sense of how our world is about to change? Do we have the resources (and the willingness!) to comply with the legal and audit requirements of the Sarbanes–Oxley Act of 2002—the landmark legislation that set higher standards for all U.S. public boards and accounting firms and added millions of dollars to the cost of going public? Will our financial team be able to produce quarterly financial statements in the required form and time frame? Are we prepared for the potential liabilities, the requirement for transparency and full disclosure, and the short-term focus of the analysts who follow our stocks?

Assuming that your answers to these kinds of questions keep pointing toward an IPO, then you'll need to go out and hire the best possible legal and accounting help you can find. In fact, you actually should do this well *before* you make the decision to go public, so that you can give them the chance to prepare you properly. They will groom you for your negotiations with the underwriter; pull together a good, clear, clean registration statement for the SEC; and get you ready for a grueling road trip that is likely to last several weeks, during which your biggest potential investors will listen to your pitch, grill you mercilessly, and decide your fate based on what they hear.

The whole process will take about three months. It will require endless amounts of time, money, and energy. During that time, the CEO will hold two full-time jobs. It's critically important to carefully plan the road trip. This aspect is crucial. It is basically a sales trip; the biggest and most interested potential investors are your audience. You only get one chance to impress them.

Of course, it's also critically important to keep the business firing on all cylinders, because all of your efforts will be wasted if your earnings dip just before the IPO. The deal will be off, and you and your colleagues will be hugely embarrassed.

I'm definitely not trying to talk you out of an IPO. I'm just trying to underscore the fact that when you consider everything that has to go into a successful IPO, you may decide that staying private has its virtues. Some of the strongest companies in the world—companies like Bechtel, Cargill, and PricewaterhouseCoopers—are happily private. They stay out from under the plethora of burdensome regulations to which public companies are subject. These companies also have the great luxury of ignoring Wall Street. In many cases, they are dominated by one or more families, and those families get to exert an influence on the company in a way that is almost never true for public companies.

The Truth about Underwriters

Underwriters are absolutely essential to the financial needs of a rapidly growing company that wants an IPO. They are the institutions that, to speak precisely, "administer the public issuance and distribution of securities from a corporation or other issuing body."[2]

First, some ancient and recent history that explains the structure of the underwriting market as it pertains to the startup game. During the early years of the venture capital industry, companies were blossoming as if every month was May or June. In Silicon Valley, liquidity for small companies was readily available because of what we called "the Four Horsemen," four smaller investment banks—Alex. Brown Inc., Hambrecht & Quist Group, Robertson Stephens & Co., and Montgomery Securities—who took a big interest in launching entrepreneurial companies into the public market through small IPOs. Back then, when the brokerage fee was 5 percent, these firms could afford to hire one or two analysts who really understood technological products and the companies that made them. Those analysts served a very important purpose. They could explain why each of these companies would grow and how they would compete successfully with larger, more mundane companies. Roy Rogers worked as an analyst for Hambrecht & Quist; on a regular basis, I would see him pop up in the president's office of our best portfolio companies. When we were ready to take a company public, Rogers was always on top of it.

Another favorite "horseman" of ours was Sandy Robertson, who founded Robertson Stephens. Now running a large private equity fund, Sandy recently told me that Robbie Stephens, as the company was referred to back then in their vernacular, took 500 companies public. All of these small investment banks performed well and were profitable because at that time, Merrill Lynch and Goldman Sachs were not interested in following the little tech companies in far off Silicon Valley. A small underwriting did not have much effect on their bottom line but was very meaningful to these smaller banks who catered to the "next tier" of institutional investors and local individuals.

Then, a major mistake was made in Washington DC in 1999. U.S. regulators and Congress were overwhelmed by Wall Street pressure to repeal the Glass–Steagall Act, a very sensible 1932 law that separated commercial banks from investment banks. When that wall came down, the Four Horsemen were swallowed up by the commercial banks. Bank of America bought Robertson Stephens; Bankers Trust bought Alex. Brown; JPMorgan Chase bought Hambrecht & Quist; and Bank of Boston bought

Montgomery. Although this was a satisfactory exit for the owners of those firms, the venture capitalists and entrepreneurs of small profitable companies had the IPO door slammed in their face as one by one those Four Horsemen hit the dust and were closed down. A difference in culture, size, and regulations between commercial banks and investment banks made these marriages untenable.

A far greater problem exploded in 2008 when much larger mergers that were allowed to take place led to commercial banks risking customer deposits (which are guaranteed by the U.S. government) on cleverly devised investment banking schemes, which carry big fees but horrendous risk. Add to that risk the excessive leverage commercial banks are authorized to utilize.

In simple terms, a commercial bank was traditionally very cautious about potentially losing the principal on any loan. Mortgages required about one-third of the cost of the house for a down payment, and the homeowner had to have a salary that would cover the mortgage payments. The bank could not afford to lose principal because its only source of income was the spread of interest rates and a few related fees. It takes many years for a bank to regain lost principal.

Today, as a result of moving commercial and investment banking under the same roof, the whole country has suffered. The first tip-off that we were in for trouble came ten years ago when the Four Horsemen disappeared. The result was the loss of innovative, energetic, and productive service providers for these young, strong, but still-small companies that had been patiently nurtured by venture capitalists. Without this exit, venture capitalists cannot recycle their funds and much of the good synergy I have been discussing between the venture capitalist and entrepreneur—which leads to spectacular new products and services—stagnates and dries up.

Now let's look at some of the specifics of the underwriting process. The relationship between a company going public and the underwriter making that process happen is both simple and complex. The financial arrangements tend to be simple, and the emotional overtones tend to be complex. (How could they be otherwise? The entrepreneur is selling his *baby*.)

Underwriters sometimes agree to work on a "best efforts" basis—meaning that they are not obligated to pay for any stock that they are unable to sell. However, most strong companies insist on selling their underwriter all of the stock at a fixed price that is set the night before the public offering. The investment bank then sells it all the next day. In addition, the company pays the underwriter a fee of around 7 percent. This sometimes feels like a large amount, but if the IPO is a success, the underwriter has certainly earned that 7 percent.

The underwriters can also reserve a small amount of stock for themselves in what is called a "green shoe." It is like an option to buy without a commitment to do so. If the stock is up, they can buy and resell the same day for a quick profit.

The day a company goes public can be a happy day for the founders, the employees, the underwriters, and the brokers. If the stock rises 10, 15, or 20 percent, everyone is satisfied, including the new stockholders. If it jumps 50 percent, the company will be concerned that it had left too much on the table. That, however, is far better than any drop in the price after the underwriting. If that happens, of course no one is happy.

Ah, Wall Street!

Although the drama is mainly restricted to the first day or two after the IPO, the underwriters' work continues long afterward. They have to follow the company closely, put out reports, and inform their customers about the company's operations, revenues, and profits as the future unfolds.

When Do You Find the Exit?

Here's another generalization that I think may help explain the "exit" process better: some venture capitalists and entrepreneurs sell their stock too soon after an IPO.

It's a phenomenon that's puzzled me. After many years of nursing their companies—from birth to a healthy, self-sufficient condition—they decide to cut and run. Most don't need the money, at least in the sense of paying the electric bill and keeping a couple of nice cars on the road.

Take the example of a company that requires $2 million to start up and another $8 million in growth capital over five years. This is a theoretical example, but it's real enough. Assume, for argument's sake, that the entire $10 million comes from the same venture capital company. Also suppose that the final ownership split is 60-40 between the venture capitalist and the entrepreneur, respectively. Assume further that at the end of those five years, the company goes public. Finally, let's say that after the public buys 20 percent of the company for $20 million—establishing the company's market valuation at $100 million—the venture capitalist still owns 50 percent, and the management, 30 percent. At this $100 million market cap, the venture capitalist would have made five times her $10 million investment—a good return on her "seed" money and five years of work on behalf of the company (serving on the board, opening doors, recruiting management talent, and so on). For his part, the entrepreneur is looking at a $30 million cash payout: again, not a bad payday based on five years of incredibly hard work and a minimal cash investment.

Here's the rub: statistically speaking, there's a good chance that without a significant amount of additional work, the company's value would have doubled in just a few more years. Yahoo, Microsoft, Google, and Infosys, for example, were just beginning to gain momentum when they issued stock to the public. Those venture capitalists, entrepreneurs, and others who held on made the biggest gains. Warren Buffett would call it "the snowball effect." If you know your company well and like it, stick with it—and you should know the company well. After all, you created it and built it brick by brick.

Of course, if the stock is clearly overpriced, then good business practice is to sell it. But even then, this should be done carefully and only after any bad news is fully disclosed to the public.

In short, as either an entrepreneur or a venture capitalist, you probably *shouldn't* be in a hurry to sell your company's stock, and you probably *can't* rush to sell. So don't rush.

Staying Private

Private companies can face serious liquidity barriers. Both market conditions (a severe downturn in the economy) and regulatory requirements (Sarbanes–Oxley) have limited a company's access to capital and inhibited the ability to transfer ownership through an IPO. The hurdles to becoming and being a public company have increased. For example, between 1980 and 2010 in the United States, the average public offering skyrocketed from $20 million to $200 million, and the small companies are no longer interesting to underwriters in these post–Four Horsemen days. The average time until a liquidity event has increased from six years to eleven years, and the typical number of companies that are going public has decreased from 280 companies to fewer than 60 companies a year, respectively.

The markets for private securities have, to date, been rather inefficient. As a result, private securities have not traded broadly and have arguably been inadequately priced as well. The number of private companies in the United States dwarfs the number of public companies. On average, for each of the past six years, 3,200 private companies have raised capital (totaling an estimated $25 billion), versus only 52 venture-backed IPOs estimated at $5.62 billion. There is a large contingent of qualified institutional buyers (QIBs) and accredited investors (AIs), who have the ability and appetite to invest in privately traded securities but have refrained—for a number of reasons led by a lack of available information and a dearth of liquidity. By addressing these traditional barriers, the newly formed private stock exchanges, FinancialOS and SecondMarket, have opened up a vast market opportunity for themselves, private companies, and investors. The extent of their success remains to be seen.

Other Exits—Timing Is Everything

As implied earlier, patience is a virtue. Venture capital has to be *patient* money. This is especially true when the entrepreneur is doing well despite weak market conditions.

I learned that lesson the hard way, a decade or so ago. My partner Robin Richards and I had made a big return on a little company called LinkExchange, which we had bumped into at a computer show in Los Angeles. "Bumped into" is almost literally true: we encountered a large truck, with the LinkExchange logo printed all over it, parked at the entrance to the show. We agreed that this was a clever marketing gambit for what was presumably a small company with little or no marketing budget.

We dug deeper. Robin and I liked the founders, Tony Hsieh and Sanjay Madan, who started their entrepreneurial careers selling pizza in their college dorm and built LinkExchange on the side.[3] We also liked the product: LinkExchange provided online advertising services and maintained a free network of some 200,000 websites on which advertising banners could be placed. So we invested, along with Sequoia Capital and a couple of angels. When the company sold to Microsoft in 1998 for $265 million, we all cashed out.[4]

In 1999, we again invested in Hsieh. He sold shoes of all sorts over the internet, drop-shipping them directly from the factory to the customer. We loved the concept and his frugal management style. Robin and I also admired his almost fanatical emphasis on customer service and company culture, which he had concluded were inextricably intertwined. (Happy workforce = happy customers = happy workforce, at least in most cases.)

By 2000, however, internet companies were starting to implode all around us, and the carnage was pretty awful. Hsieh's venture was still looking somewhat speculative, and even though we believed in him, we thought that it was still possible that he and his colleagues could soon find themselves on that growing scrap heap. Meanwhile, Robin and I were concerned because so many investors had lost lots of money when the bubble burst; we were in a hunker-down-and-circle-the-wagons mentality. So when an opportunity came up to cash in our convertible debentures rather than converting them to stock, we took it.

Big mistake. Hsieh's company, Zappos.com, now a division of Amazon, brings in over $1 billion a year and is one of the best-known names in internet retail.

The lesson is simple: venture capitalists should not make a quick decision to exit a private investment just because the stock market has shaken the confidence of public stock investors. Swim against the tide.

The flip side of this strategy is illustrated by a story about Torrent Networking Technologies, a Silver Spring, Maryland–based company founded by Hemant Kanakia. Kanakia, originally from Mumbai, India, was a sophisticated Bell Labs engineer with a distinguished track record in developing an exciting new switching architecture. The product line, designed in Maryland but produced in India, included routers that were expected to be faster, better, and cheaper than Cisco's and Juniper's equivalent products. Draper International invested $2 million at the beginning— building on the India connection—and Kanakia set about recruiting a strong team, on both the engineering and marketing sides of the shop.

But there was a problem. As it turned out, our router was actually slower, more expensive, and in almost every other way worse than Cisco's and Juniper's. Quickly, Kanakia bumped himself upstairs and recruited his successor as CEO. When that new CEO—Jean-Luc Abaziou, fresh from a stint as the head of Alcatel Data Networks—called a board meeting rather suddenly in the spring of 1999, I attended by telephone from California. "We have an offer of $500 million from Ericsson to buy Torrent," Abaziou told us, "but with more time and more bidders, I think we might get a better price."

Now, seldom do I take an unyielding position, other than on things ethical, but in this case I was adamant: *sell!* We brought too little to the table, I told my fellow board members, and we were behind the eight ball. Time was not on our side. With this sale, I stressed, we could avoid an impending disaster. And on the positive side, Ericsson would get a start in the emerging router industry, which it badly wanted. Kanakia, Abaziou, and other senior managers would make a killing. And yes, Draper

International would get $20 million for its $2 million stake. The challenge and opportunity here, I told the board, is to not get greedy, especially when the handwriting is on the wall.

Fortunately, the board agreed. We immediately took the offer, and as far as I know, none of us ever looked back. Don't be greedy! If a reasonable exit presents a solution to a dicey situation, take the exit.

I think of Torrent as the exception to the rule of patient value creation and methodical harvesting of that value. More typical of the way I do business, and ultimately look for the exit, was my relationship with Skype.

Let me put you in the scene. It's the summer of 2005. I'm sitting in a cozy restaurant a few blocks away from Skype headquarters in London, having lunch with the company's two founders, Niklas Zennström and Janus Friis. The two Scandinavians were asking my advice at a crucial decision point in the company's history: sell, merge, or stay on the current course?

At this meeting, as at so many others in the past, I was impressed with the way the two founders worked closely together without stepping on each other's toes. Friis was twenty-nine years old, Danish, and Skype's foremost engineering genius. Zennström, a thirty-nine-year-old Swede, was the business brains. Several years earlier, they had come up with a software application that allowed users to make voice calls over the internet (a "voice over internet protocol," or VoIP). It was nothing short of a revolution—connecting users all over the world at little or no cost to them and throwing a hand grenade into the very heart of the stodgy and bureaucratic telecommunications industry. Zennström and Friis both knew that Skype's disruptive technology—especially its superb sound quality—was immensely valuable, and they wanted top dollar if they were going to sell their baby.

In 2002, I became one of the first seed investors in Skype. At a later stage Draper Fisher Jurvetson became the company's most substantial investor, and Tim took a seat on Skype's board. A partner of mine, Howard Hartenbaum, had helped Skype with its original business plan, and at other points along the way, Howard and I spent a lot of time and effort strengthening Skype's strategy.[5] In its first three years, Skype had demonstrated its enormous promise and potential buyers were closing in and waving large sums of money. The offer under consideration that day in London was around $2.5 billion from eBay.

"Well, gentlemen," I said at one point, "$2.5 billion is a lot of money. And yes, you've performed wonders with Skype during the past few years. But frankly, it's hard for me to believe that you will get more than that for the company."

Zennström, the company's CEO, led their side of the conversation, although it was more like the two of them thinking out loud. "What do you think of Morgan Stanley as our investment bankers?" he asked. "Do we *need* an investment banker, when I know we can get $2.5 billion from eBay? The other potential acquirers might be a better fit, but their offers aren't quite as good. Should we take a lower offer from one of them, in hopes of a better fit? How much compensation should we get for performance? We are confident in our future performance. Can a transaction be bifurcated, giving the management and others who so choose the option to receive less money and stock than other shareholders up front and more through an earn out if their future performance achieves growth projections?"

Zennström raised question after question, all of which I did my best to answer. I could see that he was carefully weighing my answers and making mental notes of those that he felt were useful. I think some of my answers *were* helpful, and at the same time, I had confidence that these two impressive young men would do the right thing both for themselves and their shareholders. My point here is that this was the *right* relationship: the venture capitalist offering (hopefully) sage counsel and the entrepreneurs weighing the different exit strategies in light of that advice.

We kept talking. By the time we got back to their office in central London, I knew that they were ready to merge the company for the right price—particularly if they could keep management control and get paid more if they hit some very optimistic performance numbers. I told them that I favored hiring Morgan Stanley and merging with eBay, which appeared to be the most flexible and interested suitor. They agreed and put the eBay proposal in front of their board.

As it turned out, my son, Tim, was the only board member to vote against the eBay proposal, believing strongly that Skype should remain independent. (Tim never likes to sell anything, especially apparent winners like Skype.) But the entrepreneurs wanted to sell, and the board respected their wishes. The final price was approximately $2.6 billion, which was comprised of $1.3 billion in cash and the value of 32.4 million shares of eBay stock.[6] The value of my seed investment in this truly great and transformative communications company multiplied by 1,000, and I donated almost all of it to various charities.

We'll return to philanthropy in Chapter 8. For now, suffice it to say that I get a very warm feeling every time I hear the name "Skype" mentioned—which seems to happen more and more frequently, as the company's technology moves to the very center of cyberspace.

One interesting aspect of this exit was the way in which DFJ, Howard Hartenbaum, and I managed to sell our eBay stock within a week or so of closing, even though most of that stock was restricted. We were convinced that eBay's stock was overpriced—an assessment that was soon borne out—and we wanted to unload it as soon as possible.

As it turned out, we sold it all in less than a week.

How did we do it? Let me hasten to say that it was all aboveboard. Steve Rehmus, my personal investment adviser at the time, and Andy Chase, the hottest broker in Silicon Valley and Smith Barney's star nationally, came up with a plan and executed it beautifully. Their plan involved a complex combination of puts and calls, whereby investors who believed that eBay would be worth more in the future, were willing to pay for options on our stock. Let me also hasten to say that this stuff was, and is, way over my head as a humble venture capitalist. In any case, eBay was selling at $44.96 a share when the Skype deal closed, and somehow, Chase and Rehmus got us $45.21 a share for 100 percent of our stock. Six months later eBay was selling for $33 a share, so our exit was a total success.

Cashing out through a merger with a larger public company as we did with Torrent and Skype is far less complicated and usually more liquid for large holdings like ours than going through the IPO or public offering route. On the other hand, an IPO allows the founders to maintain control and continue to guide the destiny of their company. A sale to or merger with a larger company usually means loss of freedom and independence.

These two very different courses of action should be studied closely and discussed thoroughly by the board and the management before moving ahead.

Of course, most venture capitalists who read this will immediately—and correctly—point out that I have assumed that the companies I am discussing have the comfort of choice. Many companies—in every venture firm's portfolio—are coming up against a deadline. Their "runway" is short because the money in the bank is drying up fast. Their venture capitalists and investors are tired. New prospects for additional rounds of investment are nonexistent. Their "burn rate" is too high, and yet if they resort to chopping their staff in half, they will look weak to the one lifeboat that they see—another company that might need their technology or their team. This is a nail-biting time for the entrepreneur and the venture capitalist. The venture capitalist has decided the dream that was so tantalizing and inviting a few years ago has now become somewhat of a nightmare. The entrepreneur sometimes resents the lack of faith that the venture capitalist is demonstrating but usually understands that the ever-receding horizon is *still* far away and so is the chance for more funding. At this point, the venture capitalist must decide if he is sending good money after bad by making another investment or offering a "bridge loan"—theoretically a bridge to the next institutional round but often a pier or a bridge to nowhere. It is at this time when venture capitalists and entrepreneurs display their inner strengths and weaknesses. It can be very revealing and is always exciting. Good judgment and goodwill are never more needed or respected.

There is another form of exit—shutting the company down—but I don't recommend it as a steady diet. You cannot be a venture capitalist, however, without experiencing some failures. It stings, but the learning experience is invaluable.

I was on the board of Blue Vector—a designer and builder of R.F.I.D. sensor networking platforms—and I was extremely impressed by the inter-actions between the board and the management during times of stress. The management was open and clear about the state of the company, and it was apparent that the cost of installation was eating us alive. A merger with Cisco was our only hope. Cisco declined, and the venture capitalists on the board unanimously agreed to keep enough money available to see that employees and suppliers were properly treated as the company was shut down in a very orderly way. The calm maturity shown by the CEO, the founder, the other members of management, and the venture capital-ists was extraordinary—especially because nearly six years of concentrated effort had been sacrificed and over $10 million of invested capital had to be written off. We are all older, wiser, and disappointed in the end result of Blue Vector, but somehow I think that we are better off for having tried.

CHAPTER 8

The Business of Philanthropy

What business entrepreneurs are to the economy, social entrepreneurs are to social change. They are the driven, creative individuals who question the status quo, exploit new opportunities, refuse to give up, and remake the world for the better.

—David Bornstein

MY FATHER WAS NEVER a rich man. Accordingly, philanthropy was not a major focus in our family when I was growing up during the Great Depression. My father and mother were on a very tight budget and that reined in their intrinsically generous natures.

Despite the financial difficulties in our family, however, my father was always very sensitive to the challenges being faced by others. I remember that at Christmas time, he would sit in our study and write out $25 checks—about twenty or thirty of them, I seem to remember—to close friends and family members who were struggling far more than we were. Without fanfare, he made it clear to me that this was a time of year when giving to the needy was more important than almost anything else.

He stretched, and stretched hard. I still think of him bent over that desk, writing note after note to go with check after check. I also knew, as I mentioned in an earlier chapter, that he was returning his own Christmas presents to the store, year after year, because our household's cash flow was so precarious.

I learned a lot from my father about the importance of philanthropy. And although I help more people and write bigger checks than he was ever able to do, somehow I still don't feel as generous as my father was.

I subscribe to the "Andrew Carnegie Dictum," which essentially states that it is important to spend the first third of one's life getting all the education one can, the next third making all the money one can, and the last third giving it all away to worthwhile causes. Building on this belief, I came up with a simple idea that has come to fruition, one which I think has already had a significant philanthropic impact and—if things continue to go well—is likely to have substantially more impact in the future.

The Foundations of Our Foundation

In retrospect, the idea seems almost self-evident. I can't remember exactly when I first talked to my partner Robin Richards about it, but I remember saying that we should think about giving back some of the money we earned in the venture capital game. We could set up a foundation to seed nonprofit organizations at their inception and in their earliest years of operation. We could use our venture capital skills to find and assess the best and brightest "social entrepreneurs"—a new phrase that was coming into vogue—in the same way we found traditional entrepreneurs who were starting up businesses. Although the line of distinction between the two types of entrepreneurs is becoming increasingly blurred, social entrepreneurs are defined as innovators who utilize entrepreneurial passion and rigor to solve societal problems.[1]

Robin and I figured that we could give selected social entrepreneurs a guaranteed sum of money for a set time period—$100,000 a year for three years—and after that, they and their good idea would be on their own.

Robin loved the concept and quickly began embellishing on it. "In those three years," she said, "we are going to have to give them lots of loving care, just as we do in our venture capital fund." I agreed, knowing exactly what she meant by "loving care." We would go on the board, help them find complementary staff, and introduce them to later-stage sources of money. As we had both learned from our venture capital experience, this targeted support and strategic guidance is often as important as the funds provided.

We would remain pretty far in the background. But even as silent partners to the success of our social entrepreneurs, we would derive satisfaction from knowing that we had helped good things happen. This new field of venture philanthropy was just getting started, and I was as excited about it as I had been forty-five years earlier when I began my venture capital career in the earliest days of the industry.

But there was a major wrinkle: given our existing commitments, including the ones that generated the money that might one day bank-roll this new venture, we didn't have the *time* to do all that. We needed someone to lead the way—someone outstanding, who in the best of worlds would turn out to be better at her business than we were at ours.

"Jenny, are you telling me you want to work in the nonprofit arena?"

The self-confident young woman standing next to me nodded vigorously.

"But you've already spent several years at an online marketing company, where you are doing great things," I continued, secretly hoping that I wouldn't succeed in dissuading her from her intentions. "You've also graduated from the Stanford University Graduate School of Business, where you learned how to be an even better businesswoman. You're in a position to write your own ticket. Are you *sure* you want to run a nonprofit operation?"

"I am *sure*," the young woman said. There was something in her tone that convinced me that this wasn't an idle decision or a passing fancy.

It was autumn of 2001. We were standing in the courtyard of the Schwab Residential Center on the Stanford campus. It's an unusual building with a strongly Spanish flavor—red tile roofs and bright yellow walls—designed by the famous Mexican architect Ricardo Legorreta. I had been daydreaming a bit, thinking about Legorreta's design, when I had bumped into Jenny—the daughter of one of my good friends, Gary Shilling—who was attending a conference at Stanford that day. I was quickly warming up to the idea that she had the skills and drive to put the "Draper Richards Foundation," still just an idea in Robin's head and my own, on the map.

A few weeks later, Jenny Shilling came to meet Robin at our office, and we talked about our respective ideas for the directions in which a foundation might go. With Robin's and my encouragement, Jenny put together a business plan that was clear, well thought-out, and very professional. We all agreed to move ahead and put the plan into action.

As I've emphasized in previous chapters, plans are important, but people are *critically* important. It was immediately evident that we had made the right decision in hiring Jenny. She almost single-handedly launched the Draper Richards Foundation and quickly built the organization's reputation for conducting in-depth research, finding superb talent, and providing brilliant coaching to the selected social entrepreneurs. Three years later, Anne Marie Burgoyne, also a graduate of the Stanford University Graduate School of Business—and the winner of the prestigious Ernest C. Arbuckle Award, as voted by her fellow students—joined our team as a full partner. Anne Marie had private-sector experience with a young software startup, and she had been executive director of United Cerebral Palsy of the Golden Gate (San Francisco). Thanks to her diligence, intellect, engaging personality, and intuitive nature, Anne Marie has substantially enhanced the Draper Richards Foundation's reputation and has helped ensure the success of our programs.

That puts several of the key players on the stage. So what does a foundation dedicated to social entrepreneurship do? As suggested above, our philanthropic model grows directly out of our business model. The Foundation funds early-stage nonprofit social entrepreneurs who have the potential to *grow*—both in terms of size and impact. We invest in social entrepreneurs who aim to change the world. We call our chosen applicants "Draper Richards Fellows."

The Foundation receives hundreds of applications each year. (We only fund about 2 percent of our applicant pool.) As we sift through this small mountain of material, which gets a little bigger every year, what we look for is not much different than what we seek in our regular business as venture capitalists. We are searching for gifted leaders with unique and scalable ideas and programs, who are determined to build a sustainable organization that creates a long-term impact for the people it serves. We look for *winners*—great leaders, great managers, great visionaries—whose work can spread rapidly and help many people.

Some aspiring Fellows self-apply after finding us through a Google search or some other web-based resource. Others are referred by members of university faculties, authors, community foundations, or peers in various sectors who are always excited to help someone taking on something new. Some of our successful applicants are mid-careerists—doctors, lawyers, teachers, or engineers. Others are MBAs or recent college graduates who have identified a market failure. All of them, based on their experience, see a way that they can effect a positive change on the world. As individuals, these diverse leaders do amazing work. As a group, they support one another during their three years in the portfolio as a Fellow, and in many cases, beyond that period of time.

Just as on the for-profit side, our diligence process tends to take several months. It focuses on the entrepreneur, the model of the program, and whether the impact of the model appears to be sustainable. We spend extensive time getting to know these social entrepreneurs. Our foundation partners want to understand their vision, as well as their capacity to manage people, strategically assess opportunities, communicate effectively, show grace under pressure, bring monetary and human resources to their organization, and exhibit the highest levels of integrity in all circumstances. We believe that these are skills that lead to the growth of extraordinary organizations.

When Draper Richards Foundation looks at a particular model, we consider its ability to scale and replicate, which includes assessing if there is demand for the model, an identifiable source of money and other resources to pay for this demand, and whether the staffing and systems needed to support the model at scale are realistic. We also consider "model impact," focusing on whether the model responds to a pressing need, whether the service fills a need that is not already being met, whether the organization and its team are positioned to fill the need, and whether the service will reach beyond the recipient and have lasting impact.

The Foundation tries to be very flexible about the sectors and geographies in which we provide support, mainly because our goal is to follow the lead of our leaders. Their job is to tell us in which arenas their skills, personal resources, and experiences are likely to come together most successfully. Our job is to help make that possible.

We also try to support as many different service- and product-delivery models as possible, in part because the resources in the philanthropic arena are limited, and because many foundations and other funders tend to behave in conservative ways. (They often go with the tried-and-true, rather than the untested and speculative.) A quick review of our past and present "portfolio ventures" makes this point.[2] Room to Read, described at length in the following pages, has a distributed fund development team that spans the world. Organizations like Little Kids Rock, Spark, Taproot Foundation, Girls for a Change, and A Home Within all use various volunteer models to bring their program to thousands of people. Others—like Kiva and Digital Wish—are technology-driven. Still others (e.g., Education Pioneers, Mapendo International, and Upwardly Global) use innovative partnership models to distribute their curricula, products, and services.

An exciting development over the past few years has been the increased prevalence of models that leverage employment and the market to unlock resources, and to incentivize individuals to better their lives through hard work. This is the model embraced by groups like Agora, Komaza, VisionSpring, and Living Goods. Finally, it has also been exciting to watch organizations use social media as a means to build networks and momentum behind social movements; these groups include Genocide Intervention Network, Global Citizen Year, and The Mission Continues.

We talk to potential Fellows multiple times. We require them and their organizations to provide detailed business plans and budgets. Because we see such a wide variety of ideas, we rely on experts to provide feedback on entrepreneurs and their models. My favorite part of the process is meeting these capable entrepreneurs and hearing the stories of how they have been inspired to do their work.

As mentioned, we give our successful applicants—our Fellows—$100,000 a year for three years. They can spend their money on whatever they decide is valuable to them and the growth of their organization. That said, I should also stress that we are a *performance-based* funder. Grantees agree to a set of financial, operational, and impact metrics at the beginning of their grants, which are then used for periodic check-ins during the life of the grant. Again, you'll recognize this from my earlier stories about working with for-profit startups. Measuring and tracking almost always makes ventures work better.

Some Fellows spend their money on staff. Others focus on infrastructure, evaluation of impact, program outreach—whatever they think it will take to build a stronger organizational foundation and spread their work further. Having guaranteed resources for three years gives them a little breathing room, but not too much of it. Those three years go by quickly. After that, they'll have to have a new funding model in place. This tends to focus the mind on that middle horizon.

As Robin anticipated back in those early discussions that led to the Foundation, we also provide different kinds of nonfinancial support to our Fellows. A member of the Foundation staff takes a board seat, which involves them in high-leverage tasks like helping to hire additional members of the leadership team, participating in strategic planning, and attracting new donors to the organization. This board seat also helps us to provide coaching to grantees, as well as to get to know other board members and grantee staff members—almost always a great help as these early-stage organizations navigate their complex landscapes.

We gather the Fellows together once a year for a three-day retreat so that they can share ideas and learn from one another. We also bring in experts on topics such as fundraising, human relations, strategy, new technologies, and financial management. Based on these interactions, they make friends and collect names of kindred spirits, whom they can contact throughout the year in order to celebrate, commiserate, and share best practices.

Our Fellows remind me in many ways of the for-profit entrepreneurs with whom I've interacted over the years. In some respects, though, these Fellows are even *more* gifted leaders, given that they so often work in incredibly resource-poor and complex environments, on problems that have resisted solutions for many years. My time at the United Nations underscored in my mind and heart the apparently intractable challenges that face the world today: grinding poverty, the AIDS pandemic, a continually degrading environment, the lack of adequate jobs for people who want and need them, and many, many more. Most people simply find these problems overwhelming and turn away. So it is a joy to meet entrepreneurs who want to address these problems as their life's work and are eager to scaffold their work with good management procedures, including operational efficiencies and strong measurement and evaluation practices.

Venture capital and venture philanthropy are similar on the surface, but those similarities mask larger differences. The key metrics are different, especially in terms of the "bottom line." The nonprofits we fund don't multiply dollars that drop to the bottom line; instead, they create social value. The rewards for star performers are also mainly outside the monetary realm, so recruiting and retaining those stars is a very different kind of challenge. Not surprisingly, our Fellows are terrific communicators, creative resource seekers, and incredibly generous of spirit.

The Draper Richards Foundation is currently at a fascinating stage in its own growth and development. Since we launched the foundation in 2002, we have invested many millions in almost three dozen social entrepreneurs. After almost a decade of testing our model and watching entrepreneurs thrive within it, we are inviting additional donors to join us in finding, funding, and supporting gifted entrepreneurs.

It turns out that there are only a handful of what might be called early- and mezzanine-stage nonprofit funders in the United States, and we have developed close relationships with several of them. We have especially strong collaboration with our friends at New York–based Echoing Green (a funder of bold and exciting ideas and leaders), San Francisco–based Mulago Foundation (standard-bearers of program design and measurement and evaluation, with a specific focus on international poverty and public health issues), Washington DC–based Ashoka (a funder of social entrepreneurs throughout the world, founded by Bill Drayton), and Palo Alto–based Skoll Foundation (a portfolio of social entrepreneurs brought together and funded by former eBay president Jeff Skoll).

Again, I think social entrepreneurship is a trend that is just starting to take hold in the broader field of philanthropy. Working with our partners, our primary goal is to build an engaged donor community that is excited about entrepreneurship and its potential to make a difference around the world. Greater collaboration—and the increased transparency and leverage that would necessarily accompany that collaboration—can only help to solve the various challenges that these talented and committed entrepreneurs take on.

Five Case Studies

Room to Read*

"Perhaps, sir, you will someday come back with books," said a Nepali school headmaster. He surveyed his empty classroom, and then looked at John Wood with hopeful eyes.

These were the words, and the eyes, that sent Wood—who in 1998 was on vacation, trekking in Nepal—down a transformative path, from

---

*Comprehensive information about all of the nonprofit organizations funded by the Draper Richards Foundation can be found in the appendix on page 236.

Microsoft magnate to social entrepreneur. They also helped serve as the catalyst for the groundbreaking organization "Room to Read."

Wood *did* return with books—thousands of books, in fact, and that was just the beginning. This year, he says, he and his colleagues will be opening more than 250 schools and ten times as many libraries:

> That's a new school every twenty-eight hours that's opening somewhere in the developing world through Room to Read. We are opening six libraries a day right now, a new library every four hours. The average library reaches 400 children, so that means every day over 2,000 kids are getting access to their first library. Yesterday, today, tomorrow, over 2,000 kids per day will have access to their first library.[3]

The goal of Room to Read is to help millions of kids to break the cycle of poverty through the power of education. The organization aims to help children in the poorest parts of the world. These are places where they face a cruel catch-22: they are too poor to afford education, but until they have education, they will always be poor. Room to Read breaks this vicious cycle by building schools and libraries in the developing world and by providing long-term scholarships for girls.

Wood approached Jenny Shilling and me for funding back in 2002, when the Draper Richards Foundation was still brand new. At that point, we had only funded one social entrepreneur—Jane Leu of Upwardly Global. Leu's organization created economic opportunities for underemployed immigrant professionals. Leu was at least on familiar turf (the east and west coasts of the United States); Wood's proposal was something else entirely.

Wood recalls his first meeting with Jenny:

> She basically tried to throw me out of her office when I first met her. Room to Read was a startup, and we didn't have any foundations investing in us. All of the other foundations had told me that the organization was too young and that it was not proven, but Jenny said the exact opposite: "You are too far advanced to be a Draper Richards fellow. We look

for organizations that are younger—organizations that are in startup mode." I somewhat frantically tried to convince her of the opposite. Nevertheless, after I had walked her through what I was up to, she liked it enough to get me a follow-up meeting with Bill.

Of course, Jenny was just doing part of her due diligence work. She wanted to see how tenacious Wood was, including whether he had what it takes to push back if somebody was trying to get rid of him. Why? Because she knew that that would happen a lot, once he started fundraising.

Within minutes of meeting Wood in his office, I was greatly impressed. He had a dynamic personality, strong leadership traits (vision, empathy, passion, etc.), high energy, mental acuity, and a good education—everything that persuades me to place a bet on a young entrepreneur. In fact, I quickly realized that he was off the charts in all of those areas. You don't have to be in a room with Wood for very long to know that he is someone special.

As Jenny and I were walking out of Wood's office after the meeting, I happened to notice a rumpled sleeping bag stashed in the corner of the room. "What's that all about?" I asked. A little sheepishly, Wood confessed that he had stayed up nearly all night tweaking (actually, writing!) his business plan in anticipation of our meeting. Not having had enough time to go home, he had slept on the floor in the sleeping bag for a couple of hours. I admit it—this display of his work ethic sealed the deal for me. I gave him a reassuring pat on the back and told him that we'd consider his application very seriously.

Part of John Wood's success lies in his ability to anoint and empower others as coleaders. For example, he brought on Erin Ganju in the earliest days of Room to Read. (She is listed on the organization's website as its "cofounder.") When I first met Wood, his outgoing and energetic personality made it apparent that he was Mr. Big Outside, and Jenny and I wondered who was going to hold down the fort. But he had already figured that out and had hired Ganju, who was as good in her own general management territory as he was in his.

Ganju took over as CEO of Room to Read in December of 2008. As Wood explains:

> There is this challenge of being an entrepreneur, where you start something up, but ultimately, you don't want to *run* it. If you haven't successfully turned it over to someone else, then you haven't succeeded as an entrepreneur. And that's why I basically decided that by our ten-year anniversary, I didn't want to be CEO of Room to Read. I wanted to have someone else be CEO, have that person surrounded by a management team, and let myself be the ambassador of Room to Read, as opposed to running things on a day-to-day basis.

Part of the organization's success can also be attributed to the fact that people all over the world feel ownership of Room to Read. Since its inception, Room to Read has incubated fundraising chapters in forty-one cities in the world, from Atlanta, Boston, Chicago, Dubai, all the way through the alphabet to Zurich. "This is not my movement," says Wood. "This is *our* movement." About 98 percent of the money that Room to Read runs on comes directly from donations, and in 2009, 53 percent of those donations came from outside of the United States. Participating cities engage in friendly competition; in one such philanthropic shoot-out, London and Hong Kong raised $1 million each in a single night in 2009. Currently, Room to Read operates in Vietnam, Sri Lanka, Laos, Thailand, Cambodia, Ghana, and Zambia. They have opened 1,128 schools and 10,000 libraries. Room to Read has distributed 8 million books—with more than half the books being in the children's native tongue (through Room to Read's local language children's publishing initiative). They have awarded over 10,000 scholarships to girls. All told, the organization has had a direct impact on the lives of more than four million children.[4] Without question, Wood has been one of the most successful entrepreneurs that I've ever funded. The $300,000 Draper Richards Foundation grant—their first significant funding—was certainly important to him back in 2002, but last year his organization raised $25 million and expects to raise $30 million this year.

In traveling around the world, John Wood has seen up close the impact that Room to Read has had. He describes one experience that was particularly meaningful to him:

> We were at a school in Vietnam, and a new library was opening. There were approximately 1,000 kids at the school, and we were all walking around after the ribbon-cutting, checking it out. This fifteen-year-old boy walked up to me, stuck out his hand, and said, "Hello, Mr. John Wood. My name is Thanh. I wish to welcome you to our library."
>
> He shook my hand, and he gave me this really firm handshake. It was like he was going to sell me an insurance policy. He said, "My goal is to read every book in this library. I am going to read every book in Vietnamese, and I want to read every book in English. What do you think of my goal?" And I said, "I think it's a great goal, but there are over 1,000 books in this library. Do you think that you can read all 1,000 books?" And he said, "It is no problem. I came in here last night with my flashlight before the library opened. I read nine books last night." I looked at the kid, and he was this little miniature Vietnamese version of me. The nerdy kid who couldn't wait to get to the library the next day. I see kids like Thanh, and I just think, we have four million kids accessing Room to Read's libraries right now.

VisionSpring

Sometimes, "vision" requires seeing what needs to be done for a single person, at a particular place, with a specific challenge.

Jordan Kassalow was a first-year student training to become an optometrist when he went to a site in rural Mexico with a student organization called Volunteer Optometric Services to Humanity (VOSH). He and his fellow optometry students—mentored by several of their professors—set up rough-and-ready clinics to help people who had never had eye care before. Some 2,000 villagers from all over the region were standing in line when the first clinic opened its "doors."

As Kassalow recalls:

My first patient was a seven-year-old boy from the local school for the
blind. I could tell right away that he was above my pay grade—he looked
like a complicated case—so I called my professor over. She examined
his eyes, and after a long look, she said, "Jordan this boy isn't blind. He's
just profoundly nearsighted."

She measured his eyes, and he had a prescription that was off the
charts—something like a minus 22, which is a crazy prescription. We
had brought 5,000 pairs of glasses. She said, "Go to the strongest box,
and see if there's anything that might match this prescription."

Sure enough, there was a pair that was 90 percent of his prescription. So I brought them back, and I was the lucky guy who got to put
them on this boy's face. As the lenses aligned with his eyes, his whole
facial expression changed from that sort of blank stare of a blind person to the face of a beautiful, animated, seven-year-old boy, and he just
smiled from ear to ear.

I was the first person he ever saw in his life.[5]

A memorable moment for a young eye-doctor-in-training, to be sure.
But Kassalow, who continued his volunteer work in developing countries
throughout his student years and afterward, had many more such revelations. On a later student-volunteer trip to Mexico, for example, he encountered a woman in her late fifties:

She had her worn-down Bible clutched to her chest. Her complaint was,
"I haven't been able to see my Bible for ten years."

This one I could handle. This was a simple one. She just needed to
put on a pair of +2.50 reading glasses. She put them on, looked at her
Bible, her eyebrows went to the crown of her head, she smiled, she hit
the floor on her knees and just hugged my knees and started to cry.

The next day, we got to the clinic, and there was that big long line,
and that lady was one of the first people in the line. She found me, and
through a translator, she said, "To you Doctor, they are just a pair of

glasses, but to me, you gave me back my God." She then handed me twenty chickens to show her appreciation.

We at the Draper Richards Foundation entered Kassalow's life several years later in 2005. He had just become the chairman and cofounder of "VisionSpring," the mission of which is to generate opportunity in the developing world through the sale of affordable eyeglasses. Although people in the developed world often take glasses for granted, most of the developing world still does not have access to them. In those countries, they are primarily available in high-priced, urban optical shops. For the rural poor in countries like India, South Africa, and El Salvador—just a few of the countries in which VisionSpring operates—the expense of buying glasses and taking several days off from work to travel back and forth to an urban center simply puts eye care out of reach. VisionSpring solves the problem by bringing the glasses to them.

Kassalow's work as an eye doctor and public-health expert has taken him on scores of medical missions to countries all over the developing world. On those trips, he gradually came to two simple but profound revelations. First, more than 40 percent of the patients he treated needed nothing more complicated than a pair of nonprescription eyeglasses—the kind found in drugstores all over the United States. Yet the people he met were losing their livelihoods simply because this affordable, mass-produced product was not available in their area. Second, there were many women who were under or unemployed and desperately needed an economic opportunity. Kassalow began to wonder if, given the proper tools and skills, these women could be provided jobs conducting eye screens and selling eyeglasses in their own communities.

Today, VisionSpring's "Business in a Bag"—a backpack filled with glasses, eye charts, marketing material, customer and inventory management tools, repair kits, and other items—empowers local Vision Entrepreneurs to sell low-cost, high-quality eyeglasses in the hardest-to-reach areas, as well as to make referrals to reputable eye hospitals for those needing advanced care. The nonprofit's "microfranchising" strategy allows entrepreneurs to purchase the $75 kit on consignment, to be paid back over a few months out of their profits, thereby lowering the risk for those new to business.

In the five years VisionSpring has been operating, the number of glasses sold has doubled or tripled every year. In 2009, the organization's Vision Entrepreneurs sold 300,000 pairs of glasses in more than a dozen countries; Kassalow hopes to cross the million-pairs-a-year mark this year. A multi-year winner of *Fast Company*'s Social Capitalist Award, VisionSpring has been recognized for its high-impact, cutting-edge work by *The Economist*, *The International Herald Tribune*, *Foreign Affairs*, and *NBC Nightly News*. Former President Bill Clinton has said that VisionSpring's work "will help hundreds of thousands of people and in the process create a whole new sector of the economy."[6]

Kassalow's long-term vision for the world's entrepreneurs is perfectly encapsulated in the organization's name. He says VisionSpring boils down to the concept "See well. Do well."

One Acre Fund

Another social entrepreneur extraordinaire who comes to mind is Andrew Youn. Founder and executive director of an organization called "One Acre Fund," Youn is a humble and visionary man, a first-generation American with several years of management consulting experience with Mercer Management in Boston.

One Acre Fund helps subsistence-farm families in East Africa "grow themselves out of poverty."[7] These families, typically a mother with between four and six children, work a plot of land roughly the size of a football field, which is often their primary source of both food and income. During the six months of the "hunger season," they need to get by on 40 percent less food, which often leads to illness and death. It's a huge problem: one in ten children in these communities dies before reaching her first birthday, often owing to malnutrition and, literally, slow starvation.

Anne Marie met Youn at a conference in late 2005 while he was an MBA student in Chicago. He described to her his desire to eradicate hunger in Africa by focusing on poor farmers and improving their access to farm inputs and markets. Youn was spurred to action after a summer working for a project in South Africa setting up rural AIDS clinics, during which time he noted that one of the greatest needs for this population was not just medicine, but food. Youn dove into the farming value chain. He spent much of his second year of business school traveling between Bungoma, Kenya (a remote agricultural town in the western part of the country), and Chicago, where he attended his classes at Kellogg (Northwestern University). In his initial pilot project, thirty farming families doubled (and in some cases, tripled) their farm output, giving them not only the unprecedented opportunity to eat consistently, but also surplus crops to sell, providing them with some money to buy other goods and services that their families desperately needed.

How does Youn's organization work? One Acre Fund believes that providing ultrapoor farmers with simple farm tools and education can significantly increase farm income. One Acre Fund supplies farmers with a "market in a box"—that is, everything they need to succeed in farming, including seed and fertilizer on loan, training, and access to markets. Families in the One Acre Fund program double farm profit per acre farmed, on average, and at the end of each growing cycle, they pay for most of the services provided to them by One Acre Fund.

Youn received Draper Richards funding in December 2006: a juncture at which he was serving one hundred farm families in Bungoma.[8] Youn himself had moved to Bungoma, where he continues to live today, convinced that being "on the ground" helps him refine his business model and scale it into additional markets. As of this writing, One Acre Fund is serving 22,000 families in seven different districts across Kenya and Rwanda, and Youn's goal is to serve 50,000 additional families in the next two years.

The Mission Continues

Eric Greitens, founder and CEO of "The Mission Continues," is an entrepreneur who applies business and leadership principles to effect social change on an intensely personal level.

As an Angier B. Duke Scholar at Duke University, Greitens studied ethics, philosophy, and public policy. Selected as a Rhodes and Truman Scholar, he attended the University of Oxford from 1996 through 2000, where he earned a master's degree in development studies and a PhD in political science. Greitens was also a White House Fellow and is a United States Navy SEAL officer who has been deployed four times on assignments related to the global struggle against terrorism.

The Mission Continues was founded in 2007, after Greitens came home from a tour of duty in Iraq. Upon his return, Greitens visited wounded Marines at Bethesda Naval Hospital in Maryland. Even though their wounds had cut their military service short, every Marine he talked to—without exception—expressed an unwavering desire to continue serving his country. Greitens recognized that although it was important to say "thank you" to our servicemen and -women, it was equally important to say *we still need you.*

When men and women return wounded and disabled from a war zone, they often lose not only their physical abilities but also their sense of purpose. They are separated from their team, their missions, and even their values.

Many people offer things *to* wounded veterans. Greitens knew that it was essential to ask something *of* them. They had been wounded, but their character had not changed. They had been disabled, but Greitens perceived them as *assets,* and he saw an innovative opportunity to challenge returning veterans to continue their service. Toward that end, he used his hard-earned combat pay to start The Mission Continues.

The Mission Continues offers competitive fellowships to engage wounded and disabled veterans who have served since 9/11 to perform service here at home. These veterans draw on leaderships skills honed on the battlefield to benefit their stateside communities. A typical fellowship lasts fourteen weeks, during which the Fellow receives a living stipend so she can serve full time at a local charitable organization. Each Fellow provides a tangible service, such as mentoring at-risk children, organizing veterans' support groups, or helping the disabled enjoy the outdoors again.

Greitens understood that what would matter most for wounded and disabled veterans was not what they were given but what they *did*. The Mission Continues does not offer charity to our returning service members. Instead, it poses a challenge to them: to continue serving here at home as leaders in their community.

By the time Greitens received the Draper Richards award for social entrepreneurship in June 2009, he had awarded twenty-two fellowships to wounded veterans, and volunteers had served 19,000 hours with the organization. One year later, The Mission Continues had awarded fifty-three fellowships, and volunteers had served nearly 40,000 hours in cities all across the country. By the end of 2011, Greitens aims to award at least one hundred fellowships per year. The organization has also seen strong financial growth, from donations of $27,000 in 2007 to $719,000 in 2009.

Wounded and disabled veterans who go through the fellowship program not only provide a tangible good to the community, but they also gain some of the experiences and skills needed to transition back to civilian life. Throughout their fellowship, veterans receive mentoring and work on an "exit strategy" to ensure postfellowship success.[9]

Kiva

Because of the recent national attention for their good work, I am constantly reminded of how proud I am of two entrepreneurs—Matt Flannery and Premal Shah—whom our foundation funded in early 2007, when Kiva was a small operation of just five employees.[10]

Kiva's mission is to connect people, through lending, for the sake of alleviating poverty. It is proving highly successful. In four short years, Kiva has blossomed from a microfinance project with seven Ugandan entrepreneurs into a global, online, person-to-person lending platform that has helped enable nearly 400,000 entrepreneurs in fifty-three countries to achieve their potential. Nearly half a million Kiva lenders from 201 countries have funded entrepreneurs on this remarkable platform, with a loan being made every thirty seconds.

An interesting Kiva innovation that sets it apart from online charities is the fact that Kiva users are truly making *loans*, not donations. More than $150 million has been loaned out in $25 increments since 2006, and more than 98 *percent* of those loans have been paid back. Kiva President Shah's previous experience at PayPal here in Silicon Valley helped enable Kiva to control and keep track of loans and interest payments over the internet.

Kiva partners with microfinance institutions (MFIs) around the globe, and these MFIs serve as the link between the Kiva lender and groups of Kiva entrepreneurs. Shah explains how this ecosystem works:

> Instead of lending to an individual, you lend to a group, and the group guarantees that loan. The microfinance institution will not give that group a future loan unless they pay back. So if one woman's cow dies, the other four women will chip in to support that. So that kind of mechanism at ground level reduces the transaction costs and reduces the risk of nonrepayment. There is a reputation collateral, rather than a financial collateral. So access to a future loan is contingent on repayment. It creates such a powerful dynamic that you get pretty high repayment rates.[11]

The average amount loaned to an individual Kiva entrepreneur is $391. This may not seem like a large amount, but in many parts of the developing world, that sum of money can be a game changer.

Matt Flannery, Kiva CEO and cofounder (he founded Kiva with Jessica Jackley), underscores and illustrates the impact that a loan of this seemingly modest size can make:

> We funded a group of people to make a water tap in a refugee camp in Kampala, Uganda. It was a $500 loan, which was an obscene amount of money for them. If you make $1 a day, a $500 capital injection is just a really different type of scenario, so people could actually build a water tap in that community and do all of the construction necessary to drill down to the water, which is actually a pretty hard thing to do. Those people were able to buy water from there instead of carrying those big jugs several kilometers to and from a water source. So that's the kind

of thing that we see happening—not once, but thousands of times—at Kiva.

Kiva is especially near and dear to my heart because it is an organization that empowers women—82 percent of its loans have been made to women—promotes entrepreneurship, and gives a chance to the hardworking poor, who otherwise would not have access to capital. Hundreds of thousands of lives have been improved through Kiva's remarkable, innovative model.

To summarize, The Draper Richards Foundation has proved that social entrepreneurs and venture capital–sponsored entrepreneurs are very much alike in that they all need to scale their organizations, and in order to do that, they need funding. The funding will only come if the ideas are good, the need for the product or services is great, and the team is strong. Regardless of the bottom line, success in the startup game depends on these factors together with "a little bit of luck," to quote the happy-go-lucky Alfred P. Doolittle in *My Fair Lady*. I think that Robin would agree with me that starting up Draper Richards Foundation was our finest hour.

Tim and the BizWorld Foundation

Before I close this chapter, I want to take a look at the next generation's involvement in philanthropy. It would be nice to be able to say that I've been a positive influence on Tim in this realm, but as you'll see, he got there before I did.

Back in 1993, when my granddaughter Jesse was eight years old, she asked her father, Tim, "What do you do? Mommy stays at home during the day, but you go out."

Well, it can be difficult to explain to someone what venture capital is, especially if that person hasn't yet been exposed to the fundamentals of how business works. So instead of trying to tell Jesse what he did, Tim decided to show Jesse—and also her entire third-grade class—how business works. He didn't realize it at the time, but these were the beginnings of what evolved into the "BizWorld Foundation."

Tim knew that Jesse and her friends liked friendship bracelets, so he created a simulation exercise that revolved around an industry of friendship bracelet companies. He broke the concept of business down into four pieces—design, manufacturing, marketing, and finance—and a full school day was devoted to the understanding and execution of each of those four elements, one at a time.

On the first day, design day, the students broke into competing companies and assigned key roles such as president, VP of design, VP of manufacturing, VP of marketing, VP of sales, and VP of finance. Then they registered their companies with the state and issued stock. The children were required to "buy" all of the materials that they used for their companies, and in order to have the means to do so, they needed to raise money from either a "venture capitalist" or a "banker." They bought paper and crayons and created a theoretical design of what they wanted their bracelet to look like. Then each student created a prototype, and each group decided which prototype to manufacture.

Next, on manufacturing day, the students were told to make as many bracelets as they possibly could. Naturally, there were a few kids who could really make them very well, and a few who couldn't. The kids began the process as a job shop, with each child individually trying to make bracelets, but they soon naturally progressed to a division of labor, and set up an assembly line.

The third day was marketing day, and each group was responsible for creating a slogan, logo, sales pitch, and commercial. They also had to pay for posters and any marketing materials that they wanted to use to get people's attention. The students of another third-grade class were each given ten "BizBucks," and they played the role of customers.

The final day was finance day—although in fact, all along the way, the kids had been keeping track of their money, paying themselves salaries, and buying all of the necessary materials. On this fourth day, though, they created a full balance sheet and income statement for each team.

Tim and Jesse's teacher valued each company based on what the balance sheet and income statement looked like, and the winner was the company that was valued the highest.

The program was a great success—so much so that the principal told Tim, "I want you to teach my fourth-, fifth-, sixth-, seventh-, and eighth-grade classes, too." Tim didn't have the time to do that, but he did come back in subsequent years to teach the classes of his two sons, Billy and Adam. Again, the simulation was a great success. When Adam's teacher told Tim, "You have to come back every year," Tim decided that he had stumbled onto something, and that this was a practice that could benefit a lot of children.

In 1997, after creating a formal program guide, he established the BizWorld Foundation, a nonprofit organization that makes the BizWorld programs available to all educators and encourages community involvement in the financial education of youth. BizWorld's mission is to "challenge and engage children across the cultural and economic spectrum through experiential learning programs that teach the basics of business, entrepreneurship, and money management and promote teamwork and leadership in the classroom."[12]

The BizWorld Foundation has enjoyed astounding success, reaching students in all fifty states and eighty-four countries. It established its first international franchise in the Netherlands in 2001 and now has affiliates in both India and South Korea.

Tim played both roles in this compelling story: the social entrepreneur with a good idea that lends itself to scaling up, and the philanthropist who provided the needed resources to make that happen. I have no doubt that we'll see more great ideas—and more generosity—emerging from Tim and his contemporaries, who in my estimation are setting a new standard in terms of active engagement in philanthropy. They are determined to have an impact and make the world a better place—and I'm fully confident that they will succeed.

CHAPTER 9

Fitting It All Together

It is difficult to say what is impossible, for the dream of yesterday is the hope of today and the reality of tomorrow.

—*Robert H. Goddard*

A T THE END OF World War II, the fate of the Korean Peninsula was very much in question. As it turned out, my fate was linked to that of Korea, in ways I could not have anticipated.

The United Nations had come up with a proposal in which the United States and the Soviet Union would exercise a joint trusteeship over the country, but that plan was never pursued seriously. In 1948, Korea was divided roughly in half along the thirty-eighth parallel, with the North coming under Soviet domination and adopting a communist system, and the South allying itself with the United States and embracing a capitalist model. It was a tenuous compromise, in part because it focused the tensions of the global Cold War on a small, divided nation, and because two antagonistic economic and political systems had to operate in the closest possible proximity.

On June 25, 1950, 231,000 soldiers from the North poured across the border, initiating the Korean War and sparking the first major armed conflict of the Cold War. This action was a clear violation of the UN Charter, and the Security Council felt compelled to act. Fate intervened: normally, the Soviet Union would have vetoed any meaningful steps to protect the South, but at that time, the Soviet representative was boycotting the Security Council's meetings. The remaining Council members quickly passed Resolution 83, which endorsed member-state military assistance to South Korea. The Soviets later protested loudly and bitterly against this action, claiming that the United Nations had no right to intervene in what was effectively a civil war, but I for one think that this was a dramatic and shining moment in the history of the United Nations. At that point, the organization was only three years old; the fact that it could craft and pass an unambiguous call for intervention against an invading army was quite remarkable.

I first heard about North Korea's invasion one summer day while I was driving down the Hudson River Parkway, listening to the radio in the first car that I ever owned. I planned to start business school that September. I didn't realize it at the time, but the grim developments on the Korean Peninsula would cut my stay at business school to only six weeks because I would be called to serve in the war in Korea.

Months later I sat in my dormitory room, reading and rereading the official government-issue papers recalling me to active duty—as you may remember, I had taken a break from undergraduate school to serve for eighteen months in the 82nd Airborne. My business career was just starting, and I was slightly concerned that my second tour of duty would send me off track. At the same time however, deep down, I was thrilled at the prospect of this new adventure.

I was first assigned to Camp Edwards in Massachusetts, as an assistant personnel officer. It was fairly light duty, and six enjoyable months passed before I was ordered to Korea. My older sister, Dorothy, and my father came to say goodbye and see me off on my evening flight to Japan, where I would spend a few days before heading to Korea.

My sister recalls that farewell vividly. She says it was the only time she ever saw my father weep. I didn't see that because I was on the plane before he allowed his emotions to rise to the surface. In fact, I never saw him show his emotions in all the time I knew him. He was a soldier, and soldiers don't cry. He was a man, and men don't cry. But he was a father, and—as it turned out—fathers can cry.

I certainly wasn't crying. Quite the opposite: I was full of excitement and anticipation. It felt like I was turning a new and important page in my life.

A young man occupied the seat next to me on the flight to Japan. It's strange. I've thought of that fellow many, many times since then, but for the life of me, I can't remember his name. We got to talking. It turned out that we were both twenty-four-year-old reserve officers headed for the front lines of Korea.

We shared an army billet in Japan for a week, and then we took the train to Osaka, the port city directly across the Korea Strait from Pusan. We left Osaka late at night on a military ferry. I'll never forget the lights in the harbor that night. There was a hit song at the time, "Harbor Lights," that had been made popular by the Sammy Kaye orchestra.[1] My new-found friend and I sang it at the top of our lungs: "*I watched the harbor lights / How could I help if tears were starting / Goodbye to tender nights beside the silvery sea.*"

In Pusan, we got on a military sleeper train with bunks stacked four high. It amazes me to think of it now, but we both slept peacefully while the train closed in on the "Iron Triangle" near Kumhwa, which straddled the central part of what would later become the demilitarized zone between the two countries. In the morning, we disembarked; he was assigned to one company, and I was assigned to another, but we were both in the same regiment and so remained close together geographically.

Several days later, after I had reported to the company commander and had taken over responsibility for my platoon, I got into an army jeep and went off in search of my friend and traveling companion.

He was preparing for his first patrol. He proudly showed me his bulletproof vest, told me about his company commander and his own men, and described the purpose of the patrol on which he was about to embark. I had already taken one of my squads out on a patrol, and I talked to him in general terms about that experience. (Although, there were some things I *didn't* tell him. For example, my top sergeant had pointed out a phosphorus land mine just as I was about to step on it, and I had also seen a man screaming in agony after stepping on one of those same mines—his face glowing grotesquely in the dark.) But on this visit with my friend, we mostly joked, laughed, and—like almost every other soldier in the history of warfare—complained about the food.

It came time for me to leave. I wished him luck, got into my jeep, and went back to my post. A few days later, I learned that he had been killed on that first patrol in defense of the freedom of a country he might not have been able to find on a map a year earlier.

It very easily could have been *me* who died on that blasted and barren hillside in central Korea. I was lucky enough to go on and lead a long, varied, and interesting life, but my friend's life was snuffed out at age twenty-four. Why him and not me? At the time, we both thought we were pretty much indestructible. But how would we have acted, and what would we have talked about in our few weeks together, if we had been able to look into the future?

I know that it wouldn't come close to compensating him for his sacrifice, but I wish that somehow, he could come back and see the difference between North and South Korea today. The creativity, entrepreneurship, and resulting growth in economic productivity and social services evident in the South stand in vivid contrast to—and eloquent condemnation of-the stagnant economy, isolated paranoia, and horrific poverty in the North. I like to think that my friend would be proud of the United Nations, proud of his country, and reassured that his sacrifice was not in vain.

I include this story about my service in Korea mainly because of its redeeming bottom line: for all of its terrible costs, our intervention on the Korean Peninsula made it possible for the 48 million people in the South to prosper through entrepreneurship and private enterprise, while the millions of unfortunate people in the North—dominated first by the Soviet communists, then by the Chinese communists, and now by an oppressive North Korean family dynasty—have suffered a fate of grinding poverty and misery which continues to this day.

I've already told you that my candidate for Economic Hero of the Twentieth Century is Deng Xiaoping. By embracing foreign direct investments in China, as well as private ownership and global trade, Deng was able to awaken a sleeping economic giant. Problems remain, of course, including issues in the realm of democratic principles, freedom of speech and press, and human rights. Still, I don't hesitate to say it: by his leadership in bringing about an economic revolution and unleashing free enterprise for one-sixth of the world's population, Deng created more opportunity for more people than any other single individual in the history of the planet.

Runner-up for Economic Hero of the Twentieth Century is Manmohan Singh, current prime minister of India, whom (as recounted earlier) I first met in 1990. Back then, although staunchly democratic, he was still wavering in his commitment to economic freedom, favoring instead a "mixed economy" of both private and state-run enterprises. By the mid-1990s, however, Singh had fully recognized the power of the private sector. As India's finance minister, he led a breathtaking series of reforms, including the effective abolishment of the "License Raj" system. India's gross domestic product growth rate has since tripled, and the country has emerged as home to scores of millions of entrepreneurs.

Will these trends promoting free enterprise continue? I think they *have* to. Once people get a taste of freedom and material comfort, they want more. Throwing the engine in reverse becomes an impossibility—especially in the age of the ubiquitous internet, which gives most of the people on the planet a window into other people's lives. The number of autocratic, inward-looking countries will steadily decline. Fertile new ground in countries all over the world will continue to open up for entrepreneurs and their venture capitalist backers.

I described earlier how Draper Fisher Jurvetson has invented a new model for providing venture capital on a global basis. Tim and his colleagues point out that one way or another, you need a supportive context—including entrepreneurial colleagues, a high-powered research university, a supportive corps of professionals (e.g., smart accountants, astute lawyers), and tech-savvy media to create entrepreneurial magic. This goes a long way toward explaining why Silicon Valley, which has all of these attributes, occupies its unique position in the world.

But the world is shrinking rapidly. As a result, our future here in the United States will become more and more intertwined with that of all the other countries around the world. Therefore, it is hard for me to believe that the United States will continue to hold on to the unrivaled status that we have had in the past. The creative force of innovation, which today seems to be so centered in Silicon Valley, is already sprouting up and paying dividends in India, China, and other parts of the globe to varying degrees. Here in Silicon Valley, we've been lucky enough to bring together the talent from scientific academia with the strength of private enterprise and the power of the purse: that is, Stanford University, entrepreneurs, and venture capital. We're not entirely unique in that regard; another center of creativity is Route 128 in Boston, where MIT, entrepreneurs, and venture capitalists hang out together.

The future is clear: pockets of innovation are popping up all over the world. Skype originally came out of Estonia, Baidu out of China, and Infosys was born in India. Israel is also a technological and entrepreneurial powerhouse with a strong venture capital presence. With communication and social barriers breaking down worldwide, with governments encouraging entrepreneurship almost everywhere—in contrast to the days of hard-line communism in Russia and China and socialism in India—and with the ever-increasing focus on technology and education all over the world, the number of Silicon Valleys is likely to grow at an exponential rate over the next few decades. Russia has already dedicated several square miles of land outside of Moscow to create another Silicon Valley. (In my opinion it probably won't work because it is too far from any university.) In a world shrinking as fast as this one, I see Silicon Valleys surrounding the best engineering schools in all parts of the globe. I see a national venture capital community in each of those territories, and I see an international venture capital industry which will service entrepreneurs wherever they may be—and they will be everywhere.

The interchange of ideas will accelerate even more with the increased use across continents of webinars, Skype, Twitter, Facebook, and all the other communication systems that will surely evolve. If for no other reason than sheer numbers, creative minds in India and China will begin to "out-think" those of us in the United States and Europe.

Should we find this threatening? Absolutely not. Open competition is the healthiest environment for innovation. If we are lucky in the next few decades, we will have a lot of open competition.

On balance, I think the recent flood of money into the U.S. venture capital community has been good for the economy. Will IPOs come back in full force for speculative young companies, where profits are only a promise? Probably not. Perhaps the exchange of private stock through systems like SecondMarket and Financial OS will gain more dominance.

I am sure of one thing: venture capital is here to stay. The industry, however, is changing. Yes, returns vary radically, and today's limited partners are less and less timid about asking why returns have slipped badly over the last decade. But we have the room and the time to make it right. The industry is still young, its impact on the world has been extraordinary, and—at the end of the day—capitalist societies won't reach their potential without venture capitalists and the entrepreneurs they support.

Technological Innovation: The True Mainspring

In the late 1800s, there were then about 100,000 horses in New York, each generating between fifteen and thirty-five pounds of manure per day. In London, with similar numbers, a writer from the *London Times* predicted that within fifty years the entire city would be buried under nine feet of manure. Compounding the problem, hauling all that manure out of the city by horse-drawn wagons would require still more horses. Feeding all those horses would require ever more horse-drawn carts bringing hay into the city, which would create more manure, and so on.[2] In 1898, the first-ever international urban planning conference was abruptly called to a halt, three days into its scheduled ten-day run, because no one could come up with a plausible alternative to mountains of horse manure.

Well, Henry Ford came up with that alternative. To me, the lesson of that story is that wearing today's lenses, few can see where tomorrow's elegant solution is going to come from.

From the earliest days of venture capital—including the Rockefeller family investments in Eastern Airlines, General Georges Doriot's investments in High Voltage Engineering and a little outfit called Digital Equipment, and Draper Gaither & Anderson's investment in the world's first defibrillator—people understood that technology had a special potential to change the rules of the game and that game-changing was where the real money was to be made. They didn't always get it right, of course. (Doriot's American Research & Development invested in a large number of forgettable, low-tech businesses, including shrimp-processing concerns.) But soon, the early venture capitalists all came to concentrate their investments on businesses and industries that had a high technology quotient.

You will remember that I learned this lesson, under pressure, when DGA contemplated putting some Rockefeller money into a Hawaiian "condominium" development—an exotic-sounding new idea. A Rockefeller representative in New York soon straightened me out: "We became a limited partner in DGA," he said, none too happily, "because you told us you were going to invest in technology and honest-to-God entrepreneurs. We don't need you in Hawaii. We need you in Palo Alto."

My son, Tim, arrived at this conclusion by following his own path: he decided that Alaska—for all of its astounding riches in terms of natural resources and real estate—was not a high-potential arena for venture capital. He made a lot more money investing Alaska's money in high-tech enterprises outside of the state than he did investing its money in Alaska.

So technology is truly where the action is, and the pace of innovation is not only *accelerating,* but it is also more or less invulnerable to the year-to-year swings of the economy. This has been true for centuries, and it's still true today. Simply stated, entrepreneurs and scientists don't slow their thinking during recessions. In fact, my sense is that the startup ideas only get *better* in down markets.

Consider Moore's Law—more like a rule of thumb, actually—which predicts the doubling of computing power or data storage every eighteen months. Much has been made in recent years of the assertion that Gordon Moore's famous "law" is running out of gas. But as Ray Kurzweil and others have plotted, the smooth pace of exponential progress spans from 1890 to 2010, across countless innovations, technology substrates, and social interactions—with most of the innovators involved being completely unaware that they were fitting neatly into a larger curve. "The twenty-first century," Kurzweil concludes, "will see about a thousand times greater technological change than its predecessor."[3]

Moore's Law is a primary driver of disruptive innovation, such as the iPod stealing the seemingly invulnerable Sony Walkman franchise. The point for us today is that Moore's Law pertains not only to IT and communications, but also to genomics, medical imaging, and life sciences in general. The pace of progress is accelerating dramatically, creating opportunities for new entrants in new industries. As a result, the industries affected by the latest wave of tech entrepreneurs are more diverse. Globalization is also expanding the geography of entrepreneurship and promoting cross-border collaboration, thereby leveraging a global network of innovators.

Ideas for the Future

What are the technologies of tomorrow? Here is a summary of ideas that have sprouted from the brains of Silicon Valley's best and brightest.[4]

- We'll soon see the first scalable quantum computer. If that device follows Rose's Law of annually doubling qubits for the next decade (as it has for the past seven years), it will handily outperform all computers on the planet, *combined.*

- There will soon be the first synthetic life-form, with 100 percent of its DNA built in the lab with no animals involved. This will herald an era of intelligent design in biology, in which one writes the code of life as if it were a computer program, and the software creates its own hardware. "Industrial Biotech 2.0" compounds off Moore's Law, creating billions of novel microbes per day.

- With the digitization of myriad genomes, we are learning to decode and reprogram the information systems of biology. Like computer hackers, we can leverage a prior library of evolved code, assemblers, and subsystems. This will lead to remarkable breakthroughs in energy, cleantech, materials, nanotechnology, robotics, artificial intelligence, and complex systems development in general. If Bill Gates and Larry Ellison were undergrads today, they would likely study biology.

- The life-sciences sector is one of the most dynamic and high potential fields for entrepreneurship and venture capital involvement. Diagnostics, drug therapeutics, medical devices, healthcare information technology, and healthcare services are full of opportunities to mix science, new applications, and new modes of delivery. The most recent advancements include diagnostic tests done on patient samples (tissue or blood) to predict the course or recurrence of the disease and which drug is best in what dose for that individual patient; targeted therapeutics that intervene in disease processes at specific points in the biological network in humans (thus offering better efficacy and fewer side effects); and wearable sensors that will monitor the patient and alert doctors when it may be time to intervene, thus avoiding expensive hospitalizations.

- Voice will become free within data networks. WiFi phones running Skype and forthcoming dual-mode WiFi/cell phones will make VoIP mobile and mainstream. For these consumers, voice will become a free application that runs over a commodity data network, just like it has become for email. (Remember that before Hotmail—a venture close to Tim's heart—people used to pay for email software and monthly fees per address.) And of course, voice over a data network will continue to be more valuable and enriched than the plain old telephone service.

- Effectively free and limitless storage of information will be carried with each person. That information will be easily searched and accessed, essentially giving people near real-time access to any piece of information in the world—an external hard drive for the mind.

- We expect to see small nuclear power plants that are safe, portable, and with the ability to light up a small city. In the United States, nuclear power has been all but forgotten, but globally the technology has advanced considerably to the point where there might be entrepreneurial opportunities for innovators in nuclear physics. It is the cleanest technology available by far.

- We will see real changes in the transportation industry. Electric cars such as the Tesla and the Reva have given this sleepy industry a wake-up call. People-movers of many new types—such as electric airplanes, motorcycles, and trucks, amphibious cars, Segways, and self-navigating vehicles—are making their way to the entrepreneurial mind stream.

Closing Words

Entrepreneurship is no new thing. Struggling entrepreneurs have existed for thousands of years—since the very beginning of commercial enterprise— and our progress as a society is thanks in large part to their many efforts. Venture capitalists, although not coined as such, have also been around for centuries. I like to think of Spain's Queen Isabella as one of the truly pioneering venture capitalists. Her investment in Christopher Columbus's voyage was one of risk, and quite obviously, immeasurable reward.

So the existence of intelligent, ambitious entrepreneurs with innovative, groundbreaking visions, and well-to-do people with the means to fund those visions is not a novel concept. It wasn't until the late 1950s, however, that we first began to institutionalize, and thus effectively supersize the potential of this exciting and productive partnership between entrepreneur and venture capitalist.

The venture capitalists of the last half century have provided entrepreneurs with much more than just money. The financial aspect of any venture capital firm's investment is just one small piece of a very large puzzle. Venture capitalists are also the partners of their entrepreneurs and have a genuine interest in the success of their startups. They often take a board seat and provide key advice, mentoring. and strategic guidance; assist with hiring; and open up their expansive networks in order to help their young companies find customers, suppliers, and additional investors when needed. Although all venture capitalists undoubtedly want to see a significant financial gain on their investments, the venture capital industry is actually much more about building solid businesses that will have a positive impact, in terms of providing valuable goods and services, promoting progress, and creating new jobs. Venture capitalists are not looking for a quick buck; they are looking for unique ideas from innovative entrepreneurs that will transform our world.

Thus far, the venture capital–entrepreneur partnership has proven to be a fruitful one indeed. You may not realize it, but you likely interact with a venture-backed company every single day of your life. Today, for example, if you have done any one of the following—bought a morning coffee from Starbucks; received a FedEx Package; checked your Gmail, Yahoo, or Hotmail account; conducted a Google search; played with your iPad; bought an appliance at Home Depot; called an old friend via Skype; made a microloan on Kiva.org; updated your status on Facebook; or discovered that you have a new follower on Twitter—then you have benefitted from one of the tens of thousands of companies that came into existence as a result of this powerful ecosystem. Today, total revenue of venture capital–backed companies accounts for 21 percent of the U.S. GDP, and venture-backed companies represent 11 percent of U.S. private sector employment.

As you have seen from the stories in this book, the venture capital industry and the entrepreneurs that it serves are certainly no longer limited to the United States, and have not been for some time. U.S. venture capital firms are investing outside of the United States, particularly in hotbeds of innovation such as China and India. Foreign venture capital firms are cropping up in every corner of the globe. We are becoming an increasingly interconnected society, and the interplay between globalization and the new networking economy is fascinating. Startups can sprout up anywhere, be funded by venture capitalists from any part of the world, and these companies can provide goods and services to a diverse spectrum of customers, regardless of location.

Over fifty years ago, when I first started my venture capital career at my father's firm on the Stanford University campus, in an area nestled among the fruit orchards of what would become Silicon Valley, I had no clue—really not a clue—about the magnitude of disruptive innovations that I would see, the enormous economics that would result, and the fun that I would have in being a part of this magical startup game. Fifty years from now, what will our world look like? It's really hard to say, but the ride there will certainly be an exciting one.

Afterword

A NYTHING IS POSSIBLE. When I was growing up, the last thing in the world I wanted to do was to go into the venture capital business. My father was a great venture capitalist, having pioneered the business with Pitch Johnson and his partners at Sutter Hill Ventures, and my grandfather was a founding partner of Draper Gaither & Anderson, the first venture capital firm west of the Mississippi River.

Venture capital definitely seemed exciting and intriguing, but I really wanted to cut my own path. I went to Stanford, though my father wanted me to go to Yale, his alma mater. I wanted to be a physics major, but my father guided me toward electrical engineering. After college, I wanted to take the better-paying job at Triad Systems, but my father felt strongly that I should accept the lower-paying position at Hewlett-Packard. In the late 1980s, after completing business school, I wanted to have my own startup. My original ideas for businesses were for digitized music; a revolutionary submarine; a holographic, moving 3-D imaging system; and a non-U.S. stock market that allowed for tax payments only after repatriation of investment profits. I quickly realized that I had more ideas than could be implemented in my lifetime, so I needed a job that would allow me to play in a lot of different sandboxes.

Also, the pressure to get a "job" out of business school was too strong. So rather than attempting to start a new entrepreneurial venture, I took a position with Alex. Brown & Sons, the first investment bank in the United States. My responsibilities actually had some venture capital woven into them, and I learned a lot from my two bosses. One was Don Dixon, who would always give me a project at 6:00 P.M. to finish by 6:00 A.M. the following morning. He expected perfection, which he rarely got from me. My other boss was Steve Brooks, a true mover and shaker who had a real nose for a deal. But the person I would learn the most from at Alex. Brown & Sons was my fresh-out-of-college officemate who would later become my partner and the "F" of DFJ (Draper Fisher Jurvetson), John Fisher. We worked together on spreadsheets until we were cross-eyed and then would force each other to go down for twenty push-ups. We did a little bit of investing on the side, and both of us did pretty well. This was our life until Dad headed off to Washington DC to run the Export–Import Bank of the United States and asked if I would like to take over Draper Associates, his personal SBIC, and begin investing in startups.

Years earlier, as I pointed out, a career in venture capital was not on my professional agenda, but I quickly would become enamored with this fascinating industry. From my father and grandfather, I had learned that in the world of venture capital and entrepreneurship, *anything is possible.*

To pay his way through college, my grandfather hired himself out as the "Motorcycle Magician," riding his motorcycle to events where he would do magic tricks. His whole life seems magical in retrospect. Not only was he among the first Silicon Valley venture capitalists, but he also headed the Marshall Plan after World War II, ran the Mexican Light & Power Company, served as trustee of the Long Island Railroad, became a major general, and was undersecretary of the Army under President Truman. He was a really cool grandfather who had a dog the size of a horse, played chess with a rabid competitive spirit, and did magic tricks for his grandchildren. I watched my grandfather lead large groups of people to do extraordinary things, and I admired him as he changed the world for the better. He always gave me advice, but what really stuck was what I learned while watching him lead and motivate people to do good with their lives.

As you've read through these pages, I'm sure that you've noticed that my father also has many spectacular accomplishments—he ran for Congress;

pioneered the venture capital business; promoted free markets, women in the workforce, and environmental issues whenever he met with the leaders of the 110 countries he visited while at UNDP; ran the Export–Import Bank under President Reagan; became the first U.S. venture capitalist in India; and started the Draper Richards Foundation, in which he takes a venture capitalist approach to the nonprofit sector. He never shied away from showing me the world—for example, he took me along to Uganda, Kenya, Botswana, China, and Mongolia on UN missions. He also introduced me to the exciting realm of venture capital, which has become my passion. Dad also keeps me hopping on the tennis court to this day.

These two important men—along with their entire generation of dreamers, visionaries, and businesspeople—have shown me that *anything is possible.*

Through the venture capital business, I have seen it time and time again. Entrepreneurs prove that conventional wisdom may be conventional but is not always wise. They demonstrate that good ideas—the ones that change the world—are often initially rejected by all, save for a select group of risk takers and innovative thinkers.

The way that I live my daily life today is dramatically different from the way I did a decade or two ago. Today, life is clearly faster and more efficient. These lifestyle transformations have come about in large part because of disruptive innovations that are direct ramifications of the venture capital–entrepreneurial partnership. When I was growing up, the post office was the place to send mail, the telephone company provided the way to talk to someone remotely, the encyclopedia—published once a year—was the way to learn the newest facts, the bookstore was the place to buy books, cars only ran on gasoline, and one's friend pool consisted mostly of neighbors. But then, Sabeer Bhatia and Jack Smith created Hotmail, Niklas Zennström and Janus Friis created Skype, Sergey Brin and Larry Page created Google, Jeff Bezos created Amazon, Elon Musk designed the Tesla, and Mark Zuckerberg created Facebook. These are just a few great entrepreneurs whose companies have changed the way we live.

In 2008, through a project called "Operation Immortality," I sent my digitized DNA into space. I jokingly say it is my hope that aliens make use of my DNA so my clones can encourage entrepreneurship in galaxies throughout the universe. My DNA currently resides alongside that of Stephen Hawking at the International Space Station. Now the idea of intergalactic venture capital may seem far-fetched (although anything is possible!), but the concept of global venture capital is certainly not. It is already in full force, but this too was once a pipe dream.

Pitch Johnson, one of my father's first venture capital business partners, ranks among the wisest men I know, and years ago he told me, "A venture capitalist must be local to his entrepreneur." By that time we at DFJ knew that startups were going to happen everywhere. So we decided that we had to be "local" everywhere. I had the fortune of genetic guidance here too. My grandfather on my mother's side, William Culbertson, had been the vice chairman of Merrill Lynch and the driving force behind Merrill's setting up offices all over the United States. So genetically, I had pioneering venture capitalists on one side of the family and a network builder on the other side. It was almost preordained that I would set out to build the premier venture capital network.

And the timing was good. Investors were anxious to get into new venture capital funds. So, very quickly and somewhat quietly, Draper Fisher Jurvetson began setting up what would become the DFJ Network, the largest network of venture capital funds in the world. With the help of the Alaskan Development Authority, Jim Yarmon, and Jim Lynch, we set up the Polaris Fund. With the help of David Hemingway, my business school classmate Todd Stevens, and Zions Bank, we set up Wasatch Ventures in Utah (now called Epic). Alongside my undergraduate fraternity brother, John Backus, we set up Draper Atlantic in Washington DC. Through the help of David Cremin and Frank Creer, we set up Zone Ventures in Los Angeles. With Jay Katarencic and veteran "angel" Don Jones, we set up Draper Triangle in Pittsburgh. By the end of 1998, we had unlocked one of the greatest venture capital secrets of all time. We could share deals and intelligence, cross-invest, and connect our startups to companies all over the United States. And the network became really powerful when two very creative individuals came to us with a concept to go global.

Asad Jamal and Roderick Thomson are an unlikely pairing. Thomson is a formal, British, banker-looking guy, and Jamal is Pakistani and very slick. The two of them wanted to become our network partners for "the rest of world." Steve Jurvetson and I were enamored with the idea, but John Fisher wisely said that we didn't want anyone controlling our destiny outside of the United States. It was a big world out there. So, what we painfully negotiated was that we would create a new DFJ global fund as a joint venture with Thomson and Jamal called DFJ ePlanet, and it would be a core DFJ fund. DFJ would control the money, and the two entities would split the labor in sourcing, analyzing, and managing companies. ePlanet would hire the team with DFJ's blessing, would do their share of the labor, and would establish the legal structures in each vicinity in which we set up shop.

The working relationship was sometimes strained, as the two new members were culturally very different from the DFJ Partners. But the opportunity was vast, and the results were amazing. The worldwide footprint opened up our horizons. We didn't need to just see Silicon Valley or U.S. startups—we could invest in any startup anywhere! Our limited partners were very adventuresome at that time. It may seem counterintuitive, but the more flexibility investors give their venture capitalists, the better the returns seem to be for everyone. As it turned out, our limited partners benefited greatly from the freedom that they gave us.

Skype had Scandinavian founders, was incorporated in Luxembourg, headquartered in London, and had most of the operations in Estonia. Baidu was in Beijing and was started by a Chinese founder who had studied and worked in the United States. Successful startups could spring up anywhere, and the venture capital business had changed forever. It had evolved from the small, clubby business of my grandfather's era to the Silicon Valley–centric business that my father pioneered to this worldwide opening of the brainpower and creativity of the entire globe.

I am confident that the world's entrepreneurs will continue to build transformative companies, and global venture capital will continue to be the rocket fuel for these entrepreneurs to fly their missions. In addition, countries wanting to attract more jobs, creativity, and wealth to their people will roll out the red carpet for venture capitalists and entrepreneurs to build businesses in their countries. Tax incentives, lifting of bureaucratic barriers, improved bankruptcy laws, free repatriation, and so on, are beginning to be implemented around the planet.

Many countries are very receptive to this exciting new world. In Singapore, I discussed a new type of stock market with one government official at breakfast. By lunch, they had arranged for the head of their SEC to be on my left and the head of the Singapore stock market to be on my right. In Ukraine, I met with President Yushchenko and discussed startups. He said, "Companies used to have to wait six months and discuss their business with twenty-three bureaucrats before getting incorporated. Now it is one bureaucrat and five days." The country had also just lifted its requirement for a visa, and I was the first American to enter Ukraine without one. In South Korea, I met President Lee, and he told me how easy it had become to start and run a business in South Korea. Many other countries are following suit.

There is however one notable exception. *Ironically,* as the rest of the world expands and embraces this new group of burgeoning entrepreneurs, the United States has begun implementing regulations that hinder, rather than encourage, entrepreneurs. The United States of America, land of the free, home of the brave has recently begun creating disincentives for entrepreneurs and venture capitalists in the form of proposed additional taxes, increased accounting demands, and inappropriate requirements for small companies. If we want to continue to be the beacon of free enterprise, then it is essential that we focus on clearing the way for entrepreneurship to flourish.

My son Adam, who may become the first fourth-generation venture capitalist, is starting down a similar path to the one that I traveled over twenty-five years ago. Instinctively, he has been drawn to this exciting and volatile world. He has recently joined a friend of his to create a new vehicle for the startup game. They have set up a new alternative trading system for private securities that might allow entrepreneurs and venture capitalists the liquidity they need to keep the virtuous cycle going in this country.

So the startup game continues to evolve, and our family continues to strive and innovate to support those daring individuals who take huge risks to bring about extraordinary outcomes that improve our world. I am thankful to Grandpa and to Dad for blazing a trail that provided me with the opportunity to meet extraordinary geniuses and to see the world from a remarkable perch, while all the time knowing that what I do allows people to dream, create, invent, and pursue greatness.

Anything is possible.

—Tim Draper

Appendix

Nonprofit Organizations Sponsored by the Draper Richards Foundation

AGORA PARTNERSHIPS

www.agorapartnerships.org, Draper Richards grant 2009
Leader: Ben Powell—Presidential Management fellow and program examiner, White House Office of Management and Budget; MBA Columbia University; MS Foreign Service Georgetown University; BA Haverford College.

Impact: Founded in 2005, Agora helps small business "impact" entrepreneurs—those too big for microfinance but too small for traditional finance—create and grow businesses that generate social, environmental, and economic value for their communities. Agora provides them with the management tools, business networks, and access to long-term impact investment needed to grow successful, socially responsible companies that can create jobs in some of the world's poorest communities. The organization seeks to create a modern-day agora, where entrepreneurs, investors, passionate MBA students, and volunteer professionals come together to create and grow the businesses that will move the world forward.

Results: Agora Partnerships (2010 estimated (E) budget of $700,000) has created and sustained 1,700 jobs in Nicaragua and is a founding member of the Aspen Network for Development Entrepreneurs.

AMERICA ABROAD MEDIA

www.americaabroadmedia.org, Draper Richards grant 2004
Leader: Aaron Lobel—previously research fellow at the Brookings Institute; National Security fellow at the John M. Olin Institute for Strategic Studies at Harvard University; National Security fellow at the Belfer Center for Science and International Affairs at Harvard's Kennedy School of Government; PhD in Government at Harvard University.
Impact: Founded in 2002, America Abroad Media harnesses the power of media to inform America and the world about the critical international issues of our time. They produce radio and television programming that explores today's critical issues and connects America and the world for discussion.
Results: America Abroad Media (2011 estimated budget of $3,500,000) reaches an audience of 80 million each year on more than 200 radio stations nationwide and in more than 140 countries through NPR Worldwide. Their programs help build civil society, promote tolerance, and pluralism, strengthen independent media, and promote the free exchange and critical analysis of ideas.

BUILD CHANGE

www.buildchange.org, Draper Richards grant 2006
Leader: Elizabeth Hausler—previously a 2002 Fulbright scholar to India with a background in earthquake engineering and masonry construction; MS and PhD in civil engineering from University of California, Berkeley; MS in Environmental Science from University of Colorado.
Impact: Founded in 2004, Build Change designs earthquake-resistant houses and trains builders, homeowners, engineers, and government officials in developing nations to build them. Build Change promotes low or no-cost improvements to existing ways of building so that homeowners and builders continue to build safe houses after Build Change's intervention is complete.
Results: Build Change (2010E budget of $1,200,000) has designed and/or improved the construction of over 18,000 homes in China and Indonesia and is launching work in Haiti. Houses built to the Build Change

minimum standard in West Sumatra, Indonesia survived the 2009 earthquakes without damage. Build Change's training programs have permanently upgraded the skills of 1,000 builders, 1,000 engineers, and over 600 vocational students.

DESIGN THAT MATTERS

www.designthatmatters.org, Draper Richards grant 2004

Leader: Timothy Prestero—previously of the Peace Corps in Côte d'Ivoire, West Africa in the Urban Environmental Management program; MIT/Woods Hill Oceanographic Institute Joint Program in Applied Ocean Physics and Engineering; MS degrees in Mechanical and Oceanographic Engineering; BS in Mechanical Engineering from the University of California at Davis.

Impact: Founded in 2000, Design that Matters creates new products that support social enterprises in developing countries. They use a collaborative design process through which hundreds of volunteers in academia and industry donate their skills and expertise to the creation of breakthrough products for communities in need.

Results: Design that Matters (2009 budget of $350,000) engaged 1,000 volunteers in product design last year and has launched two products in the developing world.

DIGITAL WISH

www.digitalwish.org, Draper Richards grant 2008

Leader: Heather Chirtea—previously longstanding president of Tool Factory, an educational software publisher; BS Communications and Operations Management Statistics from Syracuse University.

Impact: Founded in 2007, Digital Wish is on a mission to solve technology shortfalls in classrooms. They enable teachers to upload technology wish lists that parents, community members, and local businesses fulfill through online donations.

Results: Digital Wish (2010E budget of $360,000) has facilitated the purchase of $4.7 million in technology products for 300,000 students in every state in the United States.

EDUCATION PIONEERS

www.educationpioneers.org, Draper Richards grant 2004

Leader: Scott Morgan—previously teacher; legal counsel for Aspire Public Schools; Government degree from University of Notre Dame; MA in Teaching from University of Portland; JD from Stanford University Law School.

Impact: Founded in 2003, Education Pioneers trains, connects, and inspires a new generation of education leaders dedicated to transforming our educational system so that all students receive a quality education. Through its Fellowship and Alumni programs, Education Pioneers increases the talent supply of education leaders outside of the classroom, prepares and supports these leaders to lead, and improves the performance of key United States education organizations such as school districts, charter school organizations, and education nonprofits.

Results: Education Pioneers (2010E budget of $5,000,000) has selected and trained over 900 fellows in seven cities across the United States; 72 percent of graduated alumni work full time in the field of education.

GENOCIDE INTERVENTION NETWORK

www.genocideintervention.net, Draper Richards grant 2006

Leader: Mark Hanis—worked in Sierra Leone at the Special Court for Sierra Leone (SCSL); Ashoka and Echoing Green Fellow; 2009 World Economic Forum Young Global Leader; grandchild of four Holocaust survivors; degree in Political Science and a minor in Public Policy from Swarthmore College.

Impact: Founded in 2005, GI-NET empowers individuals and communities with the tools to prevent and stop genocide. They are mobilizing the first permanent anti-genocide constituency committed to stopping the worst atrocities around the world.

Results: Genocide Intervention Network (2010E budget of $2,178,000) includes a worldwide coalition of investors, a national fellowship of local leaders across the United States, and over 700 student chapters at colleges and high schools.

GIRLS FOR A CHANGE

www.girlsforachange.org, Draper Richards grant 2003

Leader: Niko Everett—previously manager at Girls Scouts of Northern California; director of marketing at Soulsearching.com; cofounder of Young Women Social Entrepreneurs; BA Tufts University.

Impact: Founded in 2000, Girls for a Change empowers girls for personal and social transformation. The program inspires girls to have the voice, ability, and problem solving capacity to speak up, be decision makers, create visionary change, and realize their full potential. They invite young women to design, lead, fund, and implement social change projects that tackle issues girls face in their own neighborhoods.

Results: Girls for a Change (2010 budget of $860,000) has engaged 10,000 girls on teams in more than nineteen cities and five countries. In addition, they have empowered more than 12,000 girls through their national trainings and events.

Global Citizen Year

www.globalcitizenyear.org, Draper Richards grant 2009

Leader: Abigail Falik—previously an educator in the United States and in the developing world; developed youth leadership program at NetAid (now Mercy Corps); BA and MEd from Stanford University; MBA from Harvard Business School.

Impact: Founded in 2009, Global Citizen Year is leading a movement of young Americans who engage in a transformative global service "bridge year" between high school and college. Through intensive training and a structured apprenticeship in communities across Asia, Africa, or Latin America, each GCY Fellow will develop an ethic of service, fluency in a new language, and an intimate understanding of how the global majority lives. Working in partnership with colleges, companies, governments, and social enterprises around the world, GCY will unleash a pipeline of emerging leaders to find innovative solutions to the global challenges of the twenty-first century.

Results: Global Citizen Year (2010 budget of $1,300,000) has engaged forty-four fellows in four developing countries in Africa and Latin America.

GLOBAL HEALTH CORPS

www.ghcorps.org, Draper Richards grant 2009

Leader: Barbara Bush—previously worked for Red Cross Children's Hospital in Capetown, South Africa; interned for UNICEF in Botswana before working for the Smithsonian Institution for two years; humanities degree from Yale University. Jonny Dorsey—cofounder and former executive director of FACE AIDS; Human Biology degree from Stanford University.

Impact: Founded in 2009, Global Health Corps addresses the unjust and unsustainable disparity in health outcomes and healthcare access that exists today between the world's rich and the world's poor. They connect outstanding young leaders from the United States and developing countries in high-impact, skills-based, yearlong fellowships at organizations working for global health equity.

Results: Global Health Corps (2010 budget of $700,000) has engaged sixty fellows and has thirteen partner health organizations in five countries in Africa and the United States.

GLOBAL HERITAGE FUND

www.globalheritagefund.org, Draper Richards grant 2003

Leader: Jeff Morgan—previously a trained urban and regional planner and international sales and marketing executive in software and network computing for sixteen years; MS in Management from Stanford University Graduate School of Business; BS in City and Regional Planning from Cornell University.

Impact: Founded in 2002, Global Heritage Fund involves the local community to protect and preserve the earth's most significant and endangered cultural heritage sites in the developing world.

Results: Global Heritage Fund (2009 budget of $3,200,000) has completed six projects with twelve projects in process to save endangered global heritage sites that have generated new jobs for over 20,000 people in poor communities in ten developing countries.

GRASSROOT SOCCER

www.grassrootsoccer.org, Draper Richards grant 2006
Leader: Tommy Clark—physician and a former professional soccer player; Dartmouth College Medical School; UCSF research fellow; Dartmouth College undergraduate.
Impact: Founded in 2002, Grassroot Soccer educates African adolescents about HIV. They use the power of soccer to provide youth in Africa and Latin America with the knowledge, life skills, and support to live healthier lives.
Results: Grassroot Soccer (2010E budget of $6,000,000) has graduated 350,000 youth across twelve countries in Africa.

A HOME WITHIN

www.ahomewithin.org, Draper Richards grant 2006
Leader: Toni Heineman—previously in private practice in San Francisco as a psychologist for more than twenty-five years; MSW and Health Sciences from University of California, Berkeley; PhD in Mental Health from the University of California, San Francisco.
Impact: Founded in 2001, A Home Within provides mental-health services to current and former foster youth. They build networks of volunteer mental health professionals who provide direct, pro bono services and professional training.
Results: A Home Within (2010E budget of $850,000) has trained 2,600 therapists and expects to serve 500 youth in 2010 by delivering 25,000 hours of treatment in thirty-eight communities across the United States.

KIVA

www.kiva.org, Draper Richards grant 2007

Leader: Matt Flannery—previously a computer programmer at TiVo; BS in Symbolic Systems and Master's in Analytical Philosophy from Stanford University. Premal Shah—previously a principal product manager at PayPal; BS in Economics from Stanford University.

Impact: Founded in 2005, Kiva alleviates poverty by giving entrepreneurs in the developing world access to capital through microloans. Lenders all over the world browse entrepreneurs' profiles on Kiva's website, choose someone to lend to, and make a loan. Lenders connect to entrepreneurs on the other side of the planet, and their microfinance partners can serve more micro-entrepreneurs, more efficiently.

Results: Kiva (2010E budget of $9,600,000) has facilitated over $150 million in loans to 390,000 entrepreneurs in fifty-three countries from over 470,000 lenders in over 200 countries.

KOMAZA

www.komaza.org, Draper Richards grant 2008

Leader: Tevis Howard—performed malaria research in Kenya (2002-2005); ScB in Neuroscience from Brown University (2007); grants and fellowships from Pop!Tech and Mulago, Peery, and Jasmine Foundations.

Impact: Founded in 2008, KOMAZA helps poor rural families living on dry degraded lands earn life-changing income through microforestry: planting woodlots of fast-growing trees for sale as high-margin wood products.

Results: KOMAZA (2010E budget nearly $1,000,000) is working with 2,000 farm families and has planted over 275,000 thriving trees.

LITTLE KIDS ROCK

www.littlekidsrock.org, Draper Richards grant 2005

Leader: David Wish—previously an English as a Second Language (ESL) teacher to low-income students for ten years; guitarist; credentialed teacher in the state of California; BA in Sociology and History from Brandeis University; board member of the Quincy Jones Musiq Consortium.

Impact: Founded in 2002, Little Kids Rock restores and revitalizes music education in the academic lives of students in our public schools by providing a rich music program including free instruments, instruction, and mentor training. Through weekly music education classes that use innovative teaching methods, Little Kids Rock inspires the creativity and confidence that are critical to success for kids in school and beyond.

Results: Little Kids Rock (2010E budget of $1,500,000) is the largest free music education program in the United States, and has served 100,000 students and 1,448 teachers in twenty-five cities across the United States to date.

LIVING GOODS

www.livinggoods.org, Draper Richards grant 2007

Leader: Chuck Slaughter—founded TravelSmith Catalog and built it into the number-one brand in travel wear with over two million customers and $100 million in gross sales; former program officer at Trickle Up; led turn around for an African health franchise; BA and a Master's degree in Public and Private Management from Yale University.

Impact: Founded in 2007, Living Goods is building a sustainable system for defeating diseases of poverty and improving livelihoods. They create Avon-like networks of door-to-door health promoters who make a modest income selling the simplest, cheapest solutions for the biggest killers of young kids. They improve the lives of the health promoters, who earn a living from the sales, and the customers, who are able to live healthier lives.

Results: Living Goods (2010E budget of $1,600,000) engages over 600 health promoters a year who reach over 500,000 people in Uganda.

MAPENDO INTERNATIONAL

www.mapendo.org, Draper Richards grant 2007

Leader: Sasha Chanoff—previously consulted with the Office of the United Nations High Commissioner for Refugees (UNHCR) and worked with the International Organization for Migration throughout Africa; BA from Wesleyan University and MA in Humanitarian Assistance from the Tufts University Fletcher School of Law and Diplomacy and Friedman School of Nutrition, Science, and Policy.

Impact: Founded in 2005, Mapendo International rescues and protects at-risk refugees in Africa who have fallen through the cracks of humanitarian assistance. The organization identifies individuals, families, and groups of refugees in extreme danger and advocates for and operationalizes their resettlement to countries where they can rebuild their lives safely.

Results: Mapendo International (2010E budget of $1,900,000) has enabled the relocation of over 10,800 refugees from the Democratic Republic of Congo, Darfur, Ethiopia, Somalia, Southern Sudan, and other war-torn areas of Africa to the United States, Canada, Australia, and other refugee resettlement countries. Collaborating with the UNHCR, NGOs, and governments, Mapendo International's ideas and influence are expanding globally to protect the most at-risk refugees.

THE MISSION CONTINUES

www.missioncontinues.org, Draper Richards grant 2009

Leader: Eric Greitens—Rhodes Scholar at Oxford University serving as a humanitarian volunteer around the world; United States Navy SEAL officer; White House Fellow; Angier B. Duke Scholar at Duke University in Ethics, Philosophy, and Public Policy; Master's degree in development studies in 1998 and a PhD in politics from Oxford University.

Impact: Founded in 2007, The Mission Continues empowers wounded and disabled veterans to continue their service to their country and communities as citizen leaders here at home. They award fellowships for volunteer work to veterans, enable veterans to lead service projects with fellow service members, and enable citizens to lead service projects on behalf of fallen military men and women.

Results: The Mission Continues (2010E budget of $570,000) has engaged seventy veterans in fellowships and 8,545 volunteers in contributing almost 50,000 hours of service to their communities in thirty-eight regions of the United States.

NAYA JEEVAN

www.njfk.org, Draper Richards grant 2009

Leader: Asher Hasan—previously senior director of the U.S. Medical Affairs Obesity team for Amylin Pharmaceuticals, Inc.; MBA from New York University's Stern School of Business; Harvard Medical School.

Impact: Founded in 2007, Naya Jeevan ("new life" in Urdu/Hindi) rejuvenates the lives of low-income families throughout the emerging world by providing them with affordable access to quality healthcare. The Naya Jeevan health plan is integrated with a number of value-added services (medical screenings, 24/7 medical hotline, preventive health workshops, etc.) and is targeted towards informal workers (drivers, maids, workers in the corporate, NGO, SME) and academic sectors and children studying in NGO/public sector schools.

Results: Naya Jeevan (2010 budget of $380,000) has enrolled over 1,800 health-plan participants as individuals from twenty-two client organizations in Pakistan.

ONE ACRE FUND

www.oneacrefund.org, Draper Richards grant 2006

Leader: Andrew Youn—previously a management consultant to Fortune 500 companies with Mercer Consulting; MBA Kellogg School of Management at Northwestern University; undergraduate degree from Yale University.

Impact: Founded in 2006, One Acre Fund empowers chronically hungry farm families in East Africa to permanently lift themselves out of hunger and poverty. They provide a service bundle to farmers: farm inputs on credit, weekly farm education sessions, and access to world output markets. Their implementation doubles farm profit per acre.

Results: One Acre Fund (2010E budget of $3,500,000) currently serves 30,000 farmers in Kenya and Rwanda.

ROOM TO READ

www.roomtoread.org, Draper Richards grant 2002

Leader: John Wood—previously a senior Microsoft marketing and business development executive; MBA from the Kellogg School of Management at Northwestern University; Bachelor's degree in Finance from the University of Colorado.

Impact: Founded in 2000 to break the cycle of poverty through education, Room to Read partners with local communities throughout the developing world to establish schools, libraries, and other educational infrastructure. They intervene early in the lives of children in the belief that education is a lifelong gift that empowers people to ultimately improve socioeconomic conditions for their families, communities, countries, and future generations.

Results: Room to Read (2010E budget of $33,000,000) has reached over 4 million children in nine countries by funding over 10,000 long-term education scholarships for girls, building over 1,100 schools, and opening over 10,000 libraries with 8 million books.

SPARK

www.sparkprogram.org, Draper Richards grant 2008

Leader: Chris Balme—previously taught in urban classrooms as a National Science Foundation Fellow; graduate of University of Pennsylvania and the Wharton School of Business.

Impact: Founded in 2004, Spark addresses the dropout crisis in America, where in many urban areas such as Los Angeles and Chicago the dropout rate is over 50 percent. Spark matches at-risk students with one-on-one apprenticeships in a profession of their choice where they work with a trained mentor in a local workplace. The result: student retention and graduation increases significantly, as students become more engaged with school and use it as a launch pad for their own dreams.

Results: Spark (2010E budget of $1,200,000) has built thriving apprenticeship programs in four California cities and begins national roll-out in 2011 with a launch in Chicago.

TAPROOT FOUNDATION

www.taprootfoundation.org, Draper Richards grant 2002

Leader: Aaron Hurst—previously director of product management at iSyndicate; product manager at iOwn; associate at Chicago Foundation for Education; general studies degree he created that focused on service-learning from the University of Michigan.

Impact: Founded in 2001, Taproot makes business talent available to organizations working to improve society. They engage the nation's millions of business professionals in pro-bono service both through their award-winning programs and by partnering with companies to develop their own pro-bono programs.

Results: Taproot (2010E budget of $4,100,000) has completed 1,300 service grants and engaged 5,000 professionals in over 800,000 hours of pro bono service in five cities across the Unites States. They are also working with more than a dozen Fortune 500 companies to build scalable corporate pro bono programs that will eventually reach beyond Taproot's five core cities.

UPWARDLY GLOBAL

www.upwardlyglobal.org, Draper Richards grant 2002

Leader: Jane Leu—internationally recognized social entrepreneur and expert on global immigration and workforce issues; master's in International Affairs from Columbia University; undergraduate at Tufts University.

Impact: Founded in 2000, Upwardly Global brings refugee and immigrant professionals and U.S. employers together to help unemployed and underemployed immigrants to achieve their full career potential in the United States and to create a more globally diverse workforce.

Results: Upwardly Global (2010 budget of $2,300,000) has worked with 3,600 volunteers to coach 2,500 immigrant jobseekers from more than 105 countries, developed ongoing relationships with more than 500 employers, and increased immigrant families' income by more than $50 million.

VISIONSPRING

www.visionspring.org, Draper Richards grant 2005

Leader: Jordan Kassalow—founder and adjunct senior fellow at the Global Health Policy Program at the Council on Foreign Relations; director of the Onchocerciasis Division at Helen Keller International; doctorate of Optometry from New England College of Optometry; Fellowship in Preventive Ophthalmology; Masters degree in Public Health, Johns Hopkins University.

Impact: Founded in 2001, VisionSpring engages microentrepreneurs in selling glasses in developing countries. They improve economic gains for the sellers, who earn a living from the sales, and purchasers, who are able to productively engage in the economy for more years due to their improved eyesight.

Results: VisionSpring (2010E budget of $2,000,000) has sold 600,000 pairs of glasses by engaging 10,400 vision entrepreneurs in ten developing countries and generating an estimated $152 million in economic impact to date.

WILD4LIFE

www.wild4life.org, Draper Richards grant 2010

Leader: Kel Sheppey—previously a wildlife biologist and safari guide; Oracle Corporation's applications IT implementation director for Latin America; founder of a successful adventure travel company; two science degrees and an MBA from the University of Cape Town.

Impact: Founded in 2008, Wild4life focuses on rural African communities in sub-Saharan Africa delivering HIV/AIDS prevention and treatment programs to people previously without access to either.

Results: Wild4life (2010E budget of $250,000) has reached 2,000 people in fifteen communities across ten countries in Africa.

Notes

Introduction

1. Jamis MacNiven, *Breakfast at Buck's: Tales from the Pancake Guy* (Woodside, CA: Buck's Books, 2004), 43.
2. David Filo and Jerry Yang, *Yahoo! Unplugged* (Foster City, CA: IDG Books Worldwide, 1995) 8.
3. The exclamation point (Yahoo!) was added later to make the word trademarkable. I'll omit it here.
4. Karen Angel, *Inside Yahoo!* (New York: John Wiley & Sons, 2002), 7.

Chapter 1

1. I was, therefore, "William H. Draper III." I decided not to burden my own son with "IV."
2. "Inland Steel Company," *Wikipedia*, http://en.wikipedia.org/wiki/Inland_Steel_Company.
3. Bay Area Census, Town of Atherton (Census 2000), http://www.bayareacensus.ca.gov/cities/Atherton.htm.
4. Raychem Corporation Company History, http://www.fundinguniverse.com/company-histories/Raychem-Corporation-Company-History.html.
5. "Stanford Facts: The Stanford Lands," Stanford University official website, http://www.stanford.edu/about/facts/lands.html.

Chapter 2

1. John Taylor, "NVCA 2010 Yearbook Now Available," http://nvcaccess.nvca.org/index.php/topics/research-and-trends/79-nvca-2010-yearbook-now-available.html.

2. In his book *The Godfather of Silicon Valley: Ron Conway and the Fall of the Dot-Coms*, author Gary Rivlin describes Conway as "the man who has placed more bets on internet start-ups than anyone else in Silicon Valley." See the Conway write-up on CrunchBase, http://www.crunchbase.com/person/ron-conway.

3. "Yahoo! Acquires Online Anywhere, Enables Users to Get Their Yahoo! Anywhere, Anytime," Yahoo Press Release, http://docs.yahoo.com/docs/pr/release322.html.

4. Thomas O'Keefe, "Mergers and Acquisitions—Internet Sector," http://ezinearticles.com/?Mergers-and-Acquisitions—Internet-Sector&id=82172.

5. "Measurex," *Wikipedia*, http://en.wikipedia.org/wiki/Measurex.

6. "About Us," DivX Official Website, http://www.divx.com/en/company/about-us.

7. If you issue additional shares in a company, thereby broadening its base of ownership, you "dilute" the equity positions of the original shareholders.

8. The "cliff" means that an employee who joined the company in January and left the following December—before his first full year of employment had passed—would lose all his options.

Chapter 3

1. "Corporate Fact Sheet," athenahealth Official Website, http://www.athena-health.com/our-company/corporate-facts.php.

2. "About Us," athenahealth Official Website, http://www.athenahealth.com/our-company/about-us.php.

3. Jeffrey Fleming, "The History of Activision," *Gamasutra.com*, http://www.gamasutra.com/view/feature/1537/the_history_of_activision.php?print=1.

4. Jerry N. Hess, "Oral History Interview with General William H. Draper Jr.," Harry S. Truman Library & Museum Official Website, January 11, 1972, http://www.trumanlibrary.org/oralhist/draperw.htm.

5. D. M. Giangreco and Robert E. Griffin, *Airbridge to Berlin: The Berlin Crisis of 1948, Its Origins and Aftermath* (Novato, CA: Presidio Press, 1988).

6. Hess, "Oral History Interview with General William H. Draper Jr."

7. Ibid.

8. O'Hare International Airport," *Wikipedia*, http://en.wikipedia.org/wiki/O%27Hare_International_Airport.

9. "Laker Airways," *Wikipedia*, http://en.wikipedia.org/wiki/Laker_Airways.

10. Lyssiemay Annoh, "My Tribute to Sir Freddie Laker," *Executive Traveller, International Edition* 13 (Spring 2006): 8, http://executivetraveller.net/images/archives/Spring2006edition.pdf.

11. Richard Branson, "Sixty Years of Heroes: Freddie Laker," *Time Europe*, November 13, 2006, http://www.time.com/time/europe/hero2006/laker.html.

Chapter 4

1. For a provocative view of the Ex–Im Bank's support of the U.S. nuclear power industry, see Samantha Sparks, "The Subsidy Shuffle," *The Multinational Monitor* vol. 7, no. 9 (May 1986), http://www.multinationalmonitor.org/hyper/issues/1986/05/kats.html.
2. June Grasso, Jay Corrin, and Michael Kort, *Modernization and Revolution in China* (Armonk, NY: M. E. Sharpe, 1991).
3. English and French are the two official languages of the United Nations.
4. The current report, as well as previous issues dating back to 1990, can be found online at http://hdr.undp.org/en/reports/global/hdr2009/.
5. Ellen Johnson Sirleaf, *This Child Will Be Great: Memoir of a Remarkable Life by Africa's First Woman President* (New York: Harper Perennial, 2010), 329.

Chapter 5

1. Robin later told me that she figured that I wanted her help in getting Draper International off the ground, and that later, I'd bring in someone more senior.
2. "Our Mission," Overseas Private Investment Corporation Official Website, http://www.opic.gov/about/mission.
3. "About Us," ICICI Bank Official Website, http://www.icicibank.com/aboutus/about-us.html.
4. Biography of Mahesh Veerina, Garnett & Helfrich Capital Official Website, http://www.garnetthelfrich.com/pages/portfolio_veerina_bio.html.
5. For more on The Indus Entrepreneurs (TiE), see their website at http://www.tie.org/chapterHome/about_tie/FAQS200710180764684109/viewInnerPagePT.
6. Much of this information is derived from an article about Raj Jaswa on kaboodle.com: http://www.kaboodle.com/reviews/life-in-the-fast-lane-raj-jaswa. Also useful, and very entertaining, is the Jaswa Family website (http://www.jaswa.com/index.html), which—according to its writers—has "no commercial purpose. In fact, we are at a loss to find much purpose for it at all, other than to communicate mostly irrelevant information to family and friends." Finally, we draw heavily on Yasemin Denari's April 9, 2009, interview with Jaswa for this book.

7. Nora Macaluso, "Stock Watch: Selectica IPO Takes Off," *E-Commerce Times*, March 13, 2000, http://www.ecommercetimes.com/story/2725.html?wlc=1272804696.

Chapter 6

1. Tony Perkins, interview with Yasemin Denari, November 9, 2009.
2. Much of this information comes from conversations with Tim and his DFJ colleagues and also from the *DFJ Network Overview*, a document supplied to me by DFJ. See also the Network description on the DFJ website: http://www.dfj.com/network/.
3. Tony Perkins, interview with Yasemin Denari, November 9, 2009.
4. Again, this story comes from my own conversations with Tim over the years and also from Tim's interview with Yasemin Denari on November 9, 2009.
5. Po Bronson, "HotMale," *Wired*, December 1998, http://www.wired.com/wired/archive/6.12/hotmale.html.
6. Subscriber statistics from: Jeff Peline, "Microsoft Buys Hotmail," *CNET News*, January 3, 1998, http://news.cnet.com/2100-1033-206717.html. "The stock deal for the two-year-old company," *CNET News* reported, "has been estimated in the hundreds of millions of dollars." The *Wired* story cited above says $400 million. A *Wikipedia* article says that the price was $500 million, which would make it Microsoft's largest acquisition up to that time. See http://en.wikipedia.org/wiki/List_of_mergers_and_acquisitions_by_Microsoft.
7. "Microsoft Acquires Hotmail," Microsoft Press Release, December 31, 1997, http://www.microsoft.com/presspass/press/1997/dec97/Hotmlpr.mspx. As the press release notes, "financial terms of the transaction were not disclosed" and still can't be disclosed today. But obviously, "our side" was happy, and Microsoft got a company it badly needed.
8. David Barboza, "The Rise of Baidu (That's Chinese for Google)," *New York Times*, September 17, 2006, http://query.nytimes.com/gst/fullpage.html?res=9C01E6DE1331F934A2575AC0A9609C8B63&sec=&spon=&pagewanted=2.
9. FRiENDi Group Official Website, http://www.friendigroup.com/Board-of-Directors.aspx?page_id=7.
10. Baidu Official Website, http://ir.baidu.com/phoenix.zhtml?c=188488&p=irol-homeprofile.
11. Much of this biographical detail is from: "Elon Musk," *Wikipedia*, http://en.wikipedia.org/wiki/Elon_Musk.

12. "Seventy-Five Most Influential People of the Twenty-First Century: Elon Musk," *Esquire,* http://www.esquire.com/features/75-most-influential/elon-musk-1008.

13. Marcia Dunn, "Millionaire's Test Rocket Reaches Orbit on First Try," ABC News.com, June 4, 2010, http://abcnews.go.com/Technology/wireStory?id=10824247.

14. This section draws from three sources: my own conversations with David Lee over the years; "Oral History of George Comstock," Interviewed by Gardner Hendrie, Computer History Museum, http://archive.computerhistory.org/resources/text/Oral_History/Comstock_George/Comstock_George_1.oral_history.102658008.pdf; and "Friden EC-130 Electronic Calculator," The Old Calculator Web Museum Website, http://oldcalculatormuseum.com/friden130.html.

15. See the NCR history timeline at NCR's official website, http://www.ncr.com/about_ncr/company_overview/history.jsp.

16. Paul Strassmann, *Paul's Odyssey: America 1945–1985,* (New Canaan, CT: Information Economics Press, 2007), 248.

17. "Thankfully," Perkins wrote, "Bill Draper of Sutter Hill let us participate in one of their investments with Qume, a printer company. It proved to be a good investment, and one on which we made a respectable return." Quotation from: Tom Perkins, *Valley Boy: The Education of Tom Perkins* (New York: Gotham, 2007), 109.

18. Subsequent awards have gone to companies like Google, Yahoo, and Facebook.

19. Po Bronson, "Could Anyone Have Thought Up Hotmail?" excerpt from *The Nudist on the Late Shift* (New York: Random House, 1999), http://www.businessweek.com/smallbiz/news/coladvice/book/bk990903.htm.

20. From the June 25, 1999, issue of *AsiaWeek,* quoted in Naomi Hirahara, *Distinguished Asian American Business Leaders* (Westport, CT: Greenwood Press, 2003), 24.

21. "Sabeer Bhatia: Mr. Hotmail," Investment Analysis Website, http://invest-hunt.com/learn-from-the-best/sabeer-bhatia-mr-hotmail/.

22. "America's New Immigrant Entrepreneurs," http://www.kauffman.org/uploadedfiles/entrep_immigrants_1_61207.pdf.

23. Stuart Anderson and Michaela Platzer, "American Made: The Impact of Immigrant Entrepreneurs and Professionals on U.S. Competitiveness," Joint Study by National Venture Capital Association, National Foundation for

American Policy, and Content First, LLC, January 5, 2007, http://www.nvca.
org/index.php?option=com_content&view=article&id=254&Itemid=103.

24. Todd Halvorson, "Elon Musk Unveiled," *Florida Today*, January 29, 2005,
reprinted on the SpaceX Official Website, http://www.spacex.com/media.
php?page=36.

25. From David Lee's interview with the PBS series "Commanding Heights,"
http://www.pbs.org/wgbh/commandingheights/shared/minitext/int_dav-
idlee.html#4.

Chapter 7

1. IPO Volume—Data and Graphs, Renaissance Capital Website, http://www.
renaissancecapital.com/ipohome/press/ipovolume.aspx.

2. Definition of "underwriter," *Investopedia*, http://www.investopedia.com/
terms/u/underwriter.asp.

3. Read the interesting interview with Tony Hsieh at http://viralogy.com/blog/
hot-topics/tony-hsieh-the-ceo-of-zappos-how-a-company-grows-from-0-in-
1999-to-over-1-billion-in-2008/.

4. Link Exchange Company Information, http://www.linksv.com/company-
Summary.aspx?co_idURL=2938&partnerID.

5. It was Hartenbaum who, acting on a tip from Tim, turned up the original
Skype opportunity in Stockholm.

6. "eBay to Acquire Skype," Press Release, September 12, 2005, http://about.
skype.com/2005/09/ebay_to_acquire_skype.html.

Chapter 8

1. Commonwealth Club definition, http://www.ssireview.org/opinion/entry/
what_exactly_is_social_entrepreneurship_in_america/.

2. We will expand upon several of these examples in subsequent pages. For
more information about all of these organizations and others, visit the
Draper Richards Foundation official website: http://www.draperrichards.
org/fellows/index.html#h_537#p_home.

3. Much of this story and all of the quotations come from Yasemin Denari's
August 26, 2009, interview with John Wood. See also the Room to Read
website at http://www.roomtoread.org, and Wood's excellent book: John

Wood, *Leaving Microsoft to Change the World: An Entrepreneur's Odyssey to Educate the World's Children* (New York: HarperCollins, 2006).

4. "About Us," Room to Read Official Website, http://www.roomtoread.org/Page.aspx?pid=209.

5. Much of this story and all of the quotations come from Yasemin Denari's July 31, 2009, interview with Jordan Kassalow. See also the VisionSpring website at http://www.visionspring.org/home/home.php.

6. VisionSpring Press Release, http://www.visionspring.org/newscenter/news-detail.php?id=842.

7. See the One Acre Fund website at http://www.oneacrefund.org/.

8. I should note that Echoing Green, mentioned earlier, invested in One Acre Fund seven months before Draper Richards. You don't always have to go first to do good. If someone else finds something that is right up your philanthropic alley, you can sign up with them.

9. See The Mission Continues website at http://www.missioncontinues.org.

10. See Kiva's website at http://www.kiva.org.

11. All quotations come from Yasemin Denari's September 8, 2009, interview with Matt Flannery and Premal Shah.

12. BizWorld Official Website, http://www.bizworld.org/aboutus.html.

Chapter 9

1. The Platters and Elvis Presley also had huge hits with "Harbor Lights" much later in the decade, but here, I'm talking about Sammy Kaye.

2. See, for example: Stephen Davies, "The Great Horse-Manure Crisis of 1894," *The Freeman*, September 2004 (vol. 54, issue 9), http://www.thefreemanonline.org/columns/our-economic-past-the-great-horse-manure-crisis-of-1894/#.

3. Ray Kurzweil, "Kurzweil's Law," January 12, 2004, http://www.kurzweilai.net/kurzweils-law-aka-the-law-of-accelerating-returns.

4. These ideas came from Steve Jurvetson and Tim Draper of Draper Fisher Jurvetson and Brook Byers of Kleiner Perkins Caufield & Byers.

Index